R... ON THE RABBIS

SAGE INSIGHT INTO
FIRST-CENTURY JEWISH THOUGHT

לִימוּד הַרַבָּנִים
תוֹבָנָה חֲכָמָה עַל הַשְׁקָפָה יְהוּדִית בַּמֵּאָה הָרִאשׁוֹנָה

Brian Tice, B.Sci., M.Sci.

MJR PRESS
GRAND RAPIDS, MICH.

REFLECTING ON THE RABBIS:
Sage Insight into First-Century Jewish Thought

© 2013 - 2017 (5773 - 5777) by Brian Tice

Published by MJR Press
Grand Rapids, Michigan
https://mjrabbinate.org/publishing
email: publishing@mjrabbinate.org
Printed in the United States of America

All rights reserved. No part of this publication may be reproduced, stored in a retrieval system, or transmitted in any form or by any means – including electronic, photocopy, recording – without the prior written permission of the publisher, except brief quotations in printed or online reviews or in other works where full attribution is given.

All Scripture passages quoted from *JPS* (1917, public domain) for the *Tanakh* (OT), and from the *Aramaic English New Testament* (copyright 2008, used by permission of Netzari Press) for the *B'rit Chadasha* (NT).

Cover art © 2017/5777 by Brian Tice. All Rights Reserved.

Entered according to Act of Congress by MJR Press in April 2017 with the Librarian of Congress, Washington, D.C.

Library of Congress Control Number: 2017905754

Reflecting on the Rabbis: Sage Insight into First-Century Jewish Thought / Brian Tice.

Includes biographical references and indices.

ISBN: 1-5450-1803-0
ISBN-13: 978-1-5450-1803-3

1.   Talmud – Theology
2.   Rabbinic Literature
3.   Middle-Eastern Literature – Relation to N.T.
I.   Title.   II. Author.

BM_____   2017

PRE-PUBLICATION REVIEWS

"*Reflecting on the Rabbis* draws on the Sages of old and top modern scholars to bring 1st Century Judaism new life! Professor Tice is well-studied, thorough in his presentation, and generously provides a glossary of Jewish Jargon, a comprehensive index, and other helpful appendices. For these reasons and more, we select this treasured book to receive the *5777 Yiddishkeit 101 College-Level Literature Award* and our sincerest recommendation!"

Literary Award Panel
Yiddishkeit 101

"Brian has created a 'must have' as it pertains to studying First-Century Jewish thought! He will leave you with several 'aha' moments, a strengthened faith, and a strong desire to find out 'what else didn't I know?!'"

Rav Joshua Liggins

Educator & former Student Ministries Director
Coral Springs, Fla.

"As an Orthodox Jew, I see Brian Tice's work as necessary for the Christians and the Messianics to evaluate and make a true connection to their Jewish Roots."

Ariel Manning

Neveh Ohr Congregation
Morenci, Mich.

"For nearly 1700 years, there has been a calculated and quite successful attempt to divorce Yeshua from His Jewish context. However, great strides have been made in recent years toward rectifying that travesty. This volume presents the Sages who made the greatest impact on First-Century Jewish thought - Shammai haZaqen, Hillel haZaqen, Rabban Gamli'el I, Rabban Yochanan ben Zakkai, and Rabbi Aqiva - laying out what they taught and how they lived. Against this backdrop, it can be seen where Yeshua fits into the scene of First-Century Rabbinic context."

Carmen Welker

Author of *The Refiner's Fire* website
Host of *Reality Check* videos

DEDICATION

I dedicate this volume, first and foremost, to HaShem: May this labor of love be a sweet-smelling savor unto Him.   **לִכְבוֹד שְׁמוֹ: אָמֵן:**

I also dedicate it to all who seek to better understand the cultural-historical context of the First-Century Scriptures – especially to those of the beloved faith community I am so pleased to call my spiritual *mishpocha: Adat Eytz Chayim.*

In loving memory of my HaShem-honoring
great aunt Barb Michaels,
grandparents Ray & Joyce Baker,
and great grandmother Minnie Langeance

ACKNOWLEDGEMENTS

A research-writing project such as this is absolutely not a solo act. Therefore, I wish to bid *todah rabba* (a multitude of thanks) to the long list of those who have encouraged me – whether directly or indirectly – in endeavoring this project and seeing it through to completion:

ॐ *my family* ॐ
especially my parents Dave & Kathi Tice;
grandparents Dea. Bill & Erma Tice;
sister Amy Brink; aunts and uncles Kris & Kim Baker,
Kevin, Ken, & Kyle Baker; Wendy & Dave Conner, &
Maryln Langeance; and cousins Robert Dancz, Emily
Ek, Swenna Harger, Bethany Huffman, Jayna Hilaski,
Karleigh Strickfaden, & Adrienne & Kelcey Summers

ॐ *Adat Eytz Chayim Congregation* ॐ
especially Ben Benting, Ezekiel & Teodora
Bossenbroek, Cal DeMaagd, Jeff & Molly Dervin,
Joe & Tonya Dorwin, Zaqen John Dressel,
Garth & Nancy Felton, John & Penny Dressel,
Levota Fuller, Tamara Gonzalez, Bruce & Nancy
Isenhoff, Christene Jackman, David & Kat Jordan,
Harry & Sherry Konieczka, Chris Kubiak,
Rav Michael (of blessed memory) & Bonnie Lohrberg,
Michael Manning Jr., Michael Sr. & Ruth Manning,
David & Jennette Martonosi, Brian & Rivkah Moss,
Jason & Amber Newcomb, Christina Oakes, Kris &
Liora Rasmussen, Jenna Regan, Deb & Michelle Reid,
Larry Remaly, Isadora Russell, Jorge & Olga Sanchez,
Patricia Shijka, Derek & Lisa Sisson, Michael Smith,
Dean VanderMey, Maureen VanGessel, Michael & Jill
Vick, Bernadette Wagenaar, Dave & Cheri Wheelock,
Jack & Lonnie Wisney, and John & Adele Zelenka

❧ other close friends in faith & ministry ❦
Samantha Allababidi, Alexandrea Andrade,
Vaughn Bannister, Lindsay Barron, Sally & Rhob Bauer,
Hannah Blystra, Lisa Bratt, Sam Buchan, Kimberly
Bytwerk, Jesse & Jenn Churilla, Kim Coleman, Aaron
Cooper, Diane Ebbers, Tiffany Elmergreen, Tom &
Maureen Fischer, Michael Fravel, Orlando Garcia, Nate
Geisel, Kelly Haight, the Rev. Matt & Betsy Hickok,
Micah & Sarah Hill, Pat & Keara Hilton, Seth Horton,
Carrice Hudecz, Shena Jolliffi, Ryan Kaline, Spencer
Kasten, Dan & Val Kerwin, Jenna Kokot, Ari Lahta,
Heather Langerak, Rav Joshua & Christy Liggins,
Dr. Philip J Long, Maria & Isaiah Melinn, Natasha
Mueller, Sheri Munsell, Krissy Nordhoff, Lexie Oosse,
Angela Peaster, Bruce Scheltema, Amanda Schutte,
Peter Segovia, Matt & Patrice Simpson, Jade Suhr,
Angelea Torralva, Sarah VanGessel, Brook Veldkamp,
Eric Verstraete, Shaun Weldon, Erin Willis, Levi &
Melissa Wood, and Zane & Bonnie Ziviski

❧ my fellow faculty members ❦
David Negley, Jeremy Tindall and Carmen Welker of
Messianic Jewish Rabbinate; and Jeremy Bouma, the Rev.
Shane Cox, Lenski Llorens Monteserin, and Angel
Edgardo Rodriguez of *Take Hold Ministry School*

❧ those who instructed me in ancient & Biblical languages ❦
Dr. Dwayne H. Adams, Dr. Scott T. Carroll,
Prof. David B. Kennedy, Dr. John I. Lawlor,
Dr. Gary T. Meadors, Dr. Douglas C. Mohrmann,
Prof. Andrew L. Smith, and Dr. David L. Turner

❧ my college German instructor ❦
Richard E. Bridges, without whose language training
a large number of my research sources would have
been inaccessible to me.

❧ the professors who helped raise my Cultural Intelligence ❧
Fr. Robert Badra, Dr. Havi Dreifuss,
Dr. Oded Lipschits, Dr. David A. Livermore,
Dr. Na'ama Bela Shik, Prof. Coleen Smith-Slosberg,
Dr. Avraham Susser, Dr. Barry Scott Wimpfheimer,
and Lecturer Sarah Wolf

❧ the professors who helped in honing my writing skills ❧
Dr. Byard J. Bennett, Dr. Greg McClure,
Dr. Ron Mayers, the late Prof. Ronald Miazga,
Dr. Peter G. Osborne, Prof. Kate Villaire,
and Dr. Michael E. Wittmer

❧ the professors who helped in honing my design skills ❧
Dr. Ralph Allured, Dr. Ruth Lantinga,
and Prof. Donald Perini

❧ a handful of other encouraging professors and admins ❧
Chancellor R' Steven Berkowitz, Dr. Ed Dobson,
Dr. Douglas L. Fagerstrom, Dr. Stanley N. Gundry,
Tara Kram, Kay Landrum, Dr. William Lay,
Prof. Denise Miller, Prof. Catherine Mueller-Bell,
David Murdock, Prof. Thomas F. Obee,
Dr. Gene Peterson, Kris Warren, the late Dr. James M.
Grier, and the late Dr. W. Wilbert Welch

❧ for igniting my love of languages ❧
Sra. Caterina Kenworthy and Prof. Jade Suhr

❧ and, for proof-reading and providing peer-review ❧
Ann Fournier, David & Kat Jordan,
Rav Joshua Liggins, Rabbi Ariel Manning,
and Prof. Carmen Welker

I owe you all an immeasurable debt of gratitude!

CONTENTS

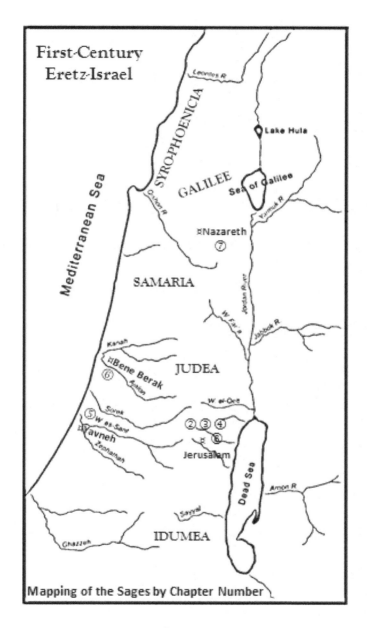

First-Century
Eretz-Israel

Mediterranean Sea

SYROPHOENICIA

GALILEE

Lake Hula

Sea of Galilee

⨯Nazareth
⑦

SAMARIA

Kanah

⨯Bene Berak
⑥

JUDEA

⑤
⨯Yavneh

②③④
⨯ ⑧
Jerusalem

Dead Sea

Arnon R.

IDUMEA

Mapping of the Sages by Chapter Number

ב

PREFACE

Allow me to open this preface with the statement that this work is not a monograph, in the sense of intending to present a new and original understanding of Judaism or Jewish thought. It is a research-based introduction to a selection of the more influential *Chakhamim* (Sages) of Israel's *Tannaitic* period. I treat just six Sages from the period, out of fifty-four named in the *Mishna*.[1] In this work, I endeavor to glean from the available sources those teachings which most influenced the Judaisms of the First Century CE, i.e. those of the two principal "schools" of the time and of the most prominent teachers to impact the religious climate. It is not the intent of this work to prove any theological (Christological) claims, but rather to paint a portrait of First-Century Jewish *hashqafah* (worldview).

I make no claim to infallibility and fully recognize the historiographical reality that a history such as this is, regardless of how earnestly I attempt to minimize it, bound to reflect some presuppositions that flavor my reading of the sources to some extent. *Errare humanum est* (to err is human). To whatever degree those presuppositions land me in error, I humbly apologize to my audience, but am hopeful that this would be as minimal as possible and that this work would offer something of value to the field of

---

[1] Shaye Cohen, "The Place of the Rabbi in Jewish Society of the Second Century," in *The Galilee in Late Antiquity* (ed. Lee I. Levine; New York, N.Y.: Jewish Theological Seminary Press, 1992), 157.

Biblical/First-Century Judaic Studies – a tool for the scholar, but also a help for any reader of the Scriptures.

My quotation of Scripture within this work, so as to provide consistency from a published translation, is from the *JPS Tanakh* (copyright 1917, Jerusalem Publication Society, public domain) for passages from the *Tanakh* (OT) and from the *Aramaic-English New Testament* (AENT; copyright 2008, used by permission of Netzari Press) for *B'rit Chadasha* (Renewed Covenant, i.e. "New Testament"[2]) references. This dual-translation approach is predicated upon my studied conviction that the *Urtext*[3] of the *B'rit Chadasha* was an Aramaic work rather than a Greek one, and thus a translation made from the Aramaic *Peshitta* is to be preferred.

The appearance of the plural form of "Judaism," i.e. "Judaisms," in this work might strike the reader as an odd choice, but it is done for good reason. It is not wholly accurate to view and/or present Judaism of the First Century CE as a monolithic entity – a belief system with only one face to it.[4] There were, in

---

[2] Note that the present author generally avoids this nomenclature due to its anti-Semitic origin and history, preferring the term *B'rit Chadasha* (Renewed Covenant), a term already introduced in this work and also treated in the glossary which follows the final chapter.

[3] Urtext: original or earliest known version of a text.

[4] Jacob Neusner, *Early Rabbinic Judaism: Historical Studies in Religion, Literature, and Art* (SJLA 13; Leiden: E. J. Brill, 1975); Douglas C. Mohrmann, course lectures, *New*

fact, at least three major sects, some of those with sub-sects beneath them, coexisting in the Holy Land during this era – some more peaceably than others. The principle sects were the Pharisees, the Sadducees, and the Zealots. Josephus also makes mention of a sect called the Therapeutae, and the Twentieth Century unveiled a unique Jewish community at Qumran called the *Yachad* now famous for their collection of significant manuscripts popularly known as the Dead Sea Scrolls. This was possibly an Essene sub-sect (but see chapter 7 for other possibilities) .

The Pharisaic Judaisms of this time could generally be classified under the schools of thought of two prominent rabbis who lived and taught in the early part of the First Century: Shammai and Hillel. These two figures are the subject of the next two chapters of this study. These two Jewish scholars, surprisingly in light of their deep impact on how First-Century Jews lived out their *halakhah*, receive not even so much as a mention in Josephus except possibly through their teachers Shemaiah (Sameas) and Avtalyon (Pollion), both of whom, ironically, were descended from Gentile converts to the Jewish faith (*b. Gittin* 57b).[5]

Besides these two was also Rabban Gamli'el haZaqen, a student and grandson of the afore-

---

Testament Survey (Grand Rapids, MI: Cornerstone University, Fall 2004).

[5] Or perhaps converts themselves, as per Emil Schürer, *Geschichte des jüdischen Volkes im Zeitalter Jesu Christi* (Leipzig, Germany: J. C. Hinrichs'sche Buchhandlung, 1898), 455.

mentioned Hillel, known fairly well in his own right, but perhaps better known through the fame achieved by his pupil Sha'ul Paulos haTarsi (Saul/Paul of Tarsus), the self-described "apostle born out of time" (1 Cor. 15:8) who wrote thirteen of the letters included in the canon of the *B'rit Chadasha*, the subject of our third study. The fourth study will center on Hillel's youngest student, Rabban Yochanan ben Zakkai, the first *Nasi* of the post-Temple era and, in many ways, the rabbi responsible for saving Judaism after the fall of Jerusalem in 70 CE.

Our fifth subject is Rabbi Aqiva ben Yosef, perhaps more of a Second Century figure but certainly not without influence in the late First Century CE. He is credited with teaching the generation of Sages which would preserve in writing much of Judaism's *Torah shebe'al peh* (oral tradition) and related commentary. The sixth and final subject of reflection will be Yeshua haNotzri, i.e. the central figure of the *B'rit Chadasha*.[6]

I have in mind that these six Jewish teachers influenced the Judaisms of the First Century more than any others, and thus their teachings, which

---

[6] The present author uses the name *Yeshua*, His given Hebrew name, for this figure to emphasize His Jewish background and character. The reader who may be more familiar with the Biblical Messiah by the name *Jesus* should be cognizant that the Yeshua who is the subject of this work's sixth chapter is the same figure, presented as Yeshua to free Him from the shackles of Hellenization that have sometimes served to obscure our ability to fully recognize His Jewish mind/worldview.

shaped the Jewish faith and the belief systems which derive therefrom, deserve some degree of reflection. Such reflection is necessary to an informed reading of the *B'rit Chadasha* in that these figures play into the clashing worldviews that comprise the backdrop of First Century Jewish life. The impact of these teachers was so deep that it can be seen in their own generation, certainly, but it is also still felt in this present age.

With the *Talmuds* (*Bavli* and *Yerushalmi*), none-theless, we are heirs to a rich history of Jewish tradition that has much to offer the student of Scripture. There are, admittedly, limitations to the reliability of the *Talmuds* for establishing historical-cultural context, as when it was codified in written form, it was several centuries removed from the Sages it presents. The *Mishna* portion took written form within the first few decades of the Third Century CE, but the *Gemara* sections were joined to that work quite a bit later. Levine rightly cautions, "To presume that the rabbinic rulings all go back to the first century and, more, that they antedate the destruction of the Temple in 70 is an act of faith, not history."[7]

The *Talmudic* literature remains, however, one of the few windows into the rabbinical teachings and politics of the First Century CE. It is lamentable that, as observed by the Rev. Roger David Aus of Berlin, Germany, "Many NT scholars today employ the

---

[7] Amy-Jill Levine, *The Misunderstood Jew: The Church and the Scandal of the Jewish Jesus* (New York, N.Y.: HarperOne, 2006), 27.

genuine problem of dating rabbinic sources… as a cheap pretext for not even considering them."[8] I have, for the most part, limited my usage of it to rulings and 'drashes attributed to the Sages presented in this present work, and to those portions which *Talmud* scholar Jacob Neusner has identified as pertaining to "Pre-70" Judaism.[9] Tyndale research fellow David Instone Brewer adds, "The most reliable details are the incidental ones, and the ones which occur in the earliest *Tannaitic* compilations (*Siphra, Siphré, Mekhiltha, Mishnah, Tosephta*),"[10] and I have also appealed to these sources. It is also incumbent upon the reader of *Talmud* to distinguish between which *sugyot* (passages) constitute legal pronouncements, which carry with them the imprimatur of Sinai, and which merely convey the opinions of the Sages. For the purposes of this work, more attention is paid to the latter.

Wherever extra-*Talmudic* material is available to support and/or clarify the *Talmudic* tradition, I have tried to consult those and make necessary adjustments or notations to reflect whatever those sources – e.g. Josephus, Philo, etc. – have to offer in augmenting or grounding the discussion. Rabbi Joseph Telushkin

---

[8] Roger David Aus, *'Caught in the Act', Walking on the Sea, and the Release of Barabbas Revisited* (South Florida Studies in the History of Judaism 157; Atlanta, Ga.: Scholars Press, 1997), x.

[9] Jacob Neusner, *The Mishnah: An Introduction* (Lanham, Md.: Jason Aronson, Inc., 2004; orig. 1989), 42-45.

[10] David Instone Brewer, "The Use of Rabbinic Material in Gospel Studies," *Tyndale Bulletin* 50.2 (1999): 289.

wisely observes, "In the ahistorical universe of the *Talmud*, followers argue down through the ages, the living argue with the dead, and followers may at times appear to precede those who influenced them."[11] In other words, it is much like the Bible in its non-linear presentation; it does not necessarily anchor itself to the western convention of chronology. My study of the rabbinical material (including both *Talmuds*, the *Tosefta*, the *Sifra* & *Sifré*, and the *Mekhiltha*) has led me to respect these sources as a history of interpretation and as a point of cultural reference. It is from this perspective that I make use of them in this work.

If reading this work leads to an interest in learning more from the *Talmud*, but tackling 63 volumes of halakhic discourse seems daunting – fear not. There are tools available to help ramp up to it slowly. There is a very good abridged version by Abraham Cohen which has been around since the 1930s called *Everyman's Talmud*. That single-volume work is a great place to start for those who are new to *Talmud*. For children who might take an interest in the *Talmudic* literature, there is also a very good series called *Talmud with Training Wheels*. *Pirqei Avot* is also a good place to begin, as it presents a series of proverb-like statements from the early Sages, which are expounded upon in a companion work called *Avot d'Rabbi Nathan*. These are all fairly easy to locate through amazon.com and other online vendors as well as through most public libraries.

---

[11] Joseph Telushkin, *Hillel: If Not Now, When?* (New York, N.Y.: Schocken Books, 2010), 83.

The reader might notice that all of the figures herein reflect some association with Pharisaic Judaism, a term which has been misunderstood by many as referring to some class of religious villain. I think and hope that after reading about these individuals and how dedicated they were to HaShem, however, that those presuppositions will fall away like scales from the eyes, and the reader will see that, like any other organization, there were both hypocrites and good role models operating under that *Weltanschauung* (worldview).

A growing number of believers, whether in the Messianic Judaism movement or in Hebrew Roots, have come to recognize the depth of the Jewish context which undergirds the whole of Scripture, including the *B'rit Chadasha*. Those who open this book with that appreciation already instilled might find the contents of the introduction to serve largely as review, but I believe the following sequence of background data to be necessary to establishing the value of such a volume as this. The hope is that the content herein would be of just as much benefit to those more learned on the subject as it is to the reader with less study in these specifics, albeit perhaps more in the way of apologetics than illumination.

As with all extra-Biblical sources, I invite and encourage my readers to "explore everything and hold fast to the good" (1 Thessalonians 5:21)... even and especially in this work, as I pray that whatever herein is good and free from interpretive misgiving would not fail to be of benefit to you in informing your reading of the Biblical text. To allow for easier accessibility for the reader, I have used standard English translations of all non-English sources. While there is a fair amount of Jewish vocabulary (whether Hebrew, Aramaic, or Yiddish) in this work, I have done my best to define any terms which might be new to a non-Jewish reader – both as they occur in

the text of this work and in a supplementary glossary at the end of this work.

I pray that this work is of value to readers as more than just a trivial pursuit of rabbinical politics, but as a tool in shaping your understanding of the cultural-historical context which underscored Jewish life in the First Century CE, including the *Netzari/ HaDerekh* movement... to inform your reading of the *B'rit Chadasha* text toward a more late-Second Temple perspective. **May HaShem be glorified.**

Brian Tice, M.Sci.
Professor of Jewish Studies
March 2014

 כ

SEMITIC TRANSLITERATION

Consonants			
א	' (but not noted at start of word)	מ, ם	m
ב	b or bb	נ, ן	n
ב	v	ס	s
ג	g or gg	ע	' (but not noted at the start of a proper name)
ג	gh		
ד	d or dd		
ד	dh	פ	p or pp
ה	h (if consonantal, but not noted if serving as a *matres lectionis*)	פ, ף	f
ו	w	צ, ץ	tz
ז	z	ק	q
ח	ch	ר	r
ט	t	שׂ	s
י	y	שׁ	sh
כּ, ךּ	k or kk	תּ	t or tt
כ, ך	kh	ת	th (if internal, but t if final)
ל	l		
Vowel Points			
ָ ַ ֲ	a	(י) ִ	i
ֶ ֱ	e	וֹ ָ ָ	o
(י) ֵ	ei	וּ	u

The Hebrew definite article is indicated by h plus the transliteration value of the attached vowel followed by a capitalized first letter of the form to which it is affixed, e.g. *haDerekh* (the way).

SIGLA & ABBREVIATIONS

General/Body

Arab.	Arabic
Aram.	Aramaic
BCE	Before Common Era (same as BC)
CE	Common Era (same as AD)
DSS	Dead Sea Scrolls
e.g.	*exempli gratia* (for example)
esp.	especially
Ger.	German
Grk.	Greek
Heb.	Hebrew
i.e.	*id est* (that is)
JPS	*Jewish Publication Society*
LXX/𝕲	*Septuagint* (Greek translation of Tanakh)
MT/𝔐	*Masoretic Text* (standard Hebrew Bible)
𝔓	Papyrus
ℚ	Qumran (location, aka S^ckhakhah)
sic.	*sic erat scriptum* (thus it had been written), meaning that the quote was transcribed as it was found in the original source, complete with errors, coloquialisms, etc.
𝕿	*Targum* (Aramaic translation) with supercript letter for version
Tanakh	Hebrew Bible (*Torah*, Prophets, & Writings)
Yid.	Yiddish
‖	parallel passage or *sugya*
ꟺ	*Samaritan Pentateuch*

Footnote Abbreviations

cf.	*confer* (contrast with, indicating a source with an opposing viewpoint)
ed./eds.	editor/editors; or sometimes also edition(s)
et al.	*et alii* (and others)
ibid.	*ibidem* (same as last footnote)
id.	*idem* (same author as in previous footnote)
loc. cit.	*loco citato* (same page/work cited previously)
op. cit.	*opere citato* (this work cited previously)
orig.	originally published
transl.	translation or translator
rev.	revised
s.v.	*sub verbo* (indicates an unattributed article in a reference work)
v. lec.	*verso lectio* (variant reading)

Books of the Tanakh (Standard SBL Abbreviations)
with transliterated Hebrew names in parenthesis

Note that the books with numerical designations, e.g. 1 Kings and 2 Kings, are not split into multiple books in the original Hebrew canon. These splits are a later development.

Gen	Genesis (*Bereshit*)
Exod	Exodus (*Shemot*)
Lev	Leviticus (*Wayyiqra*)
Num	Numbers (*B'midbar*)
Deut	Deuteronomy (*D'varim*)
Josh	Joshua (*Yehoshua*)
Judg	Judges (*Shofetim*)

1Sam	1 Samuel (*Sh'muel Alef*)
2Sam	2 Samuel (*Sh'muel Beit*)
1Kgs	1 Kings (*Malakhim Alef*)
2Kgs	2 Kings (*Malakhim Beit*)
Is	Isaiah (*Yeshayahu*)
Jer	Jeremiah (*Yirmeyahu*)
Ezek	Ezekiel (*Yechezk'el*)
Hos	Hosea (*Hoshea*)
Joel	Joel (*Yo'el*)
Amos	Amos
Obad	Obadiah (*Ovedyah*)
Jon	Jonah (*Yonah*)
Mic	Micah (*Mikhah*)
Nah	Nahum (*Nachum*)
Hab	Habakkuk (*Havakuk*)
Zeph	Zephaniah (*Tz'fanyah*)
Hag	Haggai
Zech	Zechariah (*Z'kharyah*)
Mal	Malachi
Ps	Psalms (*Tehillim*)
Job	Job (*Iyov*)
Prov	Proverbs (*Mishlei*)
Ruth	Ruth (*Rut*)
Song	Song of Songs/Solomon (*Shir haShirim*)
Eccl	Ecclesiastes (*Qoheleth*)
Lam	Lamentations (*Eikhah*)
Esth	Esther (*Ester*)
Dan	Daniel
Ezra	Ezra

Neh	Nehemiah (*Nechemyah*)
1Chron	1 Chronicles (*Divrei Hayamim Alef*)
2Chron	2 Chronicles (*Divrei Hayamim Bet*)

Books of the *B'rit Chadasha* (SBL Abbreviations)
Peshitta Order with transliterated Aramaic names in parenthesis

Matt	Matthew (*Mattityahu*)
Mark	Mark (*Marqus*)
Luke	Luke (*Luqa*)
John	John (*Yochanan*)
Acts	Acts (*Shlichim*)
Heb	Hebrews (*Ivri'im*)
Jas	James (*Ya'akov*)
Jude	Jude (*Yehudah*)
1Ptr	1 Peter (*Keefa Alef*)
2Ptr	2 Peter (*Keefa Bet*)
Rom	Romans
1Cor	1 Corinthians
2Cor	2 Corinthians
Gal	Galatians
Eph	Ephesians
Phil	Philippians
Col	Colossians
1Thess	1 Thessalonians[12]

---

[12] Note that what is commonly called 1 Thessalonians refers to a previous letter which is not in the canon, so it is actually at least the second epistle to that community, and 2 Thessalonians is likely a conflation of two later letters, either 3rd-4th or 4th-5th.

2Thess	2 Thessalonians
1Tim	1 Timothy
2Tim	2 Timothy
Titus	Titus
Phlm	Philemon
1Jn	1 John (*Yochanan Alef*)
2Jn	2 John (*Yochanan Bet*)
3Jn	3 John (*Yochanan Gimel*)
Rev	Revelation (*Hithgalut*)
Shep	Shepherd of Hermas[13]

Talmudic Abbreviations (with Translations)

b.	*Talmud Bavli* (Babylonian *Talmud*)
y.	*Talmud Yerushalmi* (Jerusalem *Talmud*)
m.	*Mishna* (*Tannaitic* teachings and rulings)

One of the above will lead an abbreviated citation, followed by one of the following 63 tractate titles. Note that the Mishna is part of Talmud Bavli, but since it has no counterpart in Talmud Yerushalmi, m. (by itself) indicates the Bavli Mishna, and b. connotes the Bavli Gemara.

---

[13] *Shepherd of Hermas* is an apocalyptic work included in every canonical list for the Christian New Testament (*B'rit Chadasha*) prior to the Council of Laodicea, which chose to exclude that book and the *Epistle of Barnabas*, presumably due to conflict between the content of those books and the Augustinian theology which prevailed at that council. It was cited as Scripture by Ecclesiastic Fathers Irenaeus, Clement of Alexandria, Athanasius, Didymus the Blind, *Papyrus Michigan* (3rd century) *Codex Sinaiticus* (4th century), and in the earlier works of Origin and Tertullian.

Arak.	*Arakin* (Estimations)
Av. Zara	*Avodah* Zarah (Strange Worship)
Bab. Qam.	*Baba Qamma* (First Gate)
Bab. Mez.	*Baba Mezia* (Middle Gate)
Bab. Bat.	*Baba Bathra* (Last Gate)
Bek.	*Bekorot* (Firstlings)
Ber.	*Berakot* (Blessings)
Bik.	*Bikkurim* (Firstfruits)
Chag.	*Chagigah* (Festival Offering)
Chul.	*Chullin* (Profane things)
Dem.	*Demai* (Doubtful)
Eduy.	*Eduyyot* (Testimonies)
Eruv.	*Eruvin* (Blendings)
Git.	*Gittin* (Bills of Divorce)
Hor.	*Horayot* (Rulings)
Kel.	*Kelim* (Vessels)
Ker.	*Keritot* (Excisions from the Community)
Ket.	*Kethubot* (Marriage Contracts)
Kil.	*Kilayim* (Mixtures)
Ma'as.	*Ma'aserot* (Tithes)
Ma'as Shen.	*Ma'aser Sheni* (Second Tithe)
Mak.	*Makkot* (Floggings)
Maksh.	*Makshirin* (Fluids rendering things Defiled)
Megill.	*Megillah* (Scroll)
Meg. Ta'an.	*Megillat* Ta'anit (Scroll of the Fast)
Meil.	*Meilah* (Defilement of Consecrated Things)
Men.	*Menachot* (Meal Offerings)
Mid.	*Middot* (Dimensions)

Miq.	*Miqvaot* (Immersion Pools)
Moed Qat.	*Moed Qatan* (Half-Holidays)
Ned.	*Nedarim* (Vows)
Neg.	*Nega'im* (They that Suffer Tzara'at)
Naz.	*Nazir* (Nazarite)
Nid.	*Niddah* (The Menstruant)
Ohol.	*Oholot* (Defilement of Tents)
Orlah	*Orlah* (Ordinances per. to Lev. 19:23)
P. Avot	*Pirqei* Avot (Ethics of the Fathers)
Par.	*Parah* (Red Heifer)
Peah	*Peah* (Harvesting)
Pes.	*Pesachim* (Passover Lambs)
Qidd.	*Qiddushin* (Consecrations)
Qinn.	*Qinnim* (Offering of Doves)
Qod.	*Qoddashim* (Holy Things)
R. haSh.	*Rosh haShanah* (Head of the Year)
Sanh.	*Sanhedrin* (Court of Justice)
Sem.	*Semachot* (Rejoicings)
Shabb.	*Shabbat* (Sabbath)
Sheb.	*Shebu'ot* (Oaths)
Shebh.	*Shebhiit* (Sabbatical Year)
Sheq.	*Sheqalim* (Sheqels, Temple-Tribute)
Sot.	*Sotah* (Adultery)
Suk.	*Sukkah* (Booth)
Ta'an.	*Ta'anit* (Fast)
Tam.	*Tamid* (The Continual Offering)
Teb. Yom.	*Tebul Yom* (Impurities requiring Same-Day Immersion)
Tem.	*Temura* (Substitution)

Ter.	*Terumot* (Heave Offerings)
Toh.	*Tohorot* (Cleannesses)
Uqtz.	*Uqtzin* (Fruits Defiled through Envelope)
Yad.	*Yada'im* (Hands)
Yeb.	*Yebamot* (Levirate)
Yom.	*Yoma* (Day of Atonement)
Zav.	*Zavim* (They that Suffer Flux)

Other Rabbinic Literature

ARN	*Avot d'Rabbi Nathan* (Midrashic literature)
Mekh.	*Mekhiltha* (Measure), 2nd Century Exodus commentary
Tos.	*Tosefta* (Additions, Supplements)

Midrash Rabbah[14]

Ber. R.	*Bereshit Rabbah* (On Genesis)
Shem. R.	*Shemot Rabbah* (On Exodus)
Wayy. R.	*Wayyiqra Rabbah* (On Leviticus)
Bem. R.	*B'midbar Rabbah* (On Numbers)
D'var. R.	*D'varim Rabbah* (On Deuteronomy)
Shir R.	*Shir haShirim Rabbah* (On Song of Songs)
Ruth R.	*Ruth Rabbah* (On Ruth)
Ester R.	*Ester Rabbah* (On Esther)
Qoh. R.	*Qoheleth Rabbah* (On Ecclesiastes)
Eikh. R.	*Eikhah Rabbathi* (On Lamentations)
Pesiq. R.	*Pesiqta Rabbathi* (On Sabbaths/Feasts)

---

[14] *Midrash Rabbah* is a collection containing both exegetical midrashim (*Bereshit Rabbah* and *Eikhah Rabbathi*) and homiletical *midrashim* (all the rest in the list).

Kallah R.	*Kallah Rabbathi* (On the Bride)
Tanch.	*Tanchuma*, aka *Yelamdenu* (On the *Torah*)[15]

Abbreviated Rabbi Names

Maimonides	Rabbi Moshe ben Maimon (12th-13th C.)
Rambam	Rabbi Moshe ben Maimon (12th-13th C.)
Rashi	Rabbi Shlomo Itzchaqi (11th – 12th C.)
Ribaz	Rabbi Yochanan ben Zakkai (1st C. CE)

Nota bene: Abbreviations like the above are common in Judaism; this list only contains those referenced in this work. There are many more in use in the rabbinic writings.

For specialized terms used in this work,
see the "Jewish Jargon" glossary at the back.

---

[15] *Tanchuma* is a homiletical midrash on the entire *Torah* composed by Rabbi Tanchuma bar Abba. Dating is uncertain, possibly 6th-7th Century; provenance seems to be most likely *Eretz-Israel*.

ת

REFLECTING ON THE RABBIS

SAGE INSIGHT INTO
FIRST-CENTURY JEWISH THOUGHT

לִימּוּד הָרַבָּנִים
תּוֹבָנָה חָכְמָה עַל הַשְׁקָפָה
יְהוּדִית בַּמֵּאָה הָרִאשׁוֹנָה

5777

CHAPTER 1

INTRODUCTION

מָבוֹא

First Century Judaism has been described as the religion's "creative period." The influences upon the Judaisms – plural – of the First Century CE come from several significant sources. Leading up into that definitive century we find ourselves in the birth epoch of modern rabbinical Judaism with the great Pharisaic *Tanna'im* Hillel and Shammai. Their respective schools continue to teach from their voices as the First Century unfolds and throughout its duration.

Aqiva is another iconic rabbi of the era, closing out the century with his endorsement of Bar Kokhba as the Messiah and then retracting that endorsement. Despite this hiccup in judgment, he remains a major influence on the politics of First Century Judaism and even into the following century. The extent to which his voice can still be heard in the rabbis of our own time puts him in the historiographical category of "great," i.e. having an impact lasting more than a century. Hillel and Aqiva constitute the bookends for the timeline pertaining to the present work, with other rabbis filling the space between them.

A rather significant rabbi emerges at the close of the Second Temple era in a quite heroic role: Rabban Yochanan ben Zakkai, who was Aqiva's rabbi/mentor. He did much in redefining Jewish observance in the absence of the Temple and was arguably the strongest catalyst for ensuring that Judaism would continue in the aftermath of Jerusalem's destruction. The teachings of Rabban Gamli'el are, in many ways, an extension of those of his famous grandfather Hillel, but we will see in our chapter on him that there is also enough uniqueness to him and his students to warrant a separate treatment. Among his most prominent students was Sha'ul haTarsi (Saul of Tarsus), who authored thirteen or fourteen epistles of the *B'rit Chadasha*.[16]

It cannot be stated strongly enough nor often enough that the Bible is, from cover to cover, a thoroughly Jewish book. It was written entirely by Jewish authors (most of them ethnic Jews, though the thirtieth chapter of Proverbs which was written by an Ishmaelite/Gentile convert named Agur[17]). Some scholars dispute the Jewishness of Luke, but if we consider the commonness in the Biblical era of the practice of taking on a "local" name, it can be reasoned that he might very well have been a Jew who adopted or accepted a Greco-Romanized name. There are certainly precedents for it even in Scripture, e.g. several biblical figures taking on Persian names while in captivity – Hadassah/Esther (Esther 2:7),

---

[16] It is uncertain who the author of Hebrews is, but some scholars believe it is Sha'ul. The style of Greek is very different from that of any other *B'rit Chadasha* book, but if the original language was a Semitic language, as asserted by Clement of Alexandria's *Hypotyposes*, the style of Greek (more Classical than Koine) says more about the translator than it does about the author and would not preclude Pauline authorship. $\mathfrak{P}^{46}$ is a collection of Pauline epistles placing Hebrews after Romans, which in agreement with Eastern Orthodoxy suggests Pauline authorship.

[17] Tewoldemedhin Habtu, "Proverbs," in Tokunboh Adayemo, ed., *Africa Bible Commentary* (Nairobi, Kenya: WordAlive, 2006), 784; Kathleen A. Farmer, *Who Knows What is Good? A Commentary on the Books of Proverbs and Ecclesiastes* (Grand Rapids, Mich.: Wm. B. Eerdmans, 1991).

Daniel/Belteshazzar, Hannaniah/Shadrach, Mishael/
Meshack, and Azariah/Abed-Nego (Daniel 1:6-7).

A similar practice can be found in the Roman
Empire of the First Century CE as well, though it was
not so much that names were changed as that a
person often had two names from birth. A well-
known example of this is Sha'ul haTarsi using both
that name and the Romanized name Paulos/Paul
(Acts 13:9). The often-preached notion that Sha'ul's
name was changed to Paulos (Paul) following his
Damascus Road encounter is unfounded.[18] The
evidence bears out that the Roman citizen's *praenomen*
(forename) being coupled with a second name — a
cognomen — began well before Sha'ul's birth and
extends well beyond it.[19] This dual-naming was
required of all Roman citizens,[20] and Sha'ul's
citizenship was both Hebrew and Roman (Acts 21:39;
22:3, 27-29).[21]

---

[18] Timothy J. Hegg, *The Letter Writer: Paul's background
and Torah Perspective* (Marshfield, Mo: First Fruits of Zion,
2002), 29-31.

[19] Benet Salway, "What's in a Name? A Survey of Roman
Onomastic Practice from c.700 B.C. to 700 A.D," *Journal of
Roman Studies 84* (1994): 124-145.

[20] E. Randolph Richards & Brandon J. O'Brien, *Misreading
Scripture with Western Eyes: Removing Cultural Blinders to
Better Understand the Bible* (Downers Grove, Ill.: IVP Books,
2012), 99.

[21] John McRay, *Paul: His Life and Teaching* (Grand Rapids,
Mich.: Baker Academic, 2003), 25-27.

Sha'ul is not the only Jew in the *B'rit Chadasha* with a Romanized name. He lists Aristarchus, Marcus (identified as a first cousin to Bar-Naba), and a "Yehoshua, who is called Justus" as being "of the circumcision," i.e. Jews, in Colossians 4:10-11. Sylvanus, aka Silas, is also identified as a Roman citizen (and thus required to have the added *cognomen*) as well (Acts 16:37; 2 Cor. 1:19; 1 Thess. 1:1; 2 Thess. 1:1). Though we do not have another name (presumably his Semitic *praenomen*) for Luke, it would not be untenable to surmise that he would not have escaped the application of that dual-name legislation.

Evidence internal to the Biblical text also points to Luke being a Jew rather than a Gentile. Romans 3:2 indicates that to the Jews (not the Gentiles) "were entrusted the words of Elohim" – which has been understood to mean that Scripture was to be penned through Jewish hands.[22] It is also apparent from Luke's historiography, i.e. what he chooses to include and what he chooses to omit, that though he has an "insider" level experience and knowledge in things Jewish – e.g. the *Tanakh*, Temple practices, Jewish traditions – he also assumes the same of his audience. A Gentile would tend to presuppose a lack of familiarity with Jewish culture, but Luke falls in line with every other (Jewish) writer of Scripture in his

---

[22] Thomas S. McCall, (Mar 1996), "Was Luke a Gentile?" *Levitt Letter* 18 (3). Online: http://www.levitt.com/essays/luke.

expectation that his readers intimately know Judaism and Jewish thought.[23]

An integral facet to the study of Scripture is the necessity of recognizing that, as a Jewish product, the Bible is *not* a Western text, that is, written with a Western mind nor with the concerns which that entails. What this means is that the Bible will not tend to be as concerned with the chronology of events or the details that comprise them as a Western world work would be. Many a misinterpretation of Scripture is directly attributable to Systematic Theology's approach to the Bible. By forcing a Western grid onto an Eastern text, i.e. asking Western world questions of the Bible which it never intended to address nor answer, the Western exegete hinders the authorial/ Authorial intent of the biblical text from becoming apparent. Goldingay goes as far as to warn, "If Systematic Theology did not exist, it might seem unwise to invent it."[24]

The Ancient Near-Eastern mind is much more concerned with observing cyclical aspects of an event

---

[23] Stephen L. Harris, *Understanding the Bible* (Palo Alto, CA: Mayfield, 1985), 266-268; Rick Strelan, "Was Luke a Jew or Gentile?" in *Luke the Priest: The Authority of the Author of the Third Gospel* (Burlington, Vt.: Ashgate Publishing, 2008), 102-110.

[24] John Goldingay, "Biblical Narrative and Systematic Theology," in *Between Two Horizons: Spanning New Testament Studies and Systematic Theology* (ed. Joel B. Green and Max Turner; Grand Rapids, Mich.: Wm. B. Eerdmans, 2000): 123-42 (138).

than plotting the details onto a timeline.[25] A good example is the repeating cycle which is so difficult to miss in the Book of Judges. Over and over, the reader sees Israel prospering... until some grievous sin creeps in (almost always idolatry), which sets in motion the "judges cycle": sin leads to Israel falling to an oppressor, followed by repentance resulting in HaShem raising up a *shofet* (judge, but in the "deliverer" sense rather than in the courtroom sense) who is successful in freeing Israel from its oppressor... only to reenter the cycle all over again after a relatively short time of prosperity.[26]

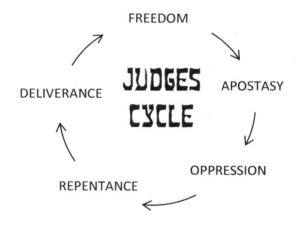

FREEDOM

JUDGES CYCLE

DELIVERANCE

APOSTASY

REPENTANCE

OPPRESSION

---

[25] The present author credits Christina Oakes for the insight presented in this paragraph; presented at Comstock Park, Mich.: *Adat Eytz Chayim*, March 2013.

[26] Marvin A. Sweeney, *Tanak: A Theological and Critical Introduction to the Jewish Bible* (Minneapolis, Minn.: Fortress Press, 2012), 197-98; chart by present author, based on Sweeney, op. cit., 193-98.

Cyclical thinking applies to more than the placement of details within the narrative of an event, however. It undergirds the workings of a Hebraic mind at the basest level. For a Jew, the statement, "I am the beginning and the end" conveys not the image of linear progression, i.e. a timeline, but rather a circle with a single point which marks the inception of a thing and its culmination – the end of the thing being not the end of all things but being simultaneously the end of the one and the start of the next... like laps on a running track. The point is not to move from point A to point B, but to continually return to the same Source of all good, i.e. HaShem.[27] It makes a difference in how we understand the biblical text to come to it with this in mind.

Now, bringing this understanding to bear on the biblical text, the reader enters a literary world where the abstract mind is alien, and concrete imagery takes its place. The imagery it takes to make a text memorable to a reader, or more likely a hearer, of the Word requires mnemonic elements such as thematic structure to trump certain things that the Western mind expects to find. It is a world that, especially for a Westerner, requires some reorientation (toward deoccidentation[28]) on the reader's part. There is a

---

[27] Thorleif Boman, *Das Hebräische Denken im Vergleich mit dem Griechischen* (2nd ed.; Göttingen: Vandenhoeck & Ruprecht, 1960; orig. 1954), 49-50.

[28] As *orientation* literally means "turning eastward," *occidentation* conveys "turning westward." The present author's coining of the term *deoccidentation* is intended to suggest to the reader that he or she set aside the presuppositional trappings of western world thinking and try to *"deoccident"*

deep, raging river of cultural difference to be crossed.[29]

With the principal players in the text of Scripture, and in particular the *B'rit Chadasha*, all being Jewish, it stands to reason that each was influenced by at least one of the Jewish teachers who impacted the who, what, when, where, and how of his or her *halakhah* – thus the imprimatur for this study is established. Not knowing the teachers behind the figures encountered in Scripture – e.g. the Pharisees, the Sadducees, the Scribes, the Sanhedrin – puts the modern Western reader at a distinct disadvantage. Understanding the *B'rit Chadasha*'s cast of characters becomes a vastly easier undertaking when the reader has an understanding of the principal influences of the time and place in view in the passage. In recent years, there has been a broadening of the realization that, as Skarsaune puts it:

> Scholars used to know a lot about the Pharisees, which did not surprise readers of the New Testament because to them the Pharisees seemed very familiar. It therefore comes as somewhat of a surprise that scholars in recent years have come to question much of established 'knowledge' about the Pharisees. But if one looks into the matter more

---

so that these texts' natural eastern world dynamics are not suppressed.

[29] J. Scott Duvall & J. Daniel Hays, *Grasping God's Word: A Hands-On Approach to Reading, Interpreting, and Applying the Bible* (2nd ed.; Grand Rapids, Mich.: Zondervan, 2005), 22.

closely, one can hardly escape the conclusion that the now widespread caution is well founded.[30]

The propensity of the First-Century Jew to prefer to follow the lead of his (or occasionally her) chosen Sage over the lead of a secular Roman mandate caused the Jewish people to be much more resistant to Hellenization than their pagan counterparts in the Empire. If a student's Sage resisted Hellenization, so also went the student. Few rabbis assented to the assimilation Rome was looking for, as a matter of religious consciousness, and so the Greek culture, though prominent all around the habitation of the Jewish people, and even to some extent among them, never successfully overtook them as it did their pagan neighbors. Hellenism failed to undermine the Jewish religious order and likewise failed to alter in any significant way the Jewish *halakhah*. Tripolitis asserts, "Neither did the Greek language, which had now become the *lingua franca* of the civilized world, ever completely replace Aramaic as the language of the people nor Hebrew as the major vehicle of literature."[31]

With the probable exception of *Beit Hillel* and *Beit Shammai*, the *Beit haMidrash* (house of study) of the late Second Temple era, both in *Eretz-Yisrael* and in the *Diaspora*, was less like a formal academy or

---

[30] Oskar Skarsaune, *In the Shadow of the Temple: Jewish Influences on Early Christianity* (Downers Grove, Ill.: IVP Academic, 2002), 117.

[31] Antonía Tripolitis, *Religions of the Hellenistic-Roman Age* (Grand Rapids, Mich.: Wm. B. Eerdmans, 2002), 64.

institution than many imagine, and much more, on the whole, like small "disciple circles."[32] Dr. Catherine Hézser, a professor of Jewish Studies at the University of London, describes the rabbinic context of the first two centuries of the common era thus: "Study houses in Roman Palestine seem to have been private houses or apartments or public buildings where people customarily met to study *Torah...* [rather than] 'rabbinic academies'."[33] In the First Century, it was generally quite easy to discern from which rabbi a student was receiving his or her religious studies. Students, or *talmidim*, were not merely apprenticed to a Sage to learn content, but to actually mirror that Sage in every detail of life. It was said that a *talmid* (apprentice or student) would follow so closely behind his rabbi, in order to imitate his every word and gesture, that he would be covered with the dust kicked up by the Sage's sandals.[34]

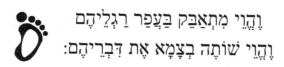

וֶהֱוֵי מִתְאַבֵּק בַּעֲפַר רַגְלֵיהֶם
וֶהֱוֵי שׁוֹתֶה בְצָמָא אֶת דִּבְרֵיהֶם:

---

[32] David Goodblatt, *Rabbinic Instruction in Sasanian Babylonia* (Leiden: E. J. Brill, 1975), 267; Catherine Hézser, *The Social Structure of the Rabbinic Movement in Roman Palestine* (Tübingen: Mohr-Siebeck, 1997), 492

[33] Hézser, op. cit., 213-14.

[34] *Talmud Bavli, Mishna, Pirqei Avot* 1:4 "Become dusty in the dust of their feet, and imbibe their words thirstily." (transl. of Aramaic text shown at the bottom of this page).

The Sages who left the deepest imprint on First Century CE Judaism, in the estimation of the present author, number six. Shammai and Hillel were contemporary to one another, each one founding a rabbinical school very different from the other on nearly every interpretive matter. Gamli'el I, mentioned by name in the *B'rit Chadasha*, was the grandson of Hillel and, as one would expect, followed very closely in his ancestor's sandal tracks. The youngest of Hillel's students was Rabban Yochanan ben Zakkai, who is said to have "saved Judaism" after the fall of Jerusalem in 70 CE. Aqiva comes on scene a bit later, closing out the First Century and spilling over into the Second – perhaps the last of the influential Second Temple Sages. All five of these have left a mark on Judaism which not only shaped some essential elements of the Jewish worldview (*hashqafah*) of their own time but continue to define Jewish thought today. The same (or greater) can be said of the sixth great Sage, Yeshua haNotzri, Who, in a sense, needs no introduction at all… yet could also be classed the most misunderstood of these figures, and thus, He needs a much more culturally-nuanced introduction than is normally availed to us.

The principal source on Yeshua is the *B'rit Chadasha* of the Bible, and for the first four Sages listed, the following:

- Flavius Josephus: a Jewish historian and author of many ancient histories with a Jewish focus, most famously *Antiquitates Judaicae* (*Antiquities of the Jews;* 20 volumes, the Aramaic originals now lost, but the content preserved in a later Greek translation thereof) and *Bellum Judaicum* (*Jewish Wars;* 7 volumes).

- *Mekhiltha* (מְכִילְתָא): an ancient *halakhic midrash* on *Shemot* (Exodus) reflecting the Aqiva tradition. Two versions exist, one compiled by his student Rabbi Shim'on bar Yochai and the other by Rabbi Ishmael. This work dates to ca. 250 CE.[35] It is sometimes also referred to by its Hebrew name *Middah*. Both titles translate to English as "measure, rule." [36]

- *Midrash Rabbah* (מִדְרָשׁ רַבָּה): About 400-450 CE, shortly after the *Talmud Yerushalmi* came to take its final form, the *Midrash Rabbah* emerged as an exegetical work on the five books of the *Torah*, as well as Ruth, Lamentations, Song of Songs, and Ecclesiastes.[37]

- *Sifra* (סִפְרָא): the companion to *Mekhiltha* covering Leviticus. Companion volumes corresponding to Numbers and Deuteronomy were called *Sifré* (סִפְרִי) but have, save a few portions, been lost. Genesis is not known to have ever had a volume. These works date to about 250 CE.

---

[35] Jacob Neusner, *Rabbinic Literature: An Essential Guide* (Nashville, Tenn.: Abingdon Press, 2005), 52.

[36] *Nota bene:* The original work is no longer extant, except in a few small fragments, but these fragments have been collected and published by Hoffman in the work cited here. Allusions to the work are found in medieval rabbinical writings. See David Zvi Hoffman, "Mechilta des R. Simon b. Jochai," *HaPeles I-IV* (1900-04).

[37] Jacob Neusner, *Rabbinic Literature*, 74-89.

- *Talmud Bavli* (תַּלְמוּד בַּבְלִי): aka the Babylonian *Talmud*, more of a history of interpretation than what a modern scholar would consider a commentary, but useful in its cataloging of rabbinical teachings from some of Judaism's most renowned Sages. Comprised of the *Mishna* (com-7piled by Yehudah the Prince ca. 200 – 220 CE and divided into six orders of seven to twelve tractates each) and the *Gemara* (named from the Aramaic verb "to study," codified ca. 600 CE). Levine observes, "The *Talmud* happily puts into conversation teachers who lived centuries and hundreds of miles apart."[38]

- *Talmud Yerushalmi* (תַּלְמוּד יְרוּשַׁלְמִי): aka Jerusalem *Talmud*, the "shorter" *Talmud*; produced in *Eretz-Yisrael*, but for whatever reason, never as popular as its Babylonian counterpart. It does, however, contain some data which the *Talmud Bavli* does not, and thus finds its value for this present project. Dating for this *Talmud* slightly predates that of the *Gemara* of its Babylonian counterpart, set at about the 375-425 CE.

- *Tosefta* (תּוֹסֶפְתָּא): Supplements to the *Mishna* compiled by Rabbi Nehemiah, a student to Rabbi Aqiva, in the late Second Century CE (*Mishnaic* Period), reportedly in 189 CE.[39] *Tosefta*

---

[38] Amy-Jill Levine, *The Misunderstood Jew: The Church and the Scandal of the Jewish Jesus* (New York, N.Y.: HarperOne, 2006), 27.

[39] Avraham ben David, *Seder HaQabbalah l'haRavad* (Jerusalem, 1971), 16; but Jacob Neusner, *Rabbinic Literature: An Essential Guide* (Nashville, Tenn.: Abingdon Press, 2005), 19 dates *Tosefta* at ca. 300 CE.

often attributes laws that are anonymous in the *Mishna* to specific *Tanna'im* (*Mishnaic* Sages). This is considered "com-mentary" on the *Mishna*, thus not enjoying the same authoritative status, though it is the standard reference work on the *Mishna* and might be classed "deuterocanonical" in the *Talmudic* corpus. It is written in *Mishnaic* Hebrew, with some Aramaic.

The *Talmud* quotes one of its Sages as saying, "To what is a scholar likened? To a flask containing aromatic ointment. When it is unstopped, the fragrance is diffused; when it is stopped, the frangrance is not diffused" (*b. Avodah Zarah* 35b). Each of the Sages presented herein has much to teach us – far more than is contained in these pages. Consult the reading recommendations at the end of each biographical chapter and the bibliography at the end of this work, and let these Sages nourish your soul. Enjoy your time **reflecting on the rabbis**.

CHAPTER 2

SHAMMAI HAZAQEN

שַׁמַּאי הַזָּקֵן

> ### *"Make Torah a fixed duty;*
> ### *say little, and do much."*
> ### *(Pirqei Avot 1:15)*

As Shammai haZaqen is the least likely from the cast of Sages in this work to be lauded from the *bimah* of the local synagogue, he shall be treated first. Shammai bears the popular reputation of being a rabble-rouser – the "revolutionary" among the Sages to be reflected upon herein. The present author would challenge the reader, however, to set aside such judgment and to consider that perhaps that reputation is the result of over-villainization. Shammai might be best understood if approached with the presupposition that he is perhaps the most misunderstood figure in Pharisaic Judaism.

Shammai was a native of *Eretz-Yisrael* – a carpenter by trade – born in about 50 CE. Apart from this, not much is known about Shammai's life prior to becoming a *Torah* scholar. The Sanhedrin in Israel had two appointed seats called *zughot*, the higher of which was the *Nasi* (president), held by Hillel (the subject of the next chapter) in Shammai's time; and the other, titled *Av Beit Din* (head of the Sanhedrin) was held by Menachem,[40] initially (i.e. about 35 BCE). Menachem,

---

[40] This Menachem is often referred to as "Menachem the Essene," but he was more likely a Zealot. He is most probably the author of the *Damascus Covenant* document, which gave definition to a community at Qumran which shared the site with the *Yachad* community. Menachem left Jerusalem and

who had fully submitted himself to the authority of Hillel, withdrew from the post in 20 BCE, and Shammai, who was not devoted to Hillel at all, was appointed to take his place (*m. Chagigah* 2:2).

Without question, Shammai held to a practice of rendering *Torah* in the strictest and most rigid possible sense.[41] An often-quoted comparison of Shammai to his contemporary rival Hillel quips, "Man should be always as meek as Hillel, and not so quick-tempered as Shammai" (*b. Shabbat* 30b). The statement has been characterized as condemning Shammai. Consider for a moment the possibility that it is, rather, a cautionary note to any who might aspire to emulate his insistence on a strict *halakhic* standard. The message is that even within the faith community, people whose motives are as pure as his are rare. It is an admonition to be certain to act from a pure *kawwanah* (כַּוָּנָה; i.e. motive) rather than from a position of prideful arrogance.

---

the mainstream Jewish community in 20 BCE, when Shammai became Nasi of the Sanhedrin, and took 160 with him in his departure. The statements in the *Damascus Covenant* document about "*Ish haKazav*" (Man of Lies) likely have Shammai in mind, and the "*Anshei Milchama*" (Men of War) would be the students of *Beit Shammai See* Harvey Falk, *Jesus the Pharisee: A New Look at the Jewishness of Jesus* (Eugene, Ore.: Wipf & Stock, 2003; orig. 1985), 53-4.

[41] H.D. Mantel, "The Development of the Oral Law during the Second Temple Period," in Michael Avi-Yonah, & Zvi Baras, eds., *The World History of the Jewish People: Sociey. and Religion in the Second Temple Period* (Jerusalem: Massada Publishing Ltd., 1977), 62; Nathan Isaacs, "The Law and the 'Law of Change,'" *University of Pennsylvania Law Review* 65 (1917): 659-79, 748-63.

Shammai was deeply devoted to the Jewish faith, and zealous to guard it against the threat of pagan contamination.[42]

Though Hillel would likely have seen Shammai's approach as akin to a doctor only willing to see healthy patients, Shammai's *hashqafah* (worldview) was more like that of Jeff, the director of a police academy which operated out of a community college, when it came to light that some of his cadets had been bullying non-academy students. He alerted the college staff that he did not approve of their conduct, and asked that we let him know who it is if we witness it. He said, "That is not the kind of person I want in my academy. We don't need any more of that kind of cop out there on there streets; there are too many already!" There would soon be at least one rabbi in *Eretz-Yisrael* who would prove Shammai's concern to be well-founded by bringing such dishonor to the First-Century rabbinic scene. The *Mishna* makes an example of one named Rabbi Elisha ben Abuyah. Like Shammai, he came from a wealthy and distinguished family. Like Shammai, hehad become a *Torah* scholar of high standing. Unlike Shammai, he deserted Biblical faith in favor of religious heresy and Roman politics, becoming an enemy of the *am segolah* (literally "treasured people;" i.e. the Israelites).[43]

So strict was Shammai's *halakhic* standard that he would have obligated his son at a very young age to

---

[42] Joseph Telushkin, *Hillel: If Not Now, When?* (New York, N.Y.: Schocken Books, 2010), 145.

[43] Ibid. 147.

observe the fast of Yom Kippur had his friends not succeeded in dissuading him from it (*b. Yoma* 77b, *Tos. Yoma* 4:2). When his grandson was just a newborn infant, Shammai took it upon himself to cut an opening in the roof over his daughter-in-law's bedroom so that his grandson's quarters would meet the definition of a *sukkah* for Sukkot (*m. Sukkah* 2:8), allowing him to look up at the stars. Whatever criticism one might muster up against Shammai, however, he could never be accused of inconsistency. The strict standatd that defined his rulings as Sage also defined him as a father and grandfather, as these two *sugyot* (passages or pericopae) have illustrated.

Shammai and Hillel became known for their very vocal and very public *halakhic* debates, and their respective students projected the same fervor in their interactions with the opposing *Beit* as did their respective Sages. Shammai's interpretation of Deuteronomy's allowance for divorce (24:1) was that the circumstances which would warrant such action were so limited that only infidelity on the part of the wife would qualify as meeting the *Torah's* "act of indecency" standard (*m. Gittin* 9:10). Ironically, the strict position that Shammai took on divorce resulted in his positions on acceptable conduct for wives being much more lenient and liberal than those held by *Beit Hillel*. In fact, in 55 of their 316 debates,[44] Shammai is judged to have ruled more leniently than Hillel.

---

[44] David Friedman, *At the Feet of Rabbi Gamaliel: Rabbinic Influence in Paul's Teachings* (Clarksville, Md.: Lederer Books, 2013), 51.

Another of Shammai's famous (albeit minor) arguments with Hillel was over whether an egg lain on the Sabbath was kosher to eat. Shammai held that it was because man (not the hen) was created for the Shabbat, but Hillel countered that it was not because the hen had violated Shabbat by laboring to lay it (*m. Beitzah* 1:1). This is another case in which Shammai is found taking the more lenient view. At times, it seems that whichever position one Sage took, the other felt an obligation to oppose it, regardless of his general inclination on the matter. So rancorous was the rivalry between the two schools at times that it is said, no doubt hyperbolically, that before the two of them, there had never been a *machaloqet* (dispute) in Israel (*y. Chagigah* 2:2). Even Shammai's practice of beginning to make prepara-tions for the Sabbath at the start of the week came under fire from Hillel, whose teaching and personal practice was to set aside only the day prior for Sabbath preparations (*b. Beitzah* 16a).

There was even disagreement over how one ought to be positioned for the daily recitations of the *Shema*. While Hillel's leniency allowed for great variation of personal interpretation to dictate the praxis, Shammai took the instructions of Deutero-nomy 6:4-9 to be precise and literal. He prescribed that its verbage mandated that the *ma'ariv* (evening) recitation be made laying down, but that one must stand when repeating it in the *shacharit* (morning) liturgy, "for it is written: 'when you lie down and when you rise up' [Deuteronomy 6:7]" (*m. Berakhot* 1:3).

It should be noted that these famous disputes were never over "moral matrix" matters like whether "you shall not murder" could in some way be side-stepped. On the most significant matters, including tithing (*m. Demai* 6:6), all of the Pharisees were in agreement.[45] These debates focused on the fine points of *halakhic* interpretation – such as on whether it was permissible to tell a bride she looked beautiful if that was untrue. Shammai insisted that a lie was a lie, and any lie is a sin. Hillel countered that every bride is beautiful on her wedding day (*b. Kethubot* 16b-17a). While on the surface, these disputes might call to mind the arguments between Moshe and Korach (Numbers 16), the *Mishna* characterizes the Hillel-Shammai debates as essential to the purpose of determining the true application of important *Torah* principles, "for the sake of Heaven" (*Pirqei Avot* 5:17). *Talmud* scholar Jacob Neusner expounds:

> In my religion, argument forms a mode of divine service, as much as prayer: reasoned debate on substantive issues, debate founded on respect for the other and made possible by shared premises. That kind of contention is not only a gesture of honor and respect for the other, but in the context

---

[45] Israel Ben-Shalom, *The School of Shammai and the Zealots' Struggle against Rome* (Jerusalem: Ben Gurion University of the Negev Press, 1993), 238-39; Ephraim. E. Urbach, *The Sages: Their Concepts and Beliefs* (Jerusalem: Hebrew University Magnes Press, 1971), 531n94.

of the *Torah*, it forms the gift of intellect on the altar of the *Torah*.[46]

Shammai and Hillel generally treated each other "with affection and friendship" (*b. Yebamot* 14b). On one matter, there is even record of *Beit Shammai* changing its ruling to align with that of *Beit Hillel*. This is presented in both the *Mishna* and the *Talmud Yerushalmi*. *Beit Shammai* initially ruled that a heave offering contaminated by an unclean *terumah* became unclean, but after hearing *Beit Hillel's* opposite ruling and the reasoning for it, they adopted the ruling of the opposing house (*m. Terumot* 5:4; *y. Terumot* 5:2). Against this one case of movement on the Shammaite side in Hillel's direction, however, stand four cases where *Beit Hillel* rescinded their rulings so as to agree with *Beit Shammai* (*m. Yebamot* 15:2-3; *m. Gittin* 4:5; *m. Kelim* 9:2; and *m. Oholot* 5:3). In another case, Shammai initially scolded Hillelite Yonathan ben Uzziel for violating the final wishes of a now-deceased man who had disinherited his sons. After ben Uzziel explained his position, however, Shammai withdrew his objection, having been convinced that ben Uzziel's action of gifting one third of the estate to the sons was not strictly against *halakha* (*b. Baba Bathra* 133b-134a).

Telushkin observes, "[T]he literalism of Shammai can at times turn out to be the more liberal path."[47]

---

[46] Jacob Neusner, *A Rabbi Talks with Jesus: An Intermillenial, Interfaith Exchange* (New York, N.Y.: Doubleday, 1993), 8.

SHAMMAI HAZAQEN · 25

This was true, in particular, on matters concerning women and slaves. Beginning with the latter, what seems to have been a case which would not arise very often finds its way into the *Mishna*. The scene is set that a hypothetical man is half slave and half free, perhaps by way of belonging to two brothers, one of whom frees him and the other of whom retains him as a servant. Hillel had reasoned that the man should work three days a week for his master and three for himself at a fair wage. On this matter, Shammai weighed in with a more humanitarian solution to the dilemma, citing the Hillelite principle of *tiqun 'olam* to make his point. He proposed that the solution offered by Hillel was not appropriate, because the man, being half free, was ineligible to marry a slave woman, and being half slave, barred from marrying a free woman – thus would he be denied the right to marry and obey Genesis 1:28 ("Be ye fruitful and multiply..."). His ruling was that the man be freed on the promise that he would pay the master back half his worth; i.e. if indentured, half what was owing (*m. Gittin* 4:5).

Hillel's liberal reading of Deuteronomy 24:1 resulted in a ruling that a man could divorce his wife "for any reason," including the provision of a sub-par meal. Shammai's more literal approach, however, presented the phrase "something unseemly" to be a euphemism for adultery, i.e. meaning a forbidden sexual act, and thus forbade a divorce sought on any other grounds. His understanding of the verse "inclined him to a view more protective of women"

---

[47] Joseph Telushkin, *Hillel: If Not Now, When?* (New York, N.Y.: Schocken Books, 2010), 97.

(*m. Gittin* 9:10).[48] In court, Hillel would not accept the testimony of a woman unless there were corroborating witnesses to confirm her testimony, even when she was merely testifying that she had been widowed. Shammai saw no reason for disallowing such testimony. Furthermore, Shammai ruled that she should be able, on her testimony alone, to receive in one lump sum the settlement of her *kethubah* (marriage contract) in case of widowdom. Hillel would have her restricted to a budgeted allowance from the estate, even with outside testimony that her husband was deceased (*m. Yebamot* 15:2-3). In these last two matters, Shammai won the day, convincing Hillel to abandon his stated rulings in favor of his.

One more matter where Shammai found himself in the minority among the voices of the *Talmud* was in his ruling that if a person committed a sin as an agent of another, he felt that both were guilty of the sin, but moreso the one who gave the order or paid the perpetrator of the deed. The overwhelming voice of the *Talmud* was that only the one who did the deed bore the guilt. Shammai appealed to the pericope of King David ordering his general Joab to "set Uriah in the forefront of the hottest battle and withdraw from him so that he may be hit and die" (2 Samuel 11:15). The *Talmud* would assign the guilt to Joab for carrying out the order, but the prophet Nathan held David accountable in 2 Samuel 12:1-10. Shammai was inclined to echo Nathan's judgment, contrary to the consensus view among his fellow Sages (*b. Qiddushin* 42b).

---

[48] Ibid., 98.

The political climate of the First Century had much to do with the drive of these two *zughot* (ruling pair) to define Jewish *halakha* down to the finest detail. Within the backdrop of the scene of these debates was the taint of Hasmonean corruption and the threat of Herodian Hellenization. The tension between the Pharisees and the Sadducees was also a factor. Judaism's future looked bleak, and it was believed that unifying all of Judaism around a common *halakhic* canon could save it, just as the common worship model devised by the *Anshei Knesset HaG'dolah* ("Men of the Great Assembly" convened by Ezra the Scribe) had done during the Babylonian Exile a few centuries before.[49] Shammai and his students were renowned for their refusal to submit to Roman rule. They were hostile not only toward the Roman administration but also to any Jewish citizen who acquiesced to Rome or to Hellenization.[50] On one occasion, Herod made a personal appearance in

---

[49] Note that the Babylonian Exile was not a complete exile of the Jewish people; it was an exile of the elites of Israel and a decimation of the walled fortress-towns, but the outlying areas were left untouched and Judaism continued to flourish both in the Land and among the Exiles. As time went on, Judaism took on two different faces until the Exiles returned and, for the most part, imposed their version on those who had remained in the Land, though some Remnant customs did find their way into the final form which carried forward through to the *Zugot* period which followed the death of the last member of the Great Assembly. See Oded Lipschits, *The Fall and Rise of Jerusalem* (Winona Lake, Ind.: Eisenbrauns, 2005) for more on this.

[50] "Shammai," *New World Encyclopedia* (online: http://www.newworldencyclopedia.org/entry/Shammai).

the Sanhedrin, intimidating the entire body into a petrified silence. One voice alone broke the silence to take a stand against the wicked Roman ruler – the voice of Shammai haZaqen.

Some scholars have found reason to link the party of the Zealots (called in Hebrew הַקַּנָּאִים; i.e. *haQana'im*) to the House of Shammai.[51] This should not be interpreted as indicating that the two groups were one and the same, but is merely a recognition that there were some commonalities between them. For instance, *Beit Shammai* was supported by the Zealots in some matters due to their shared opposition to *Beit Hillel*, as evidenced in the 18 decrees forced upon students of the Hillel faction by Shammai after Hillel's death. These decrees are no longer extant, and their exact content is no longer known, but it is believed that they aimed at complete separation between Jews and Gentiles.[52]

Of the passage of these measures, the *Talmudic* record reflects that it "was as grievous to Israel as the

---

[51] M. Stern, "Sicarii and Zealots," in Michael Avi-Yonah & Zvi Baras, eds., *The World History of the Jewish People: Society and Religion in the Second Temple Period* (Jerusalem: Massada Publishing Ltd., 1977), 297; Heinrich Grätz, *Geschichte der Juden von den ältesten Zeiten bis auf die Gegenwart* (impr. and ext. ed.; Leipzig: Leiner, 1900), III (2): 797-9; Aryeh Kasher, *Jews, Idumæans, and Ancient Arabs: Relations of the Jews in Erets-Israel with the Nations of the Frontier and Desert during the Hellenistic and Roman Era (332 BCE – 70 CE)* (Texte und Studien zum Antiken Judentum 18; Tübingen: J. C. B. Mohr, 1988), 237.

[52] Falk, *Jesus the Pharisee*, 56.

day when the [golden] calf was made" (*b. Shabbat* 17a). This may be a reference to the massacre which occurred just before the vote, wherein a number of *talmidim* from *Beit Hillel* were killed. One *sugya* (singular of *sugyot*; i.e. passage or pericope) of *Talmud* attributes the massacre to *Beit Shammai* (*y. Shabbat* 1:4), but both *Talmuds* indicate that swords were present in the *Beit haMidrash* (House of Study) that day, which more likely points to the *Sicarii* as the perpetrators.[53] It is, perhaps, no coincidence that the meaning of Shammai's name in Hebrew is "desolated."[54] Shammai's remains were interred in a humble tomb on the Meron River in *Eretz-Yisrael* (pictured below).

Tomb of Shammai haZaqen

After Shammai's death in 30 CE, *Beit Shammai* would dominate the Sanhedrin for the next forty years, although his successor as *Nasi* of the Sanhedrin was Rabban Gamli'el I, a Hillelite. Following Shammai's departure from the *'olam hazeh* (this world),

---

[53] Ibid., 57-8.

[54] James P. Boyd, *Dennison Bible Dictionary* (Baltimore, Md.: Ottenheimer Publishers, 1958), 207.

it is said that Rabbi Tarfon was traveling, and he recited the evening Shema lying down, adopting the stricture of *Beit Shammai*, and bandits took advantage of this and almost killed him. When he told what happened to the other Sages, they responded, "For violating the words of *Beit Hillel*, you really should have incurred a death penalty" (*b. Berakhot* 10).

Rabbi Moshe Chaim Luzzato explains that there was a great disagreement between *Beit Hillel* and Beit Shammai that almost split the Jewish People, and after enormous efforts and an interceding audible voice from the heavens, the law was decided in favor of *Beit Hillel*. When Rabbi Tarfon went and adopted the strict approach for all to see, he was weakening the force of this decision and causing harm to the Jewish People. "In such a case, it is more saintly to hold like *Beit Hillel*, even with the lenient view, than to be strict like *Beit Shammai*" (*b. Mesilat Yesharim* 20).

For the most part, even despite Shammai outliving Hillel and taking over his presidency of the *Beit Din*, Hillel's *halakhic* rulings have been accepted over Shammai's. This marked the second time in Israel's history that a Jewish authority from Babylon trumped a Jewish voice born within *Eretz-Yisrael*. Just as the will of the returning Exiles won the day with regard to the shape which Judaism would take in 538 BCE,[55] so also did the rulings of Babylonian-born Hillel take priority over those of Israel-born Shammai. In spite of this, however, Shammai's

---

[55] Oded Lipschits, *The Fall and Rise of Jerusalem* (Winona Lake, Ind.: Eisenbrauns, 2005).

conservative approach resonated more with the average "Jew in the pew" and was likely more practiced than that of Hillel. Telushkin suggests, "It was perhaps his misfortune in life (and even moreso in history) to be the foil of Hillel... [a]lways to be judged in comparison with Hillel."[56] *Talmud Bavli*, in anticipation of a reversal, predicts that Shammai's standard will prevail in the Messianic Age – that guilt or innocence will be as black-and-white a matter as purity versus defilement.[57]

---

[56] Joseph Telushkin, *Hillel: If Not Now, When?* (New York, N.Y.: Schocken Books, 2010), 111.

[57] David H. Stern, *Jewish New Testament Commentary* (Clarksville, Md.: JNTP. 1992), 59.

The present author highly recommends the following for those wishing to learn more about Shammai:

> Joseph Telushkin, *Hillel: If Not Now, When?* (New York, N.Y.: Shocken Books, 2010).

Though, as the title would indicate, this is obviously a work on Hillel, it also puts a fair amount of focus on his colleague Shammai. One can hardly discuss one without including the other. Part II of the recommended work – "Hillel versus Shammai: The Talmud's Most Famous Adversaries" – even contains a chapter solely devoted to the Shammai ("Shammai Beyond Stereotype"). Telushkin presents a very well-researched biographical sketch on this underappreciated Sage.

CHAPTER 3

HILLEL HAZAQEN

הִלֵּל הַזָּקֵן

Hillel was the founder of the *Beit Hillel* (School of Hillel) which arose in the First Century BCE. Much has been written about Hillel haZaqen... but how much accurate accounting is to be found amid the plethora of material is another matter. Schaff laments, "The *Talmudic* tradition has obscured their history and embellished it with many fables."[58] It is said, for instance, that Hillel had the ability to understand every language on the earth, even those unknown tongues of the animals and demons. It would certainly not be an impossible feat for HaShem to bequeath this gift to Hillel, but this more likely represents at least a slight exaggeration.

Of his early life, it is known that he was born and raised in Babylon, and thus might have been seen as an unlikely candidate for any place of prominence among the Jewish Sages in *Eretz-Yisrael* (*Tos. Negaim* 1:16; *Sifra Tazria* 9:15). It is worthy of note that while Hillel was so well studied in *Torah*, one of the greatest teachers thereof, he was not a Levite. His genealogy was of the tribe of Yehudah (Judah) – a direct descendant of King David (*y. Ta'anit* 4:2; *b. Kethubot* 62; *Tos. Sanhedrin* 5), and of course, by extension, a descendent of the Moabite proselyte Ruth as well. As a descendent of the great psalmist, it is fitting that the name Hillel is a form of the Hebrew verb *halal* ("to

---

[58] Philip Schaff, *History of the Christian Church: Volume I* (3rd rev. ed.; New York, N.Y.: Charles Scribner's Sons, 1890; orig. 1858), 160.

praise"), so his name would translate, quite appropriately, "he has praised."[59]

Hillel's Babylonian origins may contribute to the popularity the *Talmud Bavli* enjoys over the *Talmud Yerushalmi*, as he is credited with much of the content of *Talmud Bavli*. Both corpuses sing Hillel's praises, however. So also the *Tosefta* ("Supplements" to *Talmud*), in which we find him described, "so humble, so pious – a true disciple of Ezra" (*Tos. Sotah* 13:3). This comparison to Ezra is but one of several, as Hillel had come from Babylon and restored *Torah*, as Ezra had before him (*b. Sukkah* 20a). Rabbi Dr. Richard Hidary, Judaic Studies professor at Yeshiva University, observes that even the students of Hillel "had the intellectual honesty to change their minds whenever they recognized the correctness of Beth Shammai's opinion."[60] His humility is given in *Talmud Bavli* as the reason for his *halakhic* rulings gaining acceptance over those of Shammai:

> Since both [Hillel's and Shammai's rulings and teachings] are the words of the living G-d, what was it that entitled *Beth Hillel* to have the *halakha* fixed in agreement with their rulings? Because they were kindly and modest, they studied their own rulings and those of *Beit Shammai* and were even so [humble] as to mention the actions of *Beit Shammai* before theirs (*b. Eruvin* 13b).

---

[59] a Piel perfect 3rd person masculine singular of הָלַל (halal)

[60] Richard Hidary, *Dispute for the Sake of Heaven: Legal Pluralism in the talmud* (Brown Judaic Studies 353; Providence, R.I.: Brown University, 2010), 225.

When Hillel arrived in Jerusalem, he was very poor. He could not afford to attend the *Beit haMidrash* (House of Study) of Shemaiah and Avtalyon as there was a modest tuition fee of a quarter-dinar involved in that, which was above his means. So great was his desire to learn *Torah*, however, that he would sit on the roof and take in the lessons through the skylight. On one particularly cold Friday evening, he was perched on the roof and froze, passing out onto the skylight. The students noticed that the room had darkened and investigated, finding and reviving young Hillel, who was already buried beneath three cubits of snow. Despite it now being Shabbat, Shemaiah and Avtalyon, impressed by his desire to learn *Torah* – even at the risk of his life, kindled a fire to warm him, remarking, "This man deserves to have the Sabbath laws violated on his behalf!" (*b. Yoma* 35b). Several years later, Hillel would be the *tanna* (*Mishnaic* Sage) responsible for abolishing the practice of charging tuition at a *Beit haMidrash* (house of study).[61]

> **"Say not, 'When I have time I shall study,'**
> **for you may perhaps never**
> **have any leisure." (Pirqei Avot 2:4)**

Some might question how it is that saving a life was not viewed as sufficient grounds for overriding the Sabbath prohibitions, as it is now. Rabbi Joseph Telushkin suggests, "perhaps violating the Sabbath to

---

[61] Adin Steinsaltz, *Talmudic Images* (Northvale, N.J.: Jason Aronson, Inc., 1997), 11.

save a life was not yet regarded as definitely permitted in Jewish law" – though the Maccabean Revolt is cited as having established a precedent a mere century prior.[62] Nonetheless, this experience quite possibly might be the undergirding to the quality character attribute of *savlanut* (סַבְלָנוּת, i.e. patience) so thoroughly embodied by Hillel.

One of the most recited quotations from this Sage comes from the *Talmudic* account of a prospective convert to Judaism coming first to Shammai with his request for him to summarize the *Torah* while standing on one foot. Shammai was perturbed by the request, thinking it a mockery of *Torah*, and drove him off with a stick.[63] The student then brought that same request before Hillel, whose response was quite different from that of Shammai. He lifted one foot, balanced himself, and then offered the student this statement (which is comprised of a mere 15 words in Aramaic):

---

[62] Joseph Telushkin, *Hillel: If Not Now, When?* (New York, N.Y.: Schocken Books, 2010), 6.

[63] To be fair to Shammai, the way the question was posited did betray a Hellenistic Weltanschauung (worldview), which valued precision and brevity in the articulation of one's views, as opposed to the Hebraic *hashqafah* (Heb. הַשְׁקָפָה), where the impetus was on depth of understanding. See Edward M. Gershfield, "Hillel, Shammai, and the Three Proselytes," *Conservative Judaism* 31, no. 3 (Spring 1967): 29-39.

> That which is despicable to you, do not do to your
> neighbor. This is the whole of the *Torah*. The rest is
> elaboration. Go forth and study. (*b. Shabbat* 31a).

For Hillel, he may have seen in the questioner
the same eagerness to learn which had led to his *gratis*
admission into the school of Shemaiah and Avtalyon.
While Shammai was cautious to protect Judaism from
Gentile influence and was thus skeptical of Gentiles
seeking to "infiltrate" the faith;[64] Hillel was more
amenable to Gentile inclusion, perhaps owing to the
fact this his own teachers were descended from *ger-
tzedeq* (Gentile convert) ancestors (*b. Gittin* 57b). He
used to say, "If you see a generation to which *Torah* is
dear, spread it… but if you see a generation to which
Torah is not dear, gather it and keep it to yourself" (*b.
Berakhot* 63a). It could very well be that Hillel is the
inspiration behind the common expression, "Never
judge a man until you have walked a mile in his
shoes." Hillel made a very similar statement: "Judge
not thy neighbor 'til thou art in his situation" (*Pirqei
Avot* 2:4). It can certainly be deduced that he did not

---

[64] Shammai's concerns were not without grounds, as it
was still fresh in the Israelite memory the consequences of
Hasmonean king John Hyrcanus's force-conversion of the
Idumeans, one of whom was Antipas, the grand-father of
Herod. Herod was at that present time in control of Jerusalem (reigning from37 to 4 BCE). He had murdered 45 members of the Sanhedrin and removed from that body any who
questioned the validity of his ancestors' conversion to Judaism. The reader is referred to Telushkin, *Hillel,* 10 for a fuller
discussion of Herod's treachery.

rush to judgment against the prospective convert as did his colleague Shammai.

Another quotable proverb attributed to Hillel instructs, "In the place where there is not a man, be thou a man" (ibid.). The context for that statement is a discussion of what constitutes a man as opposed to a brute, thus the admonition is not to mirror the brutish behavior of those around us, but rather to stand apart as a man, i.e. a *mentsch,* or righteous and peaceable soul, in the midst of a brutish populus. This is, perhaps, what one might expect from a teacher who so epitomized the principle of *savlanut.* Few could be said to have exercised it to the degree that did Hillel. On one occasion, his *savlanut* was deliberately put to the test. A pair of young men (apparently not members of Hillel's school) made a wager which would award the sum of 400 *zuzim*[65] based on whether or not the one could rouse the ire of the great Sage. The one who thought Hillel could be made to lose his temper went to Hillel on Friday afternoon, intending to disrupt Hillel's Sabbath preparations, with a bevy of questions he considered frivolous.

---

[65] The word *zuzim* (זוּזִים) is the plural form of *zuz* (זוּז), also called a *dinar*. *Zuzim* were small silver coins struck without the consent or authorization of the Roman government, one zuz being valued at two farthings, or 1/6 of a penny. At right: two Bar Kokhba era *zuzim*.

One of these, aimed at insulting Hillel's background, was, 'Why are the heads of Babylonians so round?" Hillel responded calmly, "My son: you have asked a good question. It is because they do not have skillful midwives." After a barrage of similar questions, the young man finally asked, in hopes of irritating Hillel to the limits of his famed *savlanut*, "Are you Hillel, who they call the *Nasi* of Israel?" When Hillel answered in the affirmative, the lad said with an unmistakable tone of disgust, "May there not be many like you! Because of you, I have lost 400 *zuzim*!" Hillel's response was this: "Better it is for you to lose 400 *zuzim*, and even double that, than for Hillel to lose his temper" (*b. Sanhedrin* 31a).

For all his patience, however, Hillel took study of the *Torah* to be of unparalleled import, stating, "He who refuses to learn deserves extinction" (*Pirqei Avot* 1:13). He believed that *Torah* was not just for Jews but for "every living creature," as evidenced in *Pirqei Avot*: "… love all creatures, and bring them closer to *Torah*" (1:11). Hillel had learned *Torah* under the two most sought after Sages of the First Century BCE: Shemaiah and Avtalyon. Among adages attributed to Avtalyon was the admonition: "Scholars, be cautious of your words for they may cause you to be exiled to a place with polluted waters… and the name of the Lord will be profaned" (*Pirqei Avot* 1:10) – a teaching which is reflected in Hillel's demeanor.

The *Talmud Yerushalmi* reports that the Elders of Batera were reluctant to install him to the highest seat in the highest court of Israel, that of *Nasi* (president) of the Sanhedrin Gedolah (Great Sanhedrin) due to his Babylonian birth. He was, however, able to convince them by suggesting that the traditions he cited were handed down to him directly from his renowned teachers (y. Kilayim 9:3) Hillel's family would become a Jewish dynasty, occupying the seat of Nasi for about 400 years to follow.[66] This dynasty would begin with his grandson Gamli'el I, the subject of the next chapter (b. Shabbat 15a). In the final analysis, Hillel haZaqen was adjudged with the statement, "It was fitting that the Shekhinah should rest upon him, but his generation was not worthy of it" (b. Sotah 48b).

In about 31 BCE, Hillel ascended to the office of Nasi (president) by settling a question concerning the sacrificial ritual in a manner which demonstrated his superiority over the sons of Betheira, who were the Nasi and Av Beit Din at the time. That year, Passover was set to begin on a Friday night, and the sons of Betheira found themselves in a quandary. It is recorded that they "forgot the law and did not know whether or not slaughter of the Passover sacrifice overrode the Sabbath restrictions." They were referred to Hillel, as it was known that he had been the most impressive of the talmidim of Shemaiah and Avtalyon. After resolving the matter to their satisfaction, both through logic and tradition,[67] they

---

[66] Naomi E. Pasachoff & Robert J. Littman, *A Concise History of the Jewish People* (Lanham, Md.: Rowman & Littlefield, 2005), 66.

[67] The two *Talmuds* differ somewhat in their accounts of this episode. *Talmud Bavli* reports only the rational case presented by Hillel, i.e. that there were some 200 other

promptly relinquished control of the Sanhedrin to Hillel, appointing him *Nasi* (*b. Pesachim* 66a; *y. Pesachim* 6:1), thereafter to be known as Hillel haZaqen (the Elder).

Hillel came to be esteemed as a great teacher. As a teacher, he seems to have been approachable and relatable, as evidenced by his positive responses to pagans coming to him for conversion. Three such incidents are recorded in the *Talmud* (*b. Shabbat* 31a) — one wishing to convert without having to learn *Oral Torah*, one desiring to attain the office of *Kohen HaGadol* (High Priest), and the third demanding that his teaching be given succinctly enough that it be accomplished with the teacher standing on one foot. In all three episodes, the convert is first dismissed by Shammai, and subsequently accepted by Hillel, who eventually succeeds in overcoming their objections or misunderstandings.

The *Midrashic* literature preserves a parable from Hillel as an example of his pedagogy: the tale of an officer who cleans and polishes statues of emperors, past and present, which have been erected in common areas (rather than in temples), so the implication is that he has no direct contact with the

---

sacrifices which trumped the Sabbath; why should the Passover sacrifice be held in lesser regard than those? (*b. Pesachim* 66a). *Talmud Yerushalmi*, however, conveys that this initial response did not persuade them, and that he then appealed to the oral traditions handed down to him by the reknowned Shemaiah and Avtalyon, and by this they were convinced (*y. Pesachim* 6:1).

king. His diligence is, nonetheless, noticed by the king, and he is consequently rewarded by being elevated to noble status and paid a much-increased salary (*Wayyiqra Rabbah* 34.3). The message of this parable, i.e. performing one's given tasks with the utmost diligence, seems not to have been lost on Hillel's *talmidim*. It is said of his students that they numbered eighty, and that of these, thirty were like Moshe, thirty were like Yehoshua ben Nun (Joshua), and twenty were "average"... but even some of the least of his students obtained the title of Rabban, which is a step above the title of Rabbi (*b. Sukkah* 28a).

Hillel was also very detailed. His "Seven Rules of Hillel" are still to this day the standard principles of Jewish hermeneutics. They defined the method for the extrapolation of the *halakhic* precepts which characterized Pharisaic Judaism for the remainder of the Second Temple Era (*Avot d'Rabbi Nathan* 37.10) and laid the foundation for modern Rabbinics. These rules are:[68]

1. ***Qal w'Chomer* (light and heavy):** often, but not always, signaled by a phrase like *"how much more...."* E.g., Prov 11:31; Deut 31:27; 1 Sam 23:3; Jer 12:5; Ezek 15:5; Esth 9:12.[69] This can be sub-divided into explicit (*meforash*) and implied (*satum*).

---

[68] Note that this list also appears in *Tos. Sanhedrin* 7:11 and the *Sifra* with slightly different enumeration of the rules.

[69] Sha'ul (Paul) of Tarsus employed the *Qal w'Chomer* device in Romans 5:8-10, 15, 17; 11:12, 24; 1 Corinthians 9:11-12; 12:22; 2 Corinthians 3:7-9, 11; Philippians 2:12; Philemon 1:16.

2. *G'zerah Shavah* **(equivalence of expres-sions):** where the same words are applied to two separate cases, it follows that the same considerations apply to both. E.g., comparing Judges 13:5 to 1 Samuel 1:10, both bearing the phrase "no razor shall touch his head," could lend credence to the conclusion that Samuel, like Samson, was under a Nazirite vow.[70]

3. *Binyan av miKathub Echad* **(Building up a "family" from a single text):** a consideration which is found in one passage applies to all passages which address the same principle.

4. *Binyan av miShene Kethubim* **(Building up a "family" from two or more texts):** a principle is established by relating two texts together; the principle can then be applied to other passages.

5. *Kelal uferat* **(the general and the particular):** a general principle may be restricted by a particularization of it in another verse or, conversely, a particular rule may be extended into a general principle. E.g., Gen 1:27 makes the general statement that God created man. Gen 2:7, 21 particularizes this by giving the details of the creation of Adam and Chawwah (Eve).

6. *KaYotzei bo baMakom Acher* **(analogy made from another passage):** two passages may seem to conflict until compared with a third, which has points of general though not necessarily verbal similarity.

7. *Davar haLomed me'inyano* **(explanation obtained from context):** The total context, not just the isolated statement, must be considered for accurate exegesis.

---

[70] In similar application, comparing Psalm 95:7-11/ Hebrews 3:7-11 to Genesis 2:2 /Hebrews 4:4, the author of Hebrews reasons that there will be 6,000 years of this world followed by a 1,000 year Shabbat.

E.g., the rabbinic interpretation of the Decalogue's prohibition against theft intending to convey kidnapping with intent to sell into slavery, based on the surrounding verses indicating sins with a death penalty and deducing that this one must as well (Exodus 21:16; *b. Sanhedrin* 86a).

These rules seem to be the genesis of what would become rather quickly the "making [of] a fence around *Torah*" (וְעָשׂוּ סְיָג לַתּוֹרָה; *Pirqei Avot* 1:1), i.e. supererogatory standards which go beyond the plain sense of the Scriptural mandate.[71] The later *halakhic* principle of not combining meat and dairy is an example of *kelal uferat* in that it takes the particular prohibition against seething a kid in its mothers milk (Exodus 23:19; 34:26) and extends it into the general principle of *basar b'chalav* (*b. Chullin* 113b, 115b).[72] This requires that no meat of any kind be eaten in mixture with or even at the same meal as any dairy of any kind. Bonchek suggests that this is not what the verse intended, as the verb translated "seethe" or "boil" actually means "to become ripe or mature."[73] The Biblical account of Abraham entertaining the

---

[71] Morris Jastrow Jr., *Hebrew and Babylonian Traditions: The Haskell Lectures* (New York, N.Y.: Charles Scribner's Sons, 1914), 189-92; Hermann Lebrecht Strack & Günter Stemberger, *Einleitung in Talmud und Midrasch* (München: C. H. Beck'sche Verlagsbuchhandlung, 1921; orig. 1887), 10-11.

[72] The prohibition of *basar b'chalav* (lit. meat with milk) seems to be a rather late development in Judaism, dating no earlier than the Medieval Period.

[73] Avigdor Bonchek, *Studying the Torah: A Guide to In-Depth Interpretation* (Oxford: Jason Aronson, 1997), 55-6.

angels by serving them calf meat with cheese and milk (Genesis 18:1-8) is often cited as conflicting with the *halakhic* measure.

Hillel is described by modern scholarship as adhering to a "liberalizing tradition" of *Torah* interpretations,[74] as "he did not insist on the strict literal interpretation of the biblical text."[75] In comparison with his colleague Shammai, he certainly was the more liberal of the two in most matters. Many of his rulings reflected an easing of *Torah* from its natural reading, e.g., his view on divorce being that any reason was acceptable grounds, even as trivial a claim as the wife having burnt a meal (*m. Gittin* 9:10), as presented in the previous chapter.

Another example of this "liberalizing tradition" is Hillel's first *tannakah* (act as a *Tanna*), whereby he decreed by *pruzbul* (a rabbinic exception to a rabbinical enactment or *Torah* command)[76] that total cancellation of debts in the Sabbatical year, as ordered by *Torah* (Deuteronomy 15:1), should be overridden by Sanhedrin decision whenever they deemed that the economy warranted it (*b. Shevuot* 10:3; *m. Gittin* 4:3). One ancient commentator explained the action thus:

---

[74] Paul L. Maier, "Chronology," in Ralph P. Martin & Peter H. Davids (eds.), *Dictionary of the Later New Testament & Its Developments* (Downers Grove, Ill.: IVP, 1997), 186.

[75] Nathan Isaacs, "The Law and the 'Law of Change,'" *University of Pennsylvania Law Review* 65 (1917): 659-79, 748-63.

[76] Hillel was the first to institute the procedure of *pruzbul*, per Telushkin, *Hillel*, 51.

"Hillel haZaqen enacted the *pruzbul* to make the world better [*tiqun 'olam*] because he saw that people refrained from lending to one another and violated what was written in the *Torah*: 'Beware that there be not a base thought in thy heart' [Deuteronomy 15:9]" (*Sifré Re'eh* 113; see also *m. Shevi'it* 10:3). Both the *pruzbul* and the principle of *tiqun 'olam* have become part of Hillel's lasting contribution to Judaism. Telushkin comments, "Hillel's delicate balancing act – sustaining the *Torah* ethic without formally voiding a *Torah* law – helped the needy Jews of Hillel's time, and has helped the Jewish people ever since."[77]

In at least one matter, however, a supererogatory (rather than relaxed) standard was imposed by Hillel. On the question of eggs laid on the Sabbath, Hillel issued the decree that they were not to be eaten, presumably due to the hens having had to violate Sabbath in order to provide them (*y. Beitzah* 1:1). This took a command directed at human beings and extended it to apply to farm animals as well, despite his conviction that "man was not created for the Sabbath; the Sabbath was created for man." His position on the shedding of innocent blood and the sanctity of human life would likewise be regarded as conservative, by any standard, articulated in *Talmud Yerushalmi* thus:

> Whosoever destroys a soul, it is considered as if he destroyed an entire world; and whosoever that saves a life, it is considered as if he saved an entire world (*y. Sanhedrin* 4:1).

---

[77] Telushkin, *Hillel*, 57.

Hillel is reputed to have lived 120 years, and – just as the great biblical prophet Moshe (Deuteronomy 34:7) – lived the first 40 without *Torah*, the next 40 studying *Torah*, and the last 40 teaching it, departing from his earthly existence in about 10 CE in a state of abject poverty (*Sifré D'varim* 357). The 120 year figure is probably not factual, but merely a figure of speech to put Hillel symbolically into the footsteps of the great Hebrew prophet Moshe. His tomb in Meron (depicted on the facing page) has become a tourist site and quasi-shrine.

Cave-tomb where Hillel's remains are interred

The present author highly recommends the following to learn more about Hillel:

> Joseph Telushkin, *Hillel: If Not Now, When?* (New York, N.Y.: Shocken Books, 2010).

Yes, this is the same work recommended for Shammai, but Telushkin really does do a masterful job of presenting both.

CHAPTER 4

RABBAN GAMLI'EL HAZAQEN

רַבָּן גַּמְלִיאֵל הַזָּקֵן

The elder Gamli'el ben Shim'on, a Benjaminite by tribe, holds the distinction of being the first of the Sages of Israel to garner the title of Rabban (a higher title than Rabbi at that time). He was a grandson of the renowned Sage Hillel haZaqen, with his father Shim'on standing between the two in their genealogical chart.

An interesting theory has emerged with regard to Gamli'el haZaqen's father, about whom very little is known apart from that he served as *Nasi* for a short time. The proposition has been made that this Shim'on may be the same Shim'on about whom Luke (Luqa) spoke in his Gospel. It is therein reported that there was a man named Shim'on who was "a just and devout man of Jerusalem" who received a word of assurance from the *Ruach* that he would not die without seeing the arrival of the Messiah (Luke 2:25-35). This Shim'on had to have been a person of high repute in order to receive special mention, as it was not that uncommon a sentiment among the Jews of that time (Matthew 2:3; Luke 3:15).[78] The evidence is perhaps tenuous, but what makes the theory appealing and perhaps worthy of mention is that the same author writes about Gamli'el in another book.

---

[78] Ralph V. Harvey, *Rabban Gamaliel* (Xulon Press, 2005), 14-15.

Most who are acquainted with the *B'rit Chadasha* also know the name Gamli'el as belonging to the *Torah* teacher under whom Sha'ul haTarsi (Apostle Paul) studied (Acts 22:3). This is that same Gamli'el who taught in Jerusalem from 22 to 50 CE, i.e. Gamli'el haZaqen (d. abt. 52 CE[79]). The only record of this Rabban Gamli'el teaching in a public setting is, in fact, not the *Talmud*; it is the book of Acts (22:3). The first introduction to him in the Bible comes at Acts 5:34-35:

> And a certain (man) arose of the Pharisees whose name was Gamli'el, a teacher of *Torah* and honored by all people. And he commanded that they take the *Shlichim* [Yeshua's apostles] outside for a short time. And he said to them, "Men and sons of Israel take heed to yourselves and determine what is right to do to these men."

This intercession comes in a heated episode wherein an angry Sanhedrin is intent on killing the *Shlichim*. Gamli'el's counsel is given on the premise that if the *Shlichim* are of man, their plans would come to naught, but if they be of G-d, opposing them would be in vain (Acts 5:38-39). Timothy J. Hegg of *Torah Resource Institute* expounds on the remarkableness of the *Nasi* of the Sanhedrin being so "open-minded to the possibility that Yeshua was, in fact, the Messiah."[80] We find in Gamli'el haZaqen a picture of

---

[79] *Nota bene:* The general dating for Sha'ul's Damascus Road episode, wherein he became a disciple of Yeshua, is ca. 36 CE.

[80] Timothy J. Hegg, *The Letter Writer: Paul's Background and Torah Perspective* (Israel: First Fruits of Zion, 2002), 39.

a Sage very much in the lenient and pacifistic vein of the School of Hillel. There is good reason for that, as this Gamli'el is, in fact, the grandson of the renowned Hillel introduced in the previous chapter of this work.

Rabban Gamli'el haZaqen so reflected the teachings of his renowned grandfather that most *Talmud* scholars associate many of the teachings and rulings assigned to *Beit Hillel* specifically with him. He seems to have inherited or learned Hillel's humility, as evidenced in the account of his reaction to being posed a question to which he did not know the answer. He admitted that he didn't know and proceeded to take the question to the high court (Sanhedrin) for Rabbi Nachum to hand down the ruling based on precedents found in the oral tradition (*m. Pe'ah* 2:5-6).

Hillelite leniency in the name of maintaining *shalom* (שָׁלוֹם) is reflected in Gamli'el's approval of his daughter's marriage to Shim'on ben Netanel, a Sadducean priest. He allowed the marriage, but only with the stipulation that his daughter was not to participate with him in the kashering of *taharot*, i.e. ritually-clean Temple implements (*Tos. Avodah Zarah* 3:10). Perhaps in that instance, one can venture that Gamli'el saw in his prospective son-in-law what would manifest some time later, i.e. that he would leave his Sadducean position and become a student of the Pharisaic teachings. The *Mishna* reports that he was one of the five prime students of Rabban Yochanan ben Zakkai, and that teacher would describe him as one who "fears sin."[81] (*Pirqei Avot* 2:8).

Given the Hebraic tradition of a *Torah* student's imitation of every detail of his teacher's instruction, demeanor, and even personal idiosyncrasies, it is tenable to surmise that one might presumably be able to deduce more such data about Rabban Gamli'el by studying his pupils.

Earliest known image of Sha'ul haTarsi (4th-5th Century mosaic)

A certain Sha'ul Paulos haTarsi, perhaps better known as Saul of Tarsus or Apostle Paul, was a *talmid* of Gamli'el haZaqen (per Acts 22:3). He is credited with having written roughly half of the books of the *B'rit Chadasha*; but prior to his life-changing encounter with Yeshua haNotzri, he had harbored bitter hostility toward the His followers, displaying a venomous anti-Yeshuahite passion (Acts 8:3; 9:1-2; 22:4; Galatians 4:29). which did not at all align with the attitude demon-strated by his mentor Rabban Gamli'el I (per Acts 5:38-39, loc. cit.).

The disparity represented by the fact that Sha'ul had deviated from the example of his Hillelite teacher for an inestimable period of time, joining either with

---

[81] Rabban Yochanan ben Zakkai is treated in chapter 5 of the present work.

the more ultraconservative Shammaites or perhaps with the militaristic Zealots in their persecution of Hellenized Jews (Acts 8:1-2; 9:1-2), complicates the task of learning about one from the other. In fact, Jewish historian Dr. Yosef Klausner suggests the anonymous student of Gamli'el described in the *Talmud* as "impudent to learning" (*b. Shabbat* 30b) might have been Sha'ul haTarsi, though such query is speculative at best.[82] Further, Sha'ul's conduct after committing to Yeshua should be considered as that of a student not of Gamli'el haZaqen but of Yeshua haNotzri – his ultimate rabbi. Even if Gamli'el had become a disciple of Yeshua, as has been speculated, it seems from the available testimony unlikely that he would have taught Yeshua's teachings to Sha'ul, since Sha'ul makes a point of emphasizing that he had no other teacher but Yeshua in the teachings of *HaDerekh*, i.e. "The Way" (Galatians 1:12).

Those points aside, however, there were similarities between the two. One was that, like Rabban Gamli'el, Sha'ul frequently corresponded with his charges by way of epistle (sermonic letters). Three such letters by Gamli'el are preserved in the various rabbinical records (*b. Sanhedrin* 11a-11b; *Tos. Sanhedrin* 2:6; *y. Sanhedrin* 1:2; *y. Ma'aser Sheni* 8:5) – one to the Galilee region, one to the southern region of *Eretz-Yisrael*, and the last to the *Diaspora* in Babylon, Medea, and "other exiles of Israel."[83] In one of these,

---

[82] Yosef Gedaliah Klausner, *Mi-Yeshu ad Paulus* (London: Allen & Unwin, 1939), 310.

[83] See Appendix A for reconstructions/translations of these letters. That these letters belong to Gamli'el haZaqen

Gamli'el explains to *Diaspora* Jews the reason for the intercalary month added to leap years as occurring when signs of Spring were absent as *Pesach* (Passover) drew near, in order to ensure that there would be enough suitable lambs for the *qorban* sacrifice and new barley for the *omer:* "I have considered the matter and thought it advisable to add thirty days to the year" (*b. Sanhedrin* 11a). Sha'ul's letters reaching out to the *Diaspora* stand as an homage to his teacher's letter so addressed.

Another similarity is in the mentoring those who were younger in the faith. Paul seems to have had a small number of *talmidim* under his wing, e.g. Timothy, Titus, and Hermas;[84] while the elder Gamli'el is said to have had a few score of them. Both of these figures displayed an exceptional tolerance for Gentiles, as well. Sha'ul quoted from Greek hymns and philosophers in his writings,[85] and Gamli'el apparently also had a more-than-passing interest in Greek culture. While this is not a sin in itself, the

---

(rather than Rabban Gamli'el II) is affirmed in Dennis Pardee and S. David Sperling, *Handbook of Ancient Hebrew Letters: A Study Edition* (SBLSBS 15; Chico, Calif.: Scholars Press, 1982), 195.

[84] Author of *Shepherd of Hermas* (see page ד, fn 13).

[85] Acts 17:28 – the hymn presented is quoted from Epimenides of Crete's play "Κρητικά," followed with a line from Aratus of Celicia (both from hymns to the chief deity of the Greek pantheon); 1 Corinthians 15:33 contains a quotation from "Thais" by Menander, a pagan philosopher; and another line from Epimenides' "Κρητικά" is quoted in Titus 1:12.

pagan elements of that culture could be seen as compromising. It is reported in the *Talmud Bavli* that he studied Greek wisdom (*b. Sotah* 49b) and that he bathed in a Greek bathhouse known for its statue of the Greek goddess of love[86] (*m. Avodah Zarah* 3:4). Gamli'el would defend this practice by asserting that the statue was not dedicated to any goddess but was merely a decorative piece.[87]

Some have even accused this Sage of engaging too much in Greek sciences like astronomy, but Gamli'el credited the *Oral Torah* for his knowledge of space: "This is the tradition[88] that I received from the house of my father's father: that the renewal of the moon takes place after not less than twenty-nine days and a half, and two-thirds of an hour, and seventy-three *chalakin* [divisions]" (*b. Rosh HaShana* 25a).[89] The "seventy-three *chalakin*" refers to the ancient Hebrew division of an hour into 1080 divisions (i.e. 1080 units of 3.3 seconds, rather than dividing into 60 minutes or 3600 seconds). Gamli'el's calculation thus equates

---

[86] *Nota Bene:* The Greek deity's name is not used here in obedience to Exodus 23:13; Psalm 16:4.

[87] Louis Jacobs, *The Jewish Religion: A Companion* (Oxford: Oxford University Press, 1995).

[88] "Tradition" is a common way of referring to the content of the *Oral Torah*.

[89] Some exegetes of the *Talmud* attribute this statement to Rabban Gamli'el II, but the identification of his paternal grandfather as the source allocates its source as being Rabban Gamli'el I. If the central figure is Gamli'el I, the grandfather indicated as the tradition's source would be Hillel haZaqen. Either way, Gamli'el I is involved.

to 29.530359 days, which deviates from the modern calculation for a synodic lunar orbit cycle (29.530388 days[90]) by only six millionths of a day, or just over half a second (0.5184 seconds).[91]

The *Talmud* holds Gamli'el haZaqen in high regard. Not only did he serve as *Nasi* (president) of Israel's highest court, the Sanhedrin Gedolah,[92] but he also holds the distinction of being the first to be lauded with the title of *Rabban* ("our master") over the usual title of *Rabbi* ("my master").[93] Per his son Shim'on ben Gamli'el, this reknowned Sage had under his tutilege as head of *Beit Hillel* a thousand *talmidim* (*b. Sotah* 49b). As a teacher, he had a peculiar way of "grading" his students. One of the few *sugyot* (passages) in the literature clearly marked as his records this method, which involved his students being compared to classes of local fish. A "ritually impure fish" was a *talmid* who had memorized

---

[90] Carl Sagan, *Broca's Brain: Reflections on the Romance of Science* (New York, N.Y.: Presidio Press, 1980; orig. 1974), 157.

[91] Irv Bromberg, "Hebrew Calendar Studies: Why Divide Hours into 1080 Parts?," *University of Toronto website* (online: http://individual.utoronto.ca/kalendis/hebrew/chelek.htm; 30 Sep 2016); accuracy confirmed with Lt. Col. Bill Welker, USAF CISSP, Personal Correspondence (13 Apr 2017).

[92] Adolph Büchler, *Das Synhedrion in Jerusalem* (Vienna, 1902), 129.

[93] Paul L. Maier, "Chronology," in Ralph P. Martin & Peter H. Davids (eds.), *Dictionary of the Later New Testament & Its Developments* (Downers Grove, Ill.: IVP, 1997), 186.

everything by study, but had no understanding (and was the son of poor parents). A pupil desig-nated as a "ritually pure fish" was one who had learned and understood everything he taught (and had come from a wealthy family). A "fish from the Jordan River" was his appellation for one who had learned everything, but didn't know how to respond; and a "fish from the Mediterranean" had learned everything and did know how to respond (*Avot d'Rabbi Nathan* 40).

The name Gamli'el means "reward of G-d," and there is something of a rewarding feeling that comes from getting to know this particular Sage. As revered as he was, there is a certain amount of difficulty in identifying the teachings that can be properly con-nected to Rabban Gamli'el haZaqen, i.e. the grandson of Rabbi Hillel of earlier mention, and which are to be attributed to Rabban Gamli'el II, the grandson of Rabban Gamli'el haZaqen. Both are formally referred to in *Talmudic* reference as Gamli'el ben Shim'on (but re: Gamli'el haZaqen, only once in *b. Shabbat* 15a), as both were the sons of men named Shim'on.[94] It would be his fourth-great grandson, Yehudah haNasi, who would compile and codify the *Mishna* (the oldest portion of the *Talmud Bavli*) about 150 years after Gamli'el haZaqen's death.[95]

---

[94] Jacob Neusner, *The Rabbinic Traditions about the Pharisees before 70: Volume 1 – The Masters* (Eugene, Ore.: Wipf & Stock, 2005; orig. 1971), 341-48.

[95] Abraham ben David, *Seder haQabbalah Leharavad* (Jerusalem: 1971), 16.

A few discussions in *Talmud Bavli* do clearly identify their subject as Rabban Gamli'el haZaqen, but not many. One which does involves a description of our subject's method for sighting the new moon (*b. Rosh Chodesh* 2), and another recalls an incident wherein Gamli'el I ordered an Aramaic copy of Job to be "immured beneath the stairway" (*b. Shabbat* 16). As Gamli'el haZaqen was the head of the *Beit Hillel* (the School of Hillel), it is reasoned that many of the epithets assigned to it could actually have been uttered by the Gamli'el of this sketch,[96] but to discern which of those is or is not so attributable would be speculation.

The present author was aided by the logical approach of Dr. Jacob Neusner, Jewish Studies professor at Brown, with regard to sorting out which Gamli'el was which. His suggestion is to examine which other Sages are mentioned in close proximity to mentions of "Gamli'el." Rabbis Yehoshua, Yosi, Shim'on, Yonathan, Eliezer, Elazar, and Aqiva were contemporaries of Rabban Gamli'el II, the grandson of the present subject, as was Onqelos (known for his contributions to the *Targumim*). Dr. David Friedman, former academic dean of Jerusalem's King of Kings College, observes that the elder Rabban Gamli'el was frequently found against the backdrop of Temple functions (having died in 52 CE, before the Temple fell), so that context assists in identifying which

---

[96] s.v. "Gamaliel I," *Jewish Encylclopedia* (Frank H. Vizetelly . ed.; Funk & Wagnall, 1906).

Gamli'el is in view.[97] Neusner also notices this and adds that describing his precise location within the Temple grounds is part of the Gamli'el the Elder formula.[98]

Modern Jewish scholars continue to list Gamli'el haZaqen as a *Nasi* of the Sanhedrin, but conspicuously not listed in the chain of transmission of the oral tradition, which may indicate that he was suspected of deviating in some way from the *Oral Torah* (whether that assessment was made in his own generation or centuries afterward). Some have speculated that Gamli'el haZaqen may have secretly become a member of a Pharisaic movement called *HaDerekh*, i.e. a follower of Yeshua haNotzri. Catholic tradition insists that Gamli'el was baptized by Apostles Peter (Keefa) and John (Yochanan), but it cites no source but a vision received by the author,[99] and in Coptic Orthodoxy,[100] a *Gospel of Gamli'el*, written sometime between 300 and 600 CE, is found among their apocryphal works.[101]

---

[97] David Friedman, *At the Feet of Rabbi Gamaliel: Rabbinic Influence in Paul's Teachings* (Clarksville, Md.: Lederer Books, 2013), 8-9.

[98] Neusner, *The Rabbinic Traditions*, 344-45.

[99] Pseudo-Clement, *Recognitions of Clement* (2nd – 4th Century CE), I, lxv, lxvi; Photius, *Bibliotheca (Myriobiblos)* (9th Century CE.), Cod. 171.

[100] Egyptian Christianity, extant ca. 3rd Century to present

[101] *Gospel of Gamli'el* (300-600 CE).

The basis for the claim is circumstantial at best, but does warrant at least a few paragraphs of this study. It is observed that members of Gamli'el the Elder's Sanhedrin had come under the teaching of *HaDerekh*.[102] Yosef of Arimathea was the man in whose tomb Yeshua was buried (Mark 15:43-47; Luke 23:50-53), and the other was Naqdimon) – the "Nicodemus" whose acceptance of Yeshua's Messianic identity is established in the *Gospel of John* (chapters 3, 7, & 19).

This association by itself would make for a rather weak argument, but the presence of a burial marker at *Beit Gamli'el* inscribed "Buried here: Cheliel (Stephen) and Nasuam (Nicodemus)" raises questions.[103] There are only four persons known to be laid to rest at Gamli'el's estate (their graves having been discovered in 415 CE by Lucian and Migetius), namely, these two, Gamli'el himself, and Abibas (the son of Gamli'el haZaqen who preceded him in death at the age of twenty).[104] The Cheliel buried there is known to be Stephen the *Netzari* martyr whose account is given in Acts 6-8. Thus, half of the interments at that property were confirmed followers of Yeshua. In 415, these four bodies were removed from their resting

[102] Emil Schürer, *Geschichte des jüdischen Volkes im Zeitalter Jesu Christi* (Leipzig, Germany: J. C. Hinrichs'sche Buchhandlung, 1898), II(1): 172.

[103] Nelson L. Price, *The Chronicles of Nicodemus* (Metairie, La.: Journey Publications, 2008).

[104] M L'abbe Fleury, *Ecclesiastical History* (transl. John Henry Parker; London: J. F. G. & J. Rivington, 1843, orig. 429), Book VIII, 260-1.

place and by 428 CE were put on display in a Contantinoplitan church.

Next in order would be an examination of the evidence *against* the tradition. *Talmud Bavli* records that it was Rabban Gamli'el who ordered the prayer against the heretics known as *"Birkhat haMinim"* (בִּרְכַּת הַמִּינִים) to be composed (*b. Berakhot* 28b-29a). The text of *Birkhat HaMinim* reads:[105]

> **For apostates may there be no hope** (if they do not return to Your *Torah*); **and the kingdom of insolence may You quickly uproot in our days; and may** *haNotzerim and* **the minim perish in an instant.** (And may all the enemies of Your people and their oppressors quickly be cut off.) (And along with the righteous may they not be written.) **Blessed are You, O L-rd, who** (breaks evil-doers and) **humbles the arrogant.**

It has been argued, often, that the "blessing," as it is titled (though more accurately a curse) had in mind as its target those Jewish persons who proclaimed faith in Yeshua haNotzri. The term *"haNotzerim"* is undoubtedly a reference to those who accepted Yeshua haNotzri as the Messiah, as besides being known as *HaDerekh*, they were also known by the designation *Netzarim*. This addition to the *Shemoneh Esrei* (18 Benedictions) even inspired a once-popular medieval production making a mockery of Yeshua's

---

[105] *Shemoneh Esrei* (Yavneh: Council of Yavneh, 90 CE). *Nota bene:* there are several versions of this malediction; any elements which are not common to all versions are indicated either by italics or by parenthetical offset.

death. Joseph Derenbourgh even theorized that *min* (מִין), the Hebrew root of *minim*, was perhaps an acronym for *Ma'aminei Yeshu*[106] *haNozri* (מַאֲמִינֵי יֵשׁוּ הַנּוֹצְרִי; i.e. "Believers in Yeshua haNotzri").[107] The root does have a meaning of its own in Hebrew, i.e. "kind, species." In the context of the *Birkhat HaMinim*, it has the vernacular equivalency to pejoratively saying "their kind," so the assertion that it stands for something else, especially given the absence of any evidence to that effect, is an untenable claim, and wholly unnecessary.

It is noteworthy that only two known copies, both found at the same place (Cairo, Geniza cache) contain the inclusion "*haNotzerim* and," thus the evidence weighs heavily against its being original to the text (and hence its italicization in the quotation of the malediction above).[108] In fact, *b. Berakhot* 28b actually gives the composition the name "*Birkhat HaTzduqim*"

---

[106] *Nota bene:* though in some contexts, "Yeshu" is used as a pejorative term, here it reflects the probable Galilean pronunciation of Yeshua (Aramaic lacks the furtive *pathach*). See David Flusser, "Jesus, His Ancestry, and the Commandment of Love," in James H. Charleswork, ed., *Jesus' Jewishness: Exploring the Place of Jesus within Early Judaism* (New York, N.Y.: Crossroad Herder, 1996; orig. 1991), 156.

[107] Joseph Naftali Derenbourgh, "Mélanges Rabbiniques III: Quelques Observations sur le Rituel," *Revue des Études Juives* 14 (1893):26-32.

[108] Marvin R. Wilson, *Our Father Abraham: Jewish Roots of the Christian Faith* (Grand Rapids, Mich.: Wm. B. Eerdmans, 1989), 68.

(בִּרְכַּת הַצָּדוּקִים; i.e. "blessing of the Sadducees") rather than "Birkhat haMinim" (בִּרְכַּת הַמִּינִים).[109]

Some insist that this reading is a later gloss, but there is a reasonable case to be made for הַצָּדוּקִים being the reading native to the Urtext. The late David Flusser, who was a professor of Second Temple Judaism at Hebrew University, takes this position, convincingly contending that the original intent was to curse the Sadducees rather than the *Netzarim*.[110] Scholar William D. Davies concurs, insisting, "it appears more reasonable to suspect that *haNotzerim* [or in some medieval versions *haMotzerim*[111]] was added to a pre-existing

---

[109] Reading from "Berakhot 28b," *Sefaria.org* (online: http://www.sefaria.org/Berakhot.28b.23?lang=bi&with=RashR&lang2=en; niqqudot added by present author).

[110] David Flusser, "The War Against Rome;" in Doris Lambers-Petry & Peter J. Tomson (eds.), *The image of the Judaeo-Christians in ancient Jewish and Christian literature* (Tübingen: Mohr Siebeck, 2003), 15; also in agreement are Reuven Kimelman, "Birkhat Ha-Minim and the Lack of Evidence for an anti-Christian Prayer in Late Antiquity," in E. P. Sanders, et al., eds., *Jewish and Christian Self-Definition Volume 2: Aspects of Judaism in the Greco-Roman Period* (London, 1981), 233; Ruth Langer, *Cursing the Christians? A History of the Birkat HaMinim* (Oxford: Oxford University Press, 2012), 342n15; Pieter Willem van der Horst, "The Birkat ha-minim in Recent Research," van der Horst, Pieter Willem. "The Birkat ha-minim in Recent Research," in *Hellenism – Judaism – Christianity: Essays on their Interaction* (2nd ed.; Leuven: Peeters, 1998), 367.

[111] Two versions of the text with the otherwise unattested word *haMotzerim* are found in the quite late textual witness *Ms. Rome Biblioteca Casanatense 3085* (14th-15th Century CE).

malediction after the period of Yavneh – and most likely after the Bar Kokhba Revolt (or later)."[112] Considering the fact that *minim* is defined in rabbinic literature as those who "reject the duality of *Torah*" (*b. Qiddushin* 66a-b),[113] the only contemporary sects which fit that nuanced definition are the Sadducees of previous mention and the Samaritans, who were not interested in Jerusalem politics. As late as the Twelfth Century CE, it was widely asserted that "the *Minim* for whose destruction we pray" in the *Birkhat HaMinim* was the sect of the Sadducees and Boethusians.[114]

It is tenable that after the disappearance of the Sadducees as a threat to the Pharisaic *hashqafah*, the text might have been amended to indicate some other present threat. Though the Sadducees were linked to the Temple in function, recent research suggests that they may have continued to antagonize the Pharisees beyond 70 CE. Josephus' descriptions of the Sadducees, written from the late-70s into the 90s, are

[112] William David Davies, Louis Finkelstein, Steven T. Katz (eds.), *The Cambridge History of Judaism* (vol. 4: The Late Roman-Rabbinic Period; Cambridge: Cambridge University Press, 2006; orig. 1984), 291.

[113] In Jacob Neusner, *Judaism When Christianity Began: A Survey of Belief and Practice* (Louisville, Ky.: Westminster John Knox Press, 2002), 165, the following is appended to that definition (based on b. Sanhedrin 90a): "...*minim, that is,* heretic Jews, wished to deny that claim [i.e. the Resurrection] and to demonstrate that the *Torah* contains no such teaching."

[114] Yehudah haLevi, 12th Century CE; cited in David Instone Brewer, "The Eighteen Benedictions and the *Minim* before 70 CE," *Journal of Theological Studies* (2003) 54 (1): 25-44.

framed in the present tense.[115] Dr. Martin Goodman, Oxford Jewish Studies professor, reflects that Josephus "does not hint for a moment in any of his writings that two of the main *haireseis* [αἱρέσεις, i.e. factions or heresies] of the Jews, through which he himself claimed to have passed, had ceased or were ceasing to exist."[116] If they had dissolved within the first few years after the destruction of the Temple, their mention in any version of a text penned in 90 CE, i.e. *Birkhat HaMinim*, would make no sense.

Dr. John Lightfoot, a mid-Seventeenth-Century Hebraist, might have supposed an earlier origin in his statement, "... if he [Rabban Gamli'el] was not the author, yet did he approve and recommend that prayer entitled ברכת המינים *a prayer against the heretics*."[117] To associate the curse with Rabban Gamli'el haZaqen, however, is certainly an error, as that Rabban Gamli'el died in 52 CE. Most *Talmud* scholars link the *Birkhat haMinim* to the Council of Yavneh in 90 CE (*b. Berakhot* 28b), which would make the Rabban Gamli'el in view here his grandson,

---

[115] Flavius Josephus, *Bellum Judaicum* (75 CE), 2.119–166; Antiquitates Judaicae (94 CE), 18.11–22.

[116] Martin David Goodman, "Sadducees and Essenes after 70 CE." 1994; repr. pp. 153-162 in Martin David Goodman, *Judaism in the Roman World: Collected Essays* (Leiden: Brill, 2007), 153.

[117] John Lightfoot, *Horæ Hebraicæ et Talmudicæ: Hebrew and Talmudical Exercitations Upon the Gospels, the Acts, Some Chapters of St. Paul's Epistle to the Romans, and the First Epistle to the Corinthians* (Oxford: Oxford University Press, 1859; orig. 1675), IV: 53.

Gamli'el II, who also bore the title of Rabban and served as *Nasi* from about 80 – 120 CE. Gamli'el II's association with liturgical developments is perhaps his greatest legacy, the *Talmud* ascribing to him rules pertaining to the recitation of the *Shema* (*m. Berakhot* 1:1), the text for *Birkhat haMazon* (*m. Berakhot* 6:8), and the establishment of the Passover liturgy (*m. Pesachim* 10:5). The present author finds the case for Gamli'el haZaqen actively opposing the *Netzarim* uncompelling, but is content to let the question of Gamli'el's allegiance to Yeshua remain a mystery until more conclusive evidence emerges.

Gamli'el haZaqen was known to relax certain standards, usually in order to alleviate burdens from the disadvantaged. Though the established standard for releasing a woman from her marriage when her husband was presumed lost in battle required two witnesses to his demise, Gamli'el required only one (*m. Yebamot* 16:7). This was because of the increasing number of widows in *Eretz-Yisrael* that Roman swords were causing.[118] He also increased the distance one could walk on Shabbat for people in certain public service roles, such as midwives (*b. Rosh HaShanah* 23b).

Gamli'el haZaqen made a name for himself as one who looked after the best interests of women and orphans. He ruled that if a man with both sons and daughters dies, the daughters are to receive maintenance provisions from his estate whether he was rich or poor, even if doing so means the sons

---

[118] Hegg, op. cit., 38.

receive no inheritance (*m. Baba Bathra* 9:1). In another ruling, he ordered that orphans have priority over widows, i.e. that a widow could not take her *kethuba* (marriage) settlement out of what is left to orphaned children, unless such was pre-arranged on oath (*m. Gittin* 4:2-3).

Gamli'el haZaqen's teachings on the subject of marriage comprise the majority of what statements are attributed to him in the *Mishna* (compiled by his descendent Yehudah haNasi). On other subjects, we know much less about his positions, but might safely assume some degree of alignment with the views of his famous grandfather Hillel haZaqen. Later rulings attributed to *Beit Hillel* likely reflect Gamaliel's voice as well. Rather than drawing criticism for taking liberal measures, however, Gamli'el I is looked upon with favor for tending to the needs of marginalized in a way which fits very well with the definition of "pure and Set Apart" religion offered by Ya'aqov ben Yosef, the brother of Yeshua haNotzri (James 1:27).[119]

---

[119] "For the worship that is pure and Set Apart before Elohim the Father, is this: to visit the fatherless and the widow in their affliction; and: that one keep himself without blemish from the world." Note that in the First Century, the two groups most vulnerable to poverty were widows and orphans, so indicating these two groups is a Semitic idiom meaning "all the needy, even down to the neediest – widows and orphans." While Gamli'el I epitomized the first part of this verse, his depth of engagement with Greek culture might be held as being in conflict with the latter nuance, i.e. "keep himself without blemish from the world."

During Rabban Gamli'el's time, funerals were being conducted in such a lavish way as to impose great expense on the surviving family members. So great was the burden that it had become commonplace for people to abandon the body and flee from their homes in order to escape paying so hefty a cost for the burial of their loved ones. It is said: "When they would bring out the deceased for burial, the rich would be carried on dargashes ornamented with rich covers, the poor on a plain bier, and the poor felt ashamed" (*b. Moed Qatan* 27a-b).

Gamli'el requested that his own funeral be administered at the least possible expense, including that he be laid to rest in simple flaxen garments worth no more than a *zuz* (dinar) as an example to others to eschew the wanton practice of "heaping expensive shrouds on the dead." Ever thereafter, "a law was passed that all should be brought out on a plain bier, out of concern for the honor of the poor" (*b. Moed Qatan* 27b).[120] Gamli'el haZaqen's example is cited as the reason Jews are buried in plain pine boxes to this day, rather than lacquered coffins, or often in *Eretz-Yisrael* with no box at all – just a burial shroud.[121]

---

[120] Caveat: There is some degree of uncertainty as to whether this paragraph pertains to Rabban Gamli'el I or to his eponymous grandson, Rabban Gamli'el II. The scholarly consensus seems to favor its attribution to the elder Gamli'el, though, and for this reason the present author includes it in this biographical sketch.

[121] Joseph Telushkin, *A Code of Jewish Ethics Volume 2: Love Your Neighbor as Yourself* (New York, N.Y.: Bell Tower, 2009), 112 (8.18).

Gamli'el haZaqen passed from this earth in the year 52 CE., eighteen years before the destruction of Jerusalem, but not before establishing a laudable legacy. From his term as *Nasi* to the abolishment of that office in 426 CE, that seat would never be occupied by any except a descendant of Rabban Gamli'el haZaqen. He could, thus, be said to have founded a dynasty whereby the office of *Nasi* became a hereditary one, anchored for nearly 400 years to *Beit Hillel*. When Gamli'el died, the *Talmud* reports, "Honor for the *Torah* ceased, and purity and piety died" (*m. Sotah* 15:18; *b. Sotah* 49a).[122] Until his death, *Torah* had always been studied in a standing position, but with his death, the respect for *Torah* reflected in that tradition dissipated and students began to undertake their study of holy writ from a less honoring seated position (*b. Megillah* 21a).

Gamli'el haZaqen, in the tradition of prior generaions of *Tanna'im*, was honored with the appelation of *haZaqen* (the Elder). He was also the first *Nasi* to receive the formal title of *Rabban*, which is one elevation above the title of *Rabbi* in his time. Only six other *Nesi'im* (the plural form of *Nasi*) would ever be honored with that title, and five of them would be direct descendants of Gamli'el haZaqen.

---

[122] This is contrasted in b. Sotah 49a with what was said after the death of Rabban Yochanan ben Zakkai, i.e. "When he [R' Yochanan ben Zakkai] died, the glory of wisdom [scholarship] ceased."

The sole exception was Rabban Yochanan ben Zakkai,[123] the subject of the next chapter.

[123] Hersh Goldwurm and Meir Holder, *History of the Jewish People: The Second Temple Era* (Brooklyn, N.Y.: Publications: 1982), 322.

The present author highly recommends the following to learn more about Gamli'el haZaqen:

> Jacob Neusner, *The Rabbinic Traditions about the Pharisees before 70: Volume 1 – The Masters* (Eugene, Ore.: Wipf & Stock, 2005; orig. 1971).

This is admittedly a broader work, covering more than just the subject of this present chapter, but the wealth of information contained in Neusner's study includes ample biographical data on Gamli'el haZaqen as well.

The reader might also, in connection with this great Sage, take a specialized interst in his pupil Sha'ul haTarsi. On this subject, the present author recommends the following:

> Mark D. Nanos & Magnus Zetterholm, eds., *Paul Within Judaism: Restoring the First-Century Context to the Apostle* (Minneapolis, Minn.: Fortress Press, 2015).[124]

This work is a collection of eight scholarly articles representing the "Paul within Judaism" view, followed by a critical analysis of the view from the New Perspective camp. Nanos is a Jewish commentator on the Pauline texts, joined on this project by a Christian professor of New Testament in Zetterholm.

---

[124] **Publisher's Note:** This selection serves as the textbook for MJR Yeshiva's BIB-401 course: Paul in Proper Perspective.

CHAPTER 5

RABBAN YOCHANAN BEN ZAKKAI

רַבָּן יוֹחָנָן בֶּן זַכַּאי

There is a fair amount of shared *hashqafah* (worldview) and tradition to be found between Rabban Gamli'el haZaqen and Rabban Yochanan ben Zakkai. David Instone Brewer, a scholar specializing in Judaisms of this era, suggests, "This may have been due to close connections between the two during their lives, or to rivalries between their disciples who both claimed the same traditions for their masters."[125] The first option seems the more tenable of the two offered, the second relying too heavily on speculation.

The present author would posit a third possibility as viable as well, i.e. that both having been students of Hillel, learning directly under his tutilege, both had received the same teachings, and thus their conduct in a given situation would be reflective of the same Hillelite *hashqafah*. This could well explain the apparent duplication of experiences, e.g. both being posed the question how many *Torot* had been given to Israel and supplying the same response (*Sifré D'varim* §351 and *Midrash Tannaim* 215, respectively). For two scholars from the same school who studied under the same rabbi and were often found presenting the same exegetical analysis for a given passage, e.g. Deuteronomy 12:3f. (*Sifré D'varim* §61 and *Avot d'Rabbi Nathan* rescension B[126] §31), it would be more surprising for them to offer vastly different responses.

---

[125] David Instone Brewer, *Techniques and Assumptions in Jewish Exegesis before 70 CE* (Tübingen: Mohr and Siebeck, 1992), 66.

[126] Note that there are two versions of *Avot d'Rabbi Nathan.* Rescension B is cited only in Spanish versions of the

Ben Zakkai's name is frequently shorthanded Ribaz (ריב"ז) in the rabbinic literature and in general Jewish parlance. As just mentioned in the previous chapter, he was the only Sage outside of the line of Rabban Gamli'el haZaqen to receive the honorific of *rabban* – a title one elevation above that of *rabbi*. Yochanan is noted for always being the first to issue a greeting in any encounter – whether with a fellow Pharisee or a Sadducee, a fellow Jew or a non-Jew. "No man ever greeted him first, even a Gentile in the marketplace" (*b. Berakhot* 17a). This did not mean, however, that every encounter could be considered a pleasant one. Yochanan was a vocal opponent to Sadducean interpretations of *Torah* (*b. Menachot* 65a; *b. Baba Bathra* 115a; *m. Yadayim* 4:5), even to the point of insistence that the Cohen HaGadol follow the Pharisaic procedure for preparation of the red heifer rather than the Sadducean interpretation, which he would have preferred (*Tos. Parah* 3:8).

Not much is known about Yochanan's father, except that his name was Zakkai (or in Greek – Zacchaeus). An interesting observation has come out of the gnostic gospels, specifically the *Gospel of Thomas*,[127] that Yeshua haNotzri, as a child, was said

---

Talmud. Any unspecified references to *Avot d'Rabbi Nathan* (or *ARN*) should be assumed to be from rescension A.

[127] The *Gospel of Thomas* is text from the gnostic Nag Hammadi cache, discovered in Egypt in 1945 and previously only extant in 3 small fragment from the *Oxyrhynchus Papyri* (P.Oxy. 654, 655). The Coptic text assigns authorship to Didymos Judas Thomas, but the dating is far too late for this to be true, i.e. mid-Second Century CE.

to have encountered a teacher and "doctor of the law" named Zaccheus. In that text, Zaccheus is teaching young Yeshua the Hebrew *alef-bet*, and Yeshua interjects a lengthy *sod*-level interpretation of the letter *alef*, to which Zaccheus responds: "He surpasseth me! I shall not attain to His understanding.... I desired to obtain a pupil, and I find I have a tutor!" (ch. vi-vii). Neusner has suggested that this may have been intended to convey Ben Zakkai rather than his father, noting the general inaccuracy of such apocryphal works. He cautions, "We cannot hope to find in them reliable information about either Yoḥanan or Jesus."[128]

He is intrigued, however, that both Ben Zakkai and the pseudo-Thomasine Zaccheus were "teachers of the *Torah*," and both were living in Galilee during Yeshua's childhood years. Yochanan lived from approximately 1 CE to 80 CE,[129] with about the first eighteen years spent in his hometown of Arav in the Galilee (*y. Shabbat* 16:7-8). If this date range is correct, he would be at least five years younger than Yeshua, who was born sometime between 4 and 7 BCE.

---

[128] Jacob Neusner, *First-Century Judaism in Crisis: Yohanan ben Zakkai and the Renaissance of Torah* (Eugene, Ore.: Wipf & Stock, 2006; orig. 1975), 65.

[129] Some place his death as late as 90 CE and his birth as early as 30 BCE (no doubt an effort to apply the 120-year formula of Moshe to him; see *b. Rosh Hashanah* 31b), but most scholars opine that his death occurred between 73 and 80 CE. Logic dictates that he needed at least seven years as *Nasi* to accomplish all that is attributed to him. His successor, Rabban Gamli'el II, had been installed as *Nasi* by 80 CE.

Neusner's ultimate conclusion is that the tale as found in the *Gospel of (Pseudo-)Thomas* was that it was most probably polemically concocted post-70 by followers of the Nazarene in order to delegitimize the authority of Yavneh.[130] His reason for leaving Arav when he did, per the rabbinical writings, is that he was dissatisfied with the low number of cases brought before him there. He handed down exactly two *halakhic* rulings during his eighteen years teaching in Arav (*m. Shabbat* 16:7, 22:3; *y. Shabbat* 16:7).

The year 70 CE is significant not only as the year of Jerusalem's destruction, but also as the year Yochanan succeeded Shim'on ben Gamli'el to the office of *Nasi* – becoming the first *Nasi* of the post-Temple era and the immediate predecessor to Rabban Gamli'el II. His rise was likely attributable, at least in part, to his brilliant escape from Jerusalem in about 68 CE during the siege by Vespasian's forces. Jewish novelist Jonathan Kirsch speculates that among the reasons for ben Zakkai wanting to escape was that the Zealots had the city in a stranglehold, inflicting a reign of terror upon those they deemed too friendly toward Rome.[131]

Since the *Talmud* laments that the cause of the fall of Jerusalem was the sin of "wanton hatred" (*b. Yoma* 9b), that assessment might be rather tenable. The story goes that Yochanan told a pair of his

---

[130] Neusner, *First-Century Judaism in Crisis*, 66.

[131] Jonathan Kirsch, *The Woman who Laughed at God: The Untold History of the Jewish People* (New York, N.Y.: Penguin Group, 2001).

talmidim to spread the (false) word that he was mortally ill and then carry him out in a death shroad and coffin (*b. Gittin* 56a-b).[132] The plan was successfully executed, and he made his way to General Vespasian's camp. Vespasian was aware, having heard it from his spies, that Yochanan had urged the Zealots (in control of Jerusalem at the time) to surrender the city. As reward for his "sage advice" (despite its not being followed), he was afforded an audience with the general.

Yochanan regaled Vespasian by greeting the general as "your Majesty," explaining that he had been shown a Divine vision of the general's coronation as Emperor. This so pleased Vespasian that he promised that were it to come to pass, he as "Emperor Vespasian" would grant Yochanan approval to continue the operation of the *beit haMidrash* he had established in Yavneh (which also served as a *beit din*), sparing the lives of his *Chakhamim* (Sages) there. Within a year, the prophecy was realized, and the Emperor's promise was honored. In Yavneh, the Ribaz reconvened the Sanhedrin and came to be known for having saved Judaism by ensuring that there would be a continuation of Jewish life even in the absence of the Temple (*Avot d'Rabbi Nathan* 4).

---

[132] Note that in Judaism, if a lie could save a life, it is not only permissible but mandatory. As the story plays out, it will be seen that multiple lives were saved through this lie. E.g. Joshua 2:1-16. Only bloodguilt, idolatry, and forbidden relations are inviolable even to save a life (*b. Yoma* 82a-b).

That request was also granted. It is said that Rabbi Aqiva criticized him for not having asked for Jerusalem to be spared, but that he believed that request would not have been granted and no Sages would be saved (*b. Gittin* 56b). Rav Joseph Soloveitchik supports Ben Zakkai's choice, writing, "Notwithstanding the sanctity and importance of the Temple, national existence is not dependent on it. However, without the Oral Law… the Jewish people would not continue to exist."[133] Rabban Yochanan had also requested of Vespasian a physician to treat Rabbi Tzadoq, who had fasted for forty years in order to delay Jerusalem's destruction, and this was also granted. Vespasian was no friend to the Jews, as evidenced by the "Iudaea Capta" denarius issued by his regime from 70-96 CE depicting a captive Jewess (image at right), but he did honor his promises to Rabban Yochanan.

Because of the timing of his ascent to the head seat of the Sanhedrin, Yochanan faced questions and dilemmas which hadn't been raised in almost six centuries, since the fall of the first Temple. Among these concerns, Rabbi Joseph Telushkin observes, was that "when the Jerusalem Temple was destroyed, many Jews feared that the path to repentance had

---

[133] Joseph B. Soloveitchik, *The Rav Speaks* (Brooklyn, N.Y.: Judaica Press, 2002), 51-2.

been permanently blocked."[134] A *midrash* recalls Rabban Yochanan's response to this fear: "My son: be not grieved. We have another atonement as effective as this [Temple sacrifice system]. And what is it? It is acts of loving-kindness, as it is said: 'For I desire mercy, and not sacrifice' [Hosea 6:6]" (*Avot d'Rabbi Nathan* 4).

Ben Zakkai was called "the greatest of the disciples" of Hillel haZaqen (*y. Nedarim* 5:6), despite being the youngest. Given the *Talmudic* description of his accomplishments as a student, it is easy to see why. It is said of him that he left nothing unstudied, whether "*Mishna, Gemara*, the *halakhot*, the *aggadot*, the exegetical details of *Torah*, the details of the Scribes, *qal w'chomer, gezara shavah*, calendrical computations, *gematria*, the speech of ministering angels, the speech of spirits, the speech of palm trees," and even topics of secular interest (*b. Sukkah* 28a). He was always the first to arrive to the *beit haMidrash*, and was never found sleeping there (*b. Berakhot* 17a, *y. Berakhot* 2:3). There is even a legend that says he was never found engaged in any activity except study (*b. Sukkah* 28a). Even so, Yochanan said of himself, "If all the heaven were parchment, all human beings scribes, and all the trees of the forest pens, it would be insufficient to write what I have learned from my teachers; and yet I only took away from them as much as a dog laps up from the ocean" (*b. Sanhedrin* 68a; *m. Soferim* 16:8)

---

[134] Joseph Telushkin, *A Code of Jewish Ethics Volume 2: Love Your Neighbor as Yourself* (New York, N.Y.: Bell Tower, 2009), 139 (10.3).

Much like his esteemed teacher, the Ribaz frequently took a more liberal approach to Scripture than many of his contemporaries. Unlike Hillel, Ben Zakkai is found far more often debating Sadducees and teaching in open air, i.e. in public settings. David Instone Brewer, a prominent research fellow at Tyndale House in Cambridge, observes, "He was known to give public answer to a question and then give a more straightforward answer to his disciples in private."[135] The destruction of the Temple might have given him license to reinterpret *Torah* and reinvent *halakha*, but he harnessed the wisdom to do so judiciously and sparingly. There were a number of ordinances which made sense when the Temple was standing but needed adjustment in the absence of that structure. The responsibility for making those changes fell upon Rabban Yochanan.

Among these were a few of edicts respecting the way that the *mo'adim* were to be convocated in the absence of the Temple. For one, he decreed that the *shofar* (ram's horn) could be sounded on *Rosh HaShanah* (*Yom Teruah*) in any locale with a *beit din* (court of justice) just as it had been in the Temple (*m. Rosh HaShanah* 4:1). Also, the four species would be taken throughout all eight days of *Sukkot* in all locales where previously that applied only in Jerusalem (with the four species taken only on day one outside the Holy City). More general extensions of Temple practices to other venues were also instituted,

---

[135] David Instone Brewer, *Divorce and Remarriage in the Bible: The Social and Literary Context* (Grand Rapids, Mich.: Wm. B. Eerdmans, 2002), 175-77.

including the requirement that a *kohen* be barefoot when pronouncing blessings. (*b. Rosh HaShanah* 31b).

In the Hillelite tradition, Ben Zakkai also made use of the *pruzbul* edict to abrogate a few *Torah* commands (*Tos. Sotah* 14:1–2). One pertained to a woman suspected of idolatry – the ritual whereby the suspect was made to drink sacral water mixed with dirt from the floor of the Tabernacle. Her body's reaction to the concoction would determine her guilt or innocence (Numbers 5:11-31). It is stated that it was done away away with "when adulterers became numerous" (*m. Sotah* 9:9), but as this ritual was linked with the *mishkan* (Temple or Tabernacle), the structure necessary to perform it was no longer there. The other was the rite of the heifer, not to be confused with the red heifer. This was a ritual sacrifice of *eglah arufah* commanded in Deuteronomy 21:1-9, wherein if the body of a murder victim was discovered and the killer was not known, absolution of bloodguilt for the community required breaking the neck of a heifer and taking it to a wadi where the elders would pronounce, "Our hands did not shed this blood, nor did our eyes see it done. Absolve, O LORD, Your people Israel whom You redeemed, and do not let guilt for the blood of the innocent remain among Your people Israel" (*Tos. Sotah* 14:1-2).

The red heifer ritual, which was for the purification rite of priests, did not cease with the fall of Jerusalem. On this matter, a Gentile who thought the ritual involved some sort of magic, asked Ben Zakkai for an explanation of the rite – a question to which he could not formulate an acceptable enough answer to appease the heathen or even his own students (they saw his answer as trivial). He retorted, that it should be sufficient that G-d had commanded it [the red heifer ritual] and that His response might likely be, "I have issued an ordinance and enacted a decree. You are not permitted to question My decree" (*Tanchuma Chukat* §8).

Like Hillel and Gamli'el before him,[136] Ben Zakkai was quite adept in the art of the parable and made good use of it. *Talmud Bavli* relays one in which a king hosts an elaborate banquet and invites all of his servants, but he does not announce the time of the feast. Those who are wise dress for the event as soon as they hear of it and await the king's call, but the foolish among them go about their usual activity, expecting to have time to prepare once the time is announced. When the king summons the invited guests, without prior warning, the wise are seated and treated to a delightful palette of fine cuisine, but the foolish are made to stand and watch, unfed. The moral is that the invitation is open to all, but those who are unprepared become uninvited (*b. Shabbat* 153a). Those familiar with the gospels may be reminded of another parable with the same message – Yeshua's tale of the prince's wedding (Matthew 22:1-14), or perhaps another – the tale of the ten virgins, five wise and five foolish (Matthew 25:1-13).

---

[136] A parable of Hillel is recorded in *Wayyiqra Rabbah* 34.3, and one from Gamli'el I is preserved in *Avot d'Rabbi Nathan* 40.10.

Ben Zakkai was also skilled at *Midrashic* exposition. His explanation for why Exodus 21:6 bears a command that a person who is eligible for freedom but chooses to remain a servant to his master is to have his master mark him by punching an awl through his ear is an example of this. Rabban Yochanan expounded: "Why was the ear singled out from all the other organs of the body? The Holy One, blessed be He, decreed: The ear heard My declaration at Mount Sinai – 'for the children of Israel are servants to Me; they are My servants' [Leviticus 25:55], which means not servants to other servants. This man, nevertheless, went ahead and [when he could have been freed, willingly] chose a master for himself. Let him be bored in the ear." (*b. Qiddushin* 22a).

Ben Zakkai was known to have had at least six *talmidim*, and more than likely several more. Of these, five comprised his inner circle, namely Rabbis Eliezer ben Hurqanus, Yehoshua  ben Chananyah, Elazar ben 'Arakh, Yosi haKohen, and Shim'on ben Netanel (*Pirqei Avot* 2:8) – depicted above. He had other students in addition to these five, including Rabbi Aqiva ben Yosef (*m. Sotah* 5:2). Yochanan thought most highly of Rabbi Eliezer and said of him: "If all the scholars of Israel were to be placed on one side of the scales and Rabbi Eliezer on the other, he [i.e. his knowledge] would outweigh them all" (*Pirqei Avot* 2:12). This disciple became like a son to him, due largely to the strained relationship Eliezer had with his own father, the Sadducean priest Hurqanus (Hyrcanus), after leaving the priesthood to study under the Ribaz.[137]

On one occasion, Rabban Yochanan saw that Eliezer's father had come to the *beit haMidrash* where the two of them studied. Unbeknown to either of them, the purpose for the elder Hurqanus's visit was to inform Eliezer that he was being disinherited. In an act of pure compassion and *chesed* (lovingkindness), ben Zakkai turned to Eliezer and said to him, "You begin and deliver the teaching." Eliezer was reluctant, but with encouragement from the Ribaz and some of the other *talmidim*, "Eliezer stood and delivered a teaching about things that no one had ever heard." Rabban Yochanan showered him with praise, commending him: "Rabbi Eliezer, my teacher! From you I have learned Truth!"

Upon hearing his son's teaching and the accolades of his teacher, Hurqanus repented of his intended message and instead informed Eliezer that he wished to bequeath to him his entire estate. Eliezer declined the offer, insisting that he be given only his proportionate share, so as not to deprive his brothers (who had actually been in favor of his own disinheritance). His real reward in the matter was that he had received (through some orchestration by his rabbi) the one thing he truly wanted – reconciliation

---

[137] Barry W. Holtz, *Rabbi Aqiva: Sage of the Talmud* (Jewish Lives; New Haven and London: Yale University Press, 2017), 51-2.

with his formerly-estranged father (*Avot d'Rabbi Nathan* 6).

Rabban Yochanan had raised a son of his own who preceded him to the grave. When his son died and the Ribaz was sitting *shiva* (i.e. mourning), he was not at all in a mood to be consoled. His leading disciples attempted the task, nonetheless, and were met with coarse reproof. Rabbi Eliezer told him, "Adam had a son who died, yet he allowed himself to be comforted... for it is said, 'And Adam knew his wife again.'" Yochanan scolded him for adding to his own grief the grief of Adam as well. Rabbi Yehoshua made a similar statement citing Job, as did Rabbi Yosi with an allusion to Aharon mourning over Nadav and Avihu and Rabbi Shim'on referencing David losing a son. Each successive visitor added to the Rabban's irritation. Just as he was about to leave his own *shiva*, Rabbi Elazar took a turn, but he spoke to justify the Rabban's grief and assuring him that his son – a student of *Torah*, *Mishna*, *halakha*, and *aggada* – had surely left this world without unatoned sin... and the Rabban was comforted by his words (*Avot d'Rabbi Nathan* 14.6).

Yochanan spent his final hours in his own bed, surrounded by his devoted *talmidim*[138] – a fitting setting for a Sage of his caliber; but sadly, weeping out of uncertainty as to how he might be judged by HaShem. He said to his disciples:

---

[138] Jacob Neusner, *A Life of Rabban Yohanan ben Zakkai: Ca. 1-80 CE* (2nd Edition. Leiden: E. J. Brill, 1970), 227.

I go to appear before the King of Kings, the Holy One, blessed be He, whose anger, if He should be angry with me, if of both this world and the world to come, and Whom I cannot appease with words nor bribe with money. Moreover, I have before me two roads – one to Paradise and one to *Gei-Hinnom*, and I know not whether He will sentence me to *Gei-Hinnom* or admit me to Paradise. (*Avot d'Rabbi Nathan* 40a, ch. 35).

His concern may have been the result of what he considered to be failures on his part, such as the time that his *talmid* Eliezer ben Hurqanus was denied food by his father because he hadn't finished plowing the field. When he was discovered in a famished state by the Ribaz, he enquired of the innkeeper whether he had eaten there that day. Upon learning that he had eaten neither there nor with Rabban Yochanan, he lamented with the innkeeper, "Between the two of us, we have left Rabbi Eliezer to perish!" (*Avot d'Rabbi Nathan* 6).

Rabban Yochanan was laid to rest in Tiberias (image on next page). Several centuries later, Moshe ben Maimon (Maimonides) would be buried very near to his grave. The last words the Ribaz uttered before his final breath had a somewhat Messianic tone about them: "Prepare a throne for Hezekiah, King of Judah, who is coming" (*b. Berakhot* 28b). Note that though some translations append something like "to accompany me to Heaven" to the end of that statement, the Hebrew does not include any such qualifier, simply: "והכינו כסא לחזקיהו מלך יהודה שבא:", as is translated above. Yochanan ben Zakkai is eulogized thus: "When he died, the glory of wisdom [scholarship] ceased" (*m. Sotah* 9:15; *b. Sotah* 49a). And, when his academy burned, it was said to be no less grievous for the Jewish people than when the Jerusalem Temple was destroyed (*y. Megillah* 3:1).

מצבת התנא הקדוש רבן יוחנן בן זכאי
הוא היה אומר: אם למדת תורה הרבה
אל תחזיק טובה לעצמך כי לכך נוצרת
אבות .ב

TOMB INSCRIPTION:
Tomb of the Holy Tanna Rabban Yochanan ben Zakkai
He used to say: If you have learned a lot of *Torah*, do not credit
it favorably for yourself, because for this you were created.
[Pirqei] Avot 2 [v. 9].

The present author found the following work to be a treasure-trove of Ben Zakkai material:

> Jacob Neusner, *First-Century Judaism in Crisis: Yohanan ben Zakkai and the Renaissance of Torah* (augmented ed.; Eugene, Ore.: Wipf & Stock, 2006; orig. 1975).

This is admittedly an older work, but should certainly be classed as a classic. Neusner, per his usual inimitably high standard, presents a thoroughly researched and laid out presentation on this pivotal late-First-Century personality.

To learn more about his *talmid* Eliezer ben Hurqanus, who featured promininently in this chaper, consider:

> Yitzhak D. Gilat, *R. Eliezer ben Hyrcanus: A Scholar Outcast* (Bar-Ilan Studies in Near Eastern Languages and Culture; Bar-Ilan University Press, 1984).

Though the present work did not delve very deeply into his life and ministry, it is, as the title of the suggested work may hint. comprised of a fascinating series of events.

CHAPTER 6

RABBI AQIVA BEN YOSEF

רַבִּי עֲקִיבָא בֶּן יוֹסֵף

Rabbi Aqiva ben Yosef, a student of Rabban Yochanan ben Zakkai (per *m. Sotah* 5:2), conducted his teaching ministry from 50 CE to his martyrdom in 135 CE. Aqiva was born of rather unwealthy parents and had very humble beginnings in life.[139] His father is reputed to have been a *ger tzedeq* (Gentile convert) who descended from the famous Roman general Sisera (*b. Sanhedrin* 96), but the claim lacks any credible evidence.[140] As he did not have the means to procure flocks of his own, he hired himself out to a wealthy rancher named Kalba Savua.[141]

"Wealthy" may be a bit of an understatement, in all truth. Substantial enough were Savua's resources to be able to feed every inhabitant of Jerusalem for a

---

[139] Ioseph ben Iacob Shalit, *Mantua Haggadah* (2nd ed.; Padua, 1568). [*Nota bene*: this is also the source of the image of Rabbi Aqiva which appears on this page.]

[140] Barry W. Holtz, *Rabbi Aqiva: Sage of the Talmud* (Jewish Lives; New Haven and London: Yale University Press, 2017), 15.

[141] *Talmud* tractate *b. Gittin 56a* suggests that the origin of Kalba Savua's name is that when poor beggars would come to his home in search of a meal, they would leave with full bellies, like "sated dogs." In Aramaic, *kalba* (כַּלְבָּא) is the word for dog and *sabua* (סָבוּא) the word for one who satisfies or causes to be sated.

decade, were the city to ever come under siege (*Qoheleth Rabbah* 7.19). In fact, he and two other men of comparable wealth – Naqdimon ben Gurion and Ben Tzitzis haKetzas – did so apply their resources during at least one Roman assault on the city (*b. Gittin* 56a). He was well-known as an exceedingly generous man.

At this point in his life, Aqiva described himself as an "ignorant shepherd" and an "ignoramus" and recalls the hatred he harbored against *Torah* scholars at that stage of his life and what he would have done with one if he had the opportunity: "Who will give me a Sage so that I can bite him like a donkey?" When asked if he had meant to say "like a dog," he responded, "No – a donkey, because a donkey bites and breaks bones; a dog bites and does not break a bone." (*b. Pesachim* 49b). Despite all of this, Kalba's daughter Rachel[142] found in Aqiva qualities which she deemed desirable, especially his modesty, and she

---

[142] *Nota bene:* the name Rachel comes from *Avot d'Rabbi Nathan* 6, an admittedly later source; in the earliest sources, Kalba's daughter appears with no indication as to her proper name. The name Rachel has become traditionally associated with her and is used in the present work for the fluidity that it adds to the retelling, but the reader should bear in mind that its accuracy might be somewhat tenuous. It is observed in Shamma Friedman, "A Good Story Deserves Retelling – the Unfolding of the Akiva Legend," *Jewish Studies: An Internet Journal* 3 (2004): 55-93; online: http://www.biu.ac.il/JS/JSIJ/3-2004/Friedman.pdf that the name Rachel (רָחֵל) means "sheep or ewe," which given the profession of her father and, initially, of Aqiva, provides a pleasant poetic element to the love story.

bargained with him that if he would take up the study of *Torah* under the tutilege of a rabbi, she would marry him (*b. Kethubot* 62b). He agreed to her proposal, and the two became secretly betrothed. When Kalba Savua learned of it, he was furious. He disowned his daughter, vowing to never assist her as long as she was Aqiva's wife, because at the time Aqiva, at the age of forty, could not recite a single portion of *Torah* or even one ruling of *halakha* (*b. Kethubot* 62b). Thus, it is plain to see that Kalba was not repelled by Aqiva's financial status, but rather by his apparent disinterest in the Word of HaShem.

The love story here is a complicated one. For the first several years of their marriage, Aqiva and Rachel lived in such abject poverty that Rachel had to sell her hair to support her husband's *Torah* studies. This was her own idea and her decision; since she had persuaded him to go study with a rabbi, she determined that she would pay the expense involved. He went off for a period of twenty-four years to study under Rabbis Yehoshua ben Hananiah and Eliezer ben Hurqanus. He told his wife that for all she had sacrificed in order to allow him to study abroad for so long, if he could ever afford it, he would make her a "Jerusalem of gold." A "Jerusalem of gold" was an elaborate gold diadem-type hair ornament with a scene of Jerusalem engraved into it. He eventually did have the means to do so, and Rachel wore that ornament with delight (*b. Nedarim* 50a; *b. Shabbat* 59a), rousing the jealousy of even Rabban Gamli'el's wife (*y. Shabbat* 86:1).[143] (An artist's depiction of Rachel wearing the diadem appears on the back cover of the present work.)

The change in Aqiva's financial situation is the result of a rather surprising twist in the story of Rachel and her father. Kalba Savua heard that an important rabbi was to be in town and went to go see this great teacher, without knowing his identity. When he realized that the acclaimed scholar was his son-in-law Aqiva, he "fell on his face, kissed Aqiva's feet, and gave him half his wealth" (*b. Kethubot* 63a). Recalling how elephantine Kalba's fortune was, this act would be comparable to a billionaire giving half of his or her worth all to one recipient in today's economy. This episode serves to verify that Kalba's original displeasure with Aqiva was as Kalba had stated, i.e. the middle-aged shepherd's lack of concern for the *Torah*. Having experienced such poverty, Aqiva harbored great compassion for the poor. It is recalled that he said, "Even the poor of Israel, we see them as if they are free people who have lost their property, because they are children of Abraham, Isaac and Jacob" (*m. Baba Qamma* 8:6).

Aqiva's love for his fellow extended beyond his selfless wife, and even beyond those with whom he had shared ethnicity and culture. Though actually "part-Jewish," the Samaritans (called *Shomrim*, i.e.

---

[143] On the back cover of this book, there is a depiction of Rachel wearing her Jerusalem of Gold diadem, designed by Israeli artist Aharon Shevo for the Israel Philatelic Service in 2008.

guardians/keepers, in Hebrew) were despised by the vast majority of First-Century Jewry. The reasons for this were not strictly ethnic, but also derived from the Samaritan rejection of the Prophets and Writings (as well as of the *Oral Torah*)[144] and their distortion of the written *Torah* into a derivative but slanted work known as the "Samaritan Pentateuch."[145] The tension which these elements roused between the Samaritans and the majority of Israelites, however, was not shared by Aqiva. He made it a point to be friendly toward them and encouraged the same attitude in

---

[144] The Samaritans rejected the Prophetic books on the grounds that their version of *Torah*, the Samaritan Pentateuch (ﬤ), allowed for only Moshe (Moses) to hold the title and office of prophet. Cf. John MacDonald, *The Theology of the Samaritans* (SCM Press, 1964), 204-11.

[145] The Samaritan Pentateuch (ﬤ) is more often in line with the Dead Sea Scrolls (DSS) than is the Hebrew Masoretic Text (𝕸) and is likely the primary source text for the Qumran (𝕼) version of the *Torah*. The differences between ﬤ and 𝕸 number around 6000, about half of which are merely orthographical, i.e. variations in the spelling of words or the embellishment of the text by the addition of extra words for clarification. The remaining 3000 are more significant, including the replacement of Jerusalem as the Temple site with Mount Gerazim in the former. Another major change is that in 𝕸 Exodus 20, the first commandment is "I am HaShem your G-d Who brought you out of Egypt," while in ﬤ that verse is viewed as an introduction to the Decalogue, and an extra commandment is add-ed as the tenth, i.e. a com-mand to establish Mount Gerazim. Per Emanuel Tov, *Textual Criticism of the Hebrew Bible* (Grand Rapids, Mich.: Wm. B. Eerdmans, 1992), 159-60, the *Septuagint* (𝕲 or LXX) favors ﬤ in 1900 of the passages where ﬤ differs from 𝕸.

others, making no qualms about sharing a meal with a Samaritan person (*m. Shevuot* 8:10). His *halakha* even allowed intermarriage between Jews and Samaritans (*b. Qiddushin* 68a). He regarded this approach as honoring the "spirit of the *Torah*" above the letter.

Aqiva's position on intermarriage was contingent on halakhic adherence. Because Roman women did not observe *kashrut* (halakhic diet), he agreed with the prohibition against Jews taking them as wives. On one occasion, Rabbi Aqiva and Rabbi Tzadok each have their virtue tested by a Roman general. He sent Tzadok a slave woman and Aqiva two beautiful young women in bridal attire to spend the night with them. Tzadok struggled with the temptation with which he had been presented, but emerges in the morning with his chastity intact by pouring himself into the study of *Torah* all through the night. Aqiva did not overcome temptation; rather, he suffered none. He found no appeal in the proposition of involving himself with pagan women. For him, his repulsion at their absence of *kashrut* standards trumps all their physical charms. Though both rabbis maintained their purity, Aqiva was judged the greater of the two, because he had tempered his *yetzer hara* (evil impulse) to the point that he was never even tempted to sin.[146]

Aqiva believed that it was a *mitzwah* (commandment) of utmost importance to visit the sick. *Biqur cholim*, as it is called in Hebrew, goes beyond just

---

[146] Jonathan Wyn Schofer, *The Making of a Sage: A Study in Rabbinic Ethics* (Madison, Wisc.: University of Wisconsin Press, 2005), 109-11.

spending time with a person who is ill; it implies providing a level of care as well. The verb *baqar* (בָּקַר) means "to care for, to make enquiry, to seek," and the fact that this word is used rather than *paqad* (פָּקַד), to visit, is significant. Rabbi Aqiva is a great exemplar of this. He once had a student who had fallen gravely ill, to the point that his life was in peril. Upon hearing that no one had been taking care of the young man or even taking time to visit him, Rabbi Aqiva made a personal visit with him. While in the young man's home, Aqiva swept and scrubbed his floors for him, believing that the unclean surroundings was contributing to the illness. The student recovered and told Rabbi Aqiva, "My teacher: you have brought me back to life!" Aqiva went out from the house and proclaimed, "Whoever does not visit the sick, it is as if he spilled blood!" (*b. Nedarim* 40a).

Another illustration of Rabbi Aqiva's compassion emerges when he returned home with twelve thousand students halfway through his studies, his wife Rachel greeted him in unelaborate attire, to the criticism of some of the *talmidim*. He was, no doubt, disappointed with the conduct of his pupils. Among his plethora of aphorisms, after all, was the oft-quoted teaching, "Mockery and levity accustom a person to immorality" (*Pirqei Avot* 3:17). A neighbor woman also scolded her for not dressing up for the occasion, in response to which Rachel quoted from Proverbs. Which verse she quoted depends on the version of the story one is reading, but several indicate Proverbs 29:7 – "A righteous man is concerned with the cause of the wretched."[147] Aqiva defended his bride, insist-ing, "Everything we are is thanks to her!" He recognized and verbalized that Rachel had sacrificed to the point of becoming "wretched and down-trodden" for the sake of Aqiva and his studies – a sacrifice from which all of them had benefited as well.[148]

Caring for the poor and needy was also a high priority for Rabbi Aqiva. On one occasion, Rabbi Tarfon handed over to him four thousand gold dinar – a rather colossal sum of money. The coins came accompanied with instructions to invest it on his behalf. Aqiva agreed to the assignment and proceeded to divide the money up among poor and needy students in his own *beit haMidrash*. Not long afterward, Tarfon asked Aqiva to show him the fruit of his investment, expecting that Aqiva had purchased a town, or maybe even two, with the money (the amount was certainly sufficient for such a task). Aqiva then introduced him to his students. One of them arose and read Psalm 112 up to verse 9 – "He hath scattered abroad, he hath given to the needy; his righteousness endureth for ever." He then told Tarfon, "This is the town you have acquired, and it shall stand forever." Tarfon kissed and embraced his colleague and exclaimed, "My teacher in wisdom,

---

[147] Others supply the text of Proverbs 12:10 – "A righteous man knows the life of his beast" – a less romantic choice.

[148] Shamma Friedman, "A Good Story Deserves Retelling – the Unfolding of the Akiva Legend," *Jewish Studies: An Internet Journal* 3 (2004): 55-93; online: http://www.biu.ac.il/JS/JSIJ/3-2004/Friedman.pdf.

my superior in right conduct!" and proceeded to give Akiva additional funds for the poor (*Kallah Rabbathi* 2; *Wayyiqra Rabbah* 34.16).

Jewish Theological Seminary professor Dr. Barry Holtz notes that "Aqiva is self-invented. He has teachers but seems mostly to be teaching himself."[149] Early in his studies, Aqiva had anchored himself to Rabban Gamli'el II (grandson of the subject of chapter 4, present work), thus continuing the influence of the School of Hillel over into a new century. Gamli'el II placed Rabbi Aqiva in charge of the distribution of the *Ma'aser Sheni* (second tithe) to the poor (*m. Ma'aser Sheni* 5:9). He is also, as noted, a *talmid* of Rabban Yochanan ben Zakkai for a time (*m. Sotah* 5:2). He would close out the First Century not in *Eretz-Yisrael*, but in Rome, locating there in about 95 CE.[150] He returned to the Land, however right around the start of the Second Century, as it was there that his voice carried the greatest authority. When he returned, it is said that he had with him 24,000 students who had discipled themselves to him (*b. Kethubot* 62b-63a).

So revered was Rabbi Aqiva, the general rule was regarding his rulings was: "The *halakha* is always in agreement with R. Akiba when he differs with his colleague" (*b. Eruvin* 46a). There is a midrash about Adam foreseeing the generation of Rabbi Aqiva. It

---

[149] Holtz, op. cit., 53.

[150] Heinrich Grätz, *Geschichte der Juden von den ältesten Zeiten bis auf die Gegenwart* (impr. and ext. ed.; Leipzig: Leiner, 1900), IV:121.

conveys that "the Holy One, blessed be He, showed him [Adam] every generation and its thinkers, every generation and its sages. When he came to the generation of Rabbi Akiba, he [Adam] rejoiced at his learning but was grieved at his death." (*b. Sanhedrin* 38b). The following story, also midrashic, speaks of how much Rabbi Aqiva contributed to the canon of Jewish *halakha*:

> When Moshe ascended on high the Holy One was found sitting and tying crowns to letters. He said in his presence, "Master of the World! Who detains your hand?" He said to him, "There is a certain man who is yet to come, at the end of many generations, his name is Aqiva ben Yosef; he will one day seek on each and every tip mounds and mounds of *halakhot*. (*b. Menachot* 29b).

This "mounds and mounds of *halakhot*" that is mentioned is most probably a reference to Aqiva's influence on what came to be our present body of *Mishnaic* literature – numerous volumes of *midrash* on the *Torah*.[151]

Some of this is due to what he perceived to be misin-terpretation of the Scriptures by prior Sages and his desire to correct those rulings borne out of faulty exegesis. Aqiva saw in Scripture a value he himself held dear and wished to defend, i.e. the dignity of women. The reader may recall from the first few paragraphs of the present chapter that his wife Rachel

---

[151] Zacharias Frankel, *Hodegetica in Mischnam: Librosque cum ea conjunctos Tosefta, Mechilta, Sifra, Sifri* (Sumptibus Henrici Hunger, 1859).

had chosen him, proposed to him, and supported him, so it might be deduced from this that his enlightened stance toward women may have been the result of his love and admiration for the resolute woman to whom he was married. Aqiva was successful in having the *halakhot* which forbade women from social interaction abolished (*Sifra Mezora'*; *b Shabbat* 64b) as well as those which allowed them to be sold as underage brides (*Mekh. Mishpatim* §3). Aqiva overturned a *halakha* which prohibited women in *niddut* (menses) from wearing makeup or otherwise adorning themselves. He ruled, "If you hold this view, you will soon make her unattractive to her husband and he will eventually divorce her" (*b. Shabbat* 64b). He is credited with being a "rescuer of Judaism," preserving the connections between the rabbinical *halakha* and the biblical text via his "mounds and mounds of *halakhot*" (*m. Sotah* 5:2).

To be a student of one who labored to add so much to the *halakhic* corpus of Israel must have been daunting. Aqiva is reputed to have required a near-perfect degree of mastery from his *talmidim*. He is quoted as teaching, "... a person is

Aqiva depicted in Rylands Haggadah

obligated to repeat a lesson for his disciple until he learns it [however many times it takes]. As it is said, 'And you shall teach the children of Israel'

[Deuteronomy 31:19]." (*b. Eruvin* 54b). Repetition was the common andragogy among the Pharisaic Sages, but some limited the number of reptitions, e.g. Rabbi Eliezer setting the maximum at four iterations (ibid.), whereas Aqiva imposed no limit. It is said that at the end of a man's life, he will be asked about his study of *Torah*. One who did not study much will hear the question: "Why did you not study *Torah* when you were in this world?" If he uses his poverty as an excuse or if he complains that his ancestors laid up no merit for him,[152] in either case, the response from HaShem will be that this was also true for Aqiva, and he studied. "Rabbi Aqiva will shame many who did not study *Torah* in this world" (*Avot d'Rabbi Nathan* §12[153]).

He could even be found studying the *Torah* when it was potentially perilous to do so. Rome was not a friend to the Jews, and under their occupation, taking up the study of *Torah* marked one for persecution or possibly even death. Aqiva was studying on one occasion where he had drawn a very large crowd. Pappos ben Yehuda, concerned for his safety, asked

---

[152] Per Holtz, op. cit., 61; the idiom "laid up no merit for him" means that he neither came from a family of remarkable lineage nor one distinguished by exemplary behavior.

[153] Note that there are two versions of *Avot d'Rabbi Nathan*. This anecdote comes from what is known as rescension B, cited only in Spanish versions of the Talmud. Any unspecified references to *Avot d'Rabbi Nathan* or *ARN* should be assumed to be from rescension A.

him, "Aqiva: Are you not afraid of the wicked government?" He responded with a parable:

> What is this situation like? To a fox who was walking along the bank of a stream and found some fishes flitting from one place to another. The fox said to them, 'From what are you fleeing?' They answered, 'From nets which men are bringing against us." The fox said to them, 'Come up on dry land, and let us – you and me – dwell together in safety, as my fathers dwelt with yours.' The fishes replied, 'Is it not said of you that you are the cleverest of all animals? Yet you are a fool. For, if we are afraid in the place which is our life-element, how much moreso would we be in a place which is our death-element!' So it is with us: while we sit and study *Torah*, of which it is written it is your life and length of days [Deuteronomy 30:20], we find ourselves in such plight, yet how much worse if we were to neglect the *Torah*! (*b. Berakhot* 61b).

Aqiva's reputation is not entirely without blemish, however. The name Aqiva, also sometimes spelled Akiva or Akiba, is a form of the Aramaic root עקב, meaning "to follow." Ironically, Aqiva is perhaps best known outside of Jewish circles for "following" the revolutionary Shim'on Bar Kokhba and regretably declaring him to be the Messiah in 135 CE and even, in his pronouncement, changing his name from Bar Koziva (בַּר כּוֹזִיבָא,[154] ironically "son of deception"[155])

---

[154] This and its Hebrew equivalent בֶּן כּוֹזִיבָא are both attested in the *Talmud Bavli* at b. Sanhedrin 93b and 97b and in the *Talmud Yerushalmi* at y. Ta'anit 4:8.

[155] Per Marcus Jastrow, *Dictionary of the Targumim, Talmud Babli and Yerushalmi, and the Midrashic Literature*

to Bar Kokhba (בַּר כּוֹכְבָא, i.e. "son of a star") and declaring him to be the "star [who] shall go forth from Ya'aqov" prophesied in Numbers 24:17 (y. Ta'anit 4:5-8). This was perhaps his greatest failing, though he did recant the proclamation not long after its initial issuance, when it became apparent that the rebellion was being led by one "with clay feet."[156] Inasmuch as his word was sufficient to garner widespread acceptance of Bar Kokhba as Israel's Messiah on the grand scale that it did, it can tenably be argued that he held significant sway in his own era, i.e. the late First Century CE, as well, his teaching ministry operating from circa 55 until his death (the result of brutal torture suffered during his Roman imprisonment) in 135 CE. This brief mis-step in discernment is by far overshadowed by his copious contributions to rabbinical scholarship.

The *midrashic* literature comments, "Things which had not been revealed even to Moshe were revealed to Rabbi Aqiva. To Aqiva we can apply the verse: 'His eyes behold every precious thing' [Job 28:10]" (*Pesiqta Rabbathi* 14.13). Rabbi Aqiva is remembered (with mostly favorable response) for defending the place of Song of Songs in the biblical canon. The debate of his day was one of interpretation, i.e. whether the plain meaning of the text was too salacious to be

(New York, N.Y.: Title Publishing, 1943; orig. 1903), 627-8, the semantic range of the verb כָּזַב is "to fail, dry up (of watercourses); to be false, to lie, to flatter... be a deceiver;" and of the noun כָּזָב: "falsehood."

[156] Berel Wein, "Rabbi Akiva," *The Voice of Jewish History* Online: http://rabbiwein.com.

considered Scripture, and whether there might be an alternative (allegorical) way to understand its messsage. The allegorical approach was not popular with some, but Aqiva insisted that both readings could be accepted, stating, "Did not Scripture say: One thing spake G-d, twofold is what I heard (Psalm 62:11), and did this not imply a twofold meaning...?" (*b. Sanhedrin* 34a). He was perhaps the most outspoken advocate there was for the allegorical hermeneutic, believing that every detail of the Biblical text, however insignificant it might seem, was important to the proper understanding of the message HaShem had delivered at Sinai.[157] He even asserted that "if all Scripture was holy, Song of Songs was the Holy of Holies" (*m. Yadayim* 3:5). Holtz recognizes, "He is unhesitant in his challenge to those in authority, and in challenging them, he upends mountains and forges a new path."[158]

A frequently-cited *sugya* of the *Talmud* relates that in 70 CE, when the ruins of Jerusalem were still yet smoldering, four rabbis passed by — all of them wailing in mourning except one. The exception was Rabbi Aqiva, who, after a few moments of somber silence, broke out in laughter. He explained his response to his confused compatriots thus:

> Seeing the fulfillment of the prophecy — 'Zion will be plowed like a field' [Zechariah 8:4-5] — I more

---

[157] Marvin A. Sweeney, *Tanak: A Theological and Critical Introduction to the Jewish Bible* (Minneapolis, Minn.: Fortress Press, 2012), 28.

[158] Holtz, op. cit., 52.

deeply internalize the knowledge that all the prophecies will be fulfilled, including those that foretell the rebuilding of Jerusalem!" (b. Makkot 24a).

In this, the other rabbis found comfort. Rabbi Aqiva saw the event in light of prophecy and trusted HaShem's Word would not fail. That is not to say that Rabbi Aqiva did *not* mourn Jerusalem's destruction; he most certainly did, and taught that all should. Though there was never placed upon the 9th of Av (the date of the destruction) any official prohibition against work, Aqiva cautioned, "Anyone who does work on *Tisha b'Av* [the 9th of Av] will never see in his work any sign of blessing" (b. Ta'anit 30b).

Aqiva was, in general, an optimist, and this demeanor soon became inextricably intertwined with his reputation. He was once on a journey which took him through a certain town where he sought lodging for the night, but hospitality was not to be found there. To each refusal, he replied, "Whatever the All-Merciful does, He does for the best." He had with him a rooster to awaken him at dawn, a donkey to ride upon, and a lamp by which to study. As he slept that night in a field outside of town, a gust of wind extinguished his lamp, a cat ate his rooster, and a lion devoured his donkey. When he awoke and discovered this, he responded, "Whatever the All-Merciful does, He does for the best." When he went back into town, he found that it had been plundered by a gang of bandits that same night... an experience he adjudged as one he was glad to have had allude him. He said, "One should always accustom himself to say,

'Whatever the All-Merciful does, He does for the best." (*b. Berakhot* 60b).

Rabbi Aqiva promoted the praxis of exercising different prayer styles in different settings, i.e. something more reserved in public so as not to draw attention, but in private, his own prayers involved "genuflexions and prostrations" so spirited that he would invariably end in a spot some distance from where he began (*b. Berakhot* 31a). This sentiment would be echoed by later rabbis (3rd/4th Century *amora'im* Rabbi Helbo and Rabbi Huna):

> Whosoever has a fixed place[in the synagogue] for his prayer has the G-d of Avraham as his helper. And when he dies, people will say of him: Where is the pious man? Where is the humble man? (*b. Berakhot* 6b).

Despite the seriousness he ascribed to the duty to pray, Aqiva was not as adamantly opposed to the popular notion than an abbreviated form of the *Amidah* prayer (aka *Shemoneh Esrei*) was sufficient (*m. Berakhot* 4:3) as was Gamaliel II. He ruled that "If one is fluent in his prayer, he recites the *Shemoneh Esrei*, but if not – an abridged *Shemoneh Esrei*" (*b. Berakhot* 28b). With regard to the *Shema* (Deuteronomy 6:4-9), he declared that the requirement to recite it was compulsory for all who had enough discernment to distinguish a domesticated donkey from a wild one (*b. Berakhot* 9b). He is credited with having authored the *Avinu Malkheinu* prayer, which is still included in the liturgy to this day (*b. Ta'anit* 25b).

Given Aqiva's love for the Jewish people – advocating that "every Jew is to be regarded as a prince" (*b. Baba Metzia* 113b) – it is ironic that Judaism has the name Aqiva perpetually linked to the demise of his 24,000 of students who perished in the Hadrianic Period (117-138 CE), all dying in the same year between the feasts of *Pesach* and *Shavuot* (*b. Yebamot* 62b). The number given in the text is literally phrased "12,000 pairs of disciples," perhaps suggesting that they were likely paired up for their studies – a common practice in rabbinical schools. The number is likely hyperbolic, e.g. apportioning 1000 for each year he was separated from his wife to pursue the study of *Torah*, or as Holtz suggests, "a way to express in figurative language his enormous influence."[159] To this day, it is a custom in Judaism that weddings are not performed in the time between these two feasts out of respect for Rabbi Aqiva and the students he lost in that timeframe (*Shulchan Arukh* 493:1).[160]

According to legend and math, Aqiva was over 100 years old when this occurred, but he was not deterred. He took on five new students and his *Beit haMidrash* started anew. Through those five *talmidim*, it is said, Judaism was rebuilt. They were able to accomplish what thousands of students before them could not – they conquered Rome and came to be called "the waters that beat down rock." These five were Rabbis Meïr Baal HaNes, Yehudah bar Ilai, Yosi ben Halafta, Shim'on bar Yochai, and Eleazar ben

---

[159] Holtz, op. cit., 83-4.

[160] Yosef Karo of Safed, *Shulchan Arukh* (Israel, ca. 1560), 493:1.

Shammua. When he became their rabbi, he told them, ""The previous disciples died only because they begrudged one another the knowledge of Tora. See to it that you do not act like them" (*b. Yebamot* 62b). They took his words to heart, and it is largely because of these five that Rabbi Aqiva is honored in the *Talmud* with the monikers "*Rosh laChachomim*" (Head of all the Sages) and "*Av haMishna*" (Father of the *Mishna*). Those students are credited with the four main collections of rabbinical wisdom:

> Our *Mishnah* comes directly from Rabbi Meïr, the *Tosefta* from R. Nehemiah, the *Sifra* from R. Judah, and the *Sifré* from R. Simon; but they all took Aqiva for a model in their works and followed him (*b. Sanhedrin* 86a).

Aqiva saw times of trial, even the loss of Jerusalem, as a sanctifying act of HaShem: "G-d is the *mikveh* of Israel. Just as a *mikveh* purifies the defiled, so too G-d purifies Israel" (*m. Yoma* 8:9). He used to teach, "Beloved is man, for he was created in the image of God. A special love [was shown man], for it was made known to him that he was created in the image of God.... Beloved is Israel, for they are called the children of God. But, a special love [was shown to Israel], for it was made known to them that they were called the children of God, for it is written, 'You are children to the Lord your God'" (*Pirqei Avot* 3:14). For Aqiva, thus, a "Jewish slave" was an oxymoronic concept, for every Jew is to be regarded as a prince (*b. Baba Metzia* 113b).

When Hadrian imposed anti-Semitic decrees outlawing the practice of Judaism, and declaring it a capital offense to teach *Torah*, Rabbi Aqiva defiantly began teaching *Torah* openly in a public square. When he was imprisoned for that crime, he encountered a fellow prisoner named Pappus, who said to him, "Blessed are you, Rabbi Aqiva, that you were arrested for teaching *Torah*; woe to Pappus, who was arrested for trying to make a few dollars." (*b. Berakhot* 61b). On one occasion during Aqiva's incarceration, Rabbi Yehoshua haGarsi brought water to the prison for him to drink and wash his hands. The guard said that it was too much water and poured half of it out. Aqiva's response was to use the water for the keeping of the command to wash hands before eating rather than to quench his thirst, as there was no longer enough to serve both ends (*b. Eruvin* 21b).

Much to his misfortune, Aqiva's fate was to be decided by Tineius Rufus,[161] the pagan Roman then serving as Governor of Judea,[162] who also happened to be the ex-husband of Aqiva's wife at the time — Rufina. She had observed a debate between her husband Rufus and Aqiva in which the latter clearly bested the former. Part of the exchange consisted of

---

[161] On the 9th of Av, 70 CE, this same Tineius Rufus, as a military commander, had maliciously plowed over the remains of Jerusalem after it s destruction, ensuring that anything that had survived was reduced to rubble (m. Ta'anit 4:6).

[162] David A. Fiensy and James Riley Strange, eds., *Galilee in the Late Second Temple and Mishnaic Periods: Life Culture, and Society* (Minneapolis, Minn.: Fortress Press, 2014), xv.

Rufus levying the charge that Israel's G-d must be angry with the Jews for helping the poor, operating from the assumption that they were poor by Divine design and will. Aqiva countered by quoting from Isaiah 58:7: "... deal thy bread to the hungry, and... bring the poor that are cast out to thy house" (*b. Baba Bathra* 10a).

Though this public embarrassment certainly roused Rufus's ire, what most likely made them such bitter enemies was that Aqiva foresaw through the *Ruach haQodesh* (HaShem's Holy Spirit) that Rufina would convert to Judaism and become his wife (*b. Nedarim* 50b). Aqiva kept that to himself, but it did come to pass. The final outcome was played out with Rufus ordering that Aqiva be flayed to death with iron combs (*b. Berakhot* 61b) – certainly a cruel and obscene punishment, especially given that Aqiva's Judaism forbade torture even for the vilest of offenders (*b. Kethubot* 37b).

On the eve of *Yom Kippur* (Day of Atonement), 135 CE, at the traditional time for the recitation of the *Shema*, Rabbi Aqiva was taken from his cell to be publicly executed for the crime of teaching *Torah*. As the Romans were flaying his aged body, he was asked, "Even till now? Are you still thinking about your obligations to G-d even at this horrific, tragic moment?" His response was, "All my life, I have waited for the opportunity to show how much I love G-d, and now that I have the opportunity – should I waste it? Loving G-d with all one's soul means even if He takes your life." It is recorded that this great Sage breathed his last breath with the familiar words of

Deuteronomy 6:4 emanating from his trembling lips: "*Shema Yisrael HaShem Elokeinu HaShem echad*" (Hear, O Israel: The L-rd is our G-d; The L-rd is one), drawing out the word *echad* until the moment life passed out of him. At that moment, it is recorded that a *bat qol* (בַּת קוֹל; i.e. a Divine whisper) was heard saying, "Hail to you, Rabbi Aqiva, that your soul left you with the word *echad* (one). You have a share in eternity!" (*b. Berakhot* 61b).

Like Hillel, Aqiva bears the distinction of being classed with Moshe through the idiomatic 120-year formula of forty years *Torah*-less (as a shepherd), forty years a student of *Torah*, and forty years a *Torah* teacher (*Sifré D'varim* 357). Aqiva would be remembered with great esteem and would posthumously influence the production of the *Mishna* (a substantial Third Century work).[163] Holtz bestows upon this illustrious Sage mounds and mounds of praise with the description that he "is in many ways, the apotheosis [ἀποθέωσις; i.e. glorification to a divine level] of the deepest values of 'rabbinic Judaism.'"[164]

Though *Beit Aqiva*, his academy, was located in Bene Berak, he is reputed to have been buried in Tiberias at the site depicted on the next page. That particular site has become a shrine and a popular tourist stop, but it is not known with any high degree of certainty whether or not this is actually his resting

---

[163] Emil Schürer, *Geschichte des jüdischen Volkes im Zeitalter Jesu Christi* (Leipzig, Germany: J. C. Hinrichs'sche Buchhandlung, 1898), I(1):130-31fn25.

[164] Holtz, op. cit., 2.

place. Regardless, it is the site at which Jewish people by the droves honor the memory of this beloved Sage.

Traditional Tomb of Rabbi Aqiva ben Yosef in Tiberias

The present author gives the highest of recommendations to the following study on Rabbi Aqiva:

> Barry W. Holtz, *Rabbi Akiva: Sage of the Talmud* (Jewish Lives series; New Haven and London: Yale University Press, 2017).

This work just might well be the reason that the present volume, begun in March 2014, was not completed until more than three years later. It was awaiting a compendium on Aqiva such as this! Published in March 2017, Holtz's work brings Akiva's world to life, presenting not just the beloved Sage as not just a scholar, but also reveals Aqiva, the romantic, and a legendary man of near-impeccable orthopraxy.

CHAPTER 7

RABBI YESHUA HANOTZRI

רַבִּי יֵשׁוּעַ הַנּוֹצְרִי

The reader ought not to expect to find here a full biographical *vitae* of Yeshua haNotzri (known to many as Jesus of Nazareth), as to attempt to accomplish that within the limited space of a single chapter would be an exercise in futility. Thus, the reader is referred to the *B'rit Chadasha*, and especially to the four Gospels therein, for a fuller accounting of His life and ministry. The aim here is to focus on the similarities and differences between Yeshua's teachings and those of the other popular Sages of His time.

The Jewish reader might balk at the inclusion of Yeshua haNotzri in a work on the Sages, but it should be noted that this would not be the first Jewish work to refer to Him as one. Flavius Josephus introduces this figure thus: "About this time there lived Yeshua, *a wise man*...."[165] The rest of that sentence is an obvious interpolation injected by a Christian hand, but the addition[166] stands as a verification that the phrase "a wise man" is from Josephus's own pen.[167] What is significant about his word choice, as *chakham* (חָכָם, i.e. "wise one") is the formal title for a Sage. Its

---

[165] Flavius Josephus, *Antiquitates Judaicae* (1st Century CE), 18:63-64.

[166] The addition reads, "εἴγε ἄνδρα αὐτὸν λέγειν χρή" (i.e. "if indeed one ought to call him a man").

[167] As Jewish law requires two witnesses for acceptance of testimony, the second witness here would be the Arabic translation of *Antiquitates Judaicae*, which purports to preserve the unpolluted original.

commonest Greek rendering is precisely the wording which appears in Josephus's text, i.e. σοφὸς ἀνήρ.[168]

The reader should not be too taken aback by the present author's use of the title "Rabbi" in regard to the prominent First-Century figure central to the Messianic Jewish and mainstream Christian expressions of faith. The present author intends neither to exalt Yeshua beyond what is merited nor to minimize Yeshua's claim to be the Messiah. One might take note that Yeshua's own *talmidim* called Him "Rabban" and He lauded them for it, saying, "You call me 'Our Master' [*Rabban*] and 'Our Master' [*Maran*], and well you speak, for I am." (John 13:13).[169] It was likely used here to indicate the plural voice of the *talmidim* rather than to suggest Yeshua held the higher title of *Rabban* – not that He was unworthy of it, but rather because its formal use was reserved almost solely for

---

[168] Marcus Jastrow, *Dictionary of the Targumim, Talmud Babli and Yerushalmi, and the Midrashic Literature* (New York, N.Y.: Title Publishing, 1943; orig. 1903), 968; Michael Sokoloff, *A Dictionary of Jewish Palestinian Aramaic* (Ramat-Gan: Bar-Ilan University Press, 1990), 371-72.

[169] The double 'Our Master' translation presented is not a typographical error; that is how it is rendered in AENT. The present author would be more inclined to agree with the Bauscher translation on this passage, wherein the second title *Maran* is rendered "Our L-rd" instead of "Our Master." See Glenn David Bauscher, *The Aramaic-English Interlinear New Testament* (3rd ed.; Lulu Publishing, 2009), 276. It might also be an improvement to retain the Hebraism of the first title, *Rabban*, and carry it across to English simply as "Our Rabbi." See also John 1:38 and 3:2, where Yeshua is likewise addressed as "Rabbi."

Gamli'el I and his heirs, of which clan Yeshua was not a member.[170]

Outside the Gospels, we find validation of the historicity of Yeshua and His ministry in Flavius Josephus and even in the *Talmudic* literature. The former is more neutral in its reporting, simply attesting that this Yeshua existed and had a teaching ministry which differed in some way from the established teachings of the Judaisms contemporary to His. The latter source is more biased, and unapologetically so, against Yeshua in its depiction of Him and His teachings. The negative commentary, though objectionable or even offensive to many, should not be dismissed as devoid of value, however. It actually serves as a witness validating the report of the Scriptures, echoing the hostility toward Him that we find depicted in the canonical Gospels in His interactions with some of the leaders of the various Judaisms, especially obvious in the Sadducean sect.

It should be noted that the *Tosefta* apparently confuses Yeshua haNotzri, called in Aramaic "bar Abba" (son of the Father), with the thief Bar-Abbas of John 18:40 in its commentary that Yeshua "took to robbery" and "was caught, and they crucified him on a cross. And everyone who passed to and fro said, 'It seems that the king is crucified.'" (*Tos. Sanhedrin* 9:7). The latter portion applies to Yeshua, corres-ponding to Galatians 3:13, but the only way it could be said the

---

[170] Hersh Goldwurm and Meir Holder, *History of the Jewish People: The Second Temple Era* (Brooklyn, N.Y.: Publications: 1982), 322.

Yeshua "took to robbery" would be in robbing death of its victory over Him (certainly not the meaning the Toseftist intended). There is, without a doubt, a historical Yeshua haNotzri who made a lasting impact on history. It is debated, however, exactly where His life and ministry fit within (or outside of) the Jewish climate of His own generation.

Some attempt to portray Yeshua as an outsider with respect to every form of Judaism, but given the climate of the faith at that juncture and the evidence provided by his teachings and halakhic example, such a position is tenuous. It is a relatively simple matter to establish both that Judaism was anything but monolithic, allowing for great diversity of thought and praxis, and that the definition of even Pharisaic Judaism, popularly reputed to be so strict and unbending, was sufficiently broad enough to include Yeshua and His followers.[171] Part of the reason behind the present work is to properly root Galilean Sage Yeshua haNotzri in His proper *Jewish* context.

Most Christians recognize that He was Jewish; however, as Jewish *B'rit Chadasha* scholar Amy-Jill Levine laments, "The claim… may be historically true, but it is not central to the teaching of the church."[172] That tide may be on the precipice of a

---

[171] Ronald Wayne Moseley, *Yeshua: A Guide to the Real Jesus and the Original Church* (Clarksville, Md.: Lederer Books, 1996), 113. See also "Pharisees" on pp. 256-7, present work.

[172] Amy-Jill Levine, *The Misunderstood Jew: The Church and the Scandal of the Jewish Jesus* (New York, N.Y.: HarperOne, 2006), 18.

turn as the Church's interest in its "Hebrew Roots" has been experiencing an upsurge over the past few decades. While it is becoming more popular to say, "Jesus was a Jew" from a Christian pulpit... how deep does that statement go? Many of those who utter that line have but a shallow understanding of the First-Century Jewish context. Eighteenth-Century Jewish philosopher Moses Mendelssohn, on the other hand, presented his studied opinion on the matter thus:

> "Jesus of Nazareth [Yeshua haNotzri] himself observed not only the law of Moses but also the ordinances of the rabbis; and whatever seems to contradict this in the speeches and acts ascribed to him appears to do so only at first glance. Closely examined, everything is in complete agreement not only with Scripture, but also with the tradition."[173]

Hillel, who served as *Nasi* from 31 BCE until his death in about 10 CE, would have yet been leading the Sanhedrin when Yeshua was at the Temple at age twelve (Luke 2:46-47),[174] though he did not live much beyond that. It was not atypical for a child of about twelve to enter into an intensified mode of religious studies, anchoring himself to a rabbinic mentor (*m.*

---

[173] Moses Mendelssohn, *Jerusalem, or On Religious Power and Judaism* (tr. by Allan Arkush; Waltham, Mass.: Brandeis University Press, 2013; orig. 1783), 134.

[174] *Nota bene:* Yeshua could have been born no later than 4 BCE and more likely between 5 and 7 BCE. Herod died in 4 BCE, so his decree calling for the death of Hebrew boys up to age two had to have been made before that date and allow for a birth date up to two years before the decree.

Niddah 5:6; *m. Megillah* 4:6; *Pirqei Avot* 5:12), but the Biblical text tells us that Yeshua exhibited an extraordinary depth of knowledge at that young age. The Sages who were present were "amazed by his wisdom and by his answers" (Luke 2:47), which would indicate either that his responses did not deviate from Pharisaic Judaism. What this pericope communicates more than anything is that, regardless of which rabbis were present, Yeshua was taking in not an apprenticeship to the trade of his earthly father Yosef, but rather to that of His Heavenly Father (HaShem), as He Himself stated, "Did you not realize it is necessary for me to be in the House of my Father?" (Luke 2:49). It was a proclamation, already at age twelve, of Who He was/is.

In one school of thought, it has come to be questioned by some if Yeshua, and Yochanan the Immerser (John the Baptist) along with Him, might have been a member of the Essene sect.[175] This, it is reasoned, might account for how Yeshua could come to be worshiped, i.e. that He and His followers were part of a community that was already in the practice of rendering worship to divine agents (angels). It is observed that there is a similarity in the anticipation for Yeshua's return described in 1 Thessalonians 1:9-10 and in the way Malki-Tzedeq is described in Dead Sea Scrolls manuscript *11Q13 (11QMelchizedek)*.

Another text which contributes to this theory is *4Q541*, also known as the *Apocryphon of Levi*. This text

---

[175] Edward Planta Nesbit, *Jesus an Essene* (London: Simpkin, Marshall, Hamilton, Kent, & Co., 1895).

is riddled with *lacunae* (textual gaps caused by holes in the manuscript), but some of the intact phrases seem to be describing events involving Yeshua. Among these are the lines "I [spoke] about it in parables" (fragment 2, column 1, line 3; and similar statements in column 2, lines 5-6) and "and he stilled the Great Sea" (fragment 6, column 1, line 3). This portion of the text culminates with the statement: "He will make atonement for all the children of his generation" (fragment 2, column 4, line 1). It is difficult to ascertain from the extant fragments the precise context of this work, but some other passages therein suggest this could be a text delineating differences between Yeshua and the *Moreh haTzedeq* (Teacher of Righteousness), i.e. the Messianic figure of the *Yachad* literature. For example, "let not the nail touch him" (fragment 1, column 6, line 3) is a phrase which could be interpreted as expressing the author's hope that the Teacher of Righteousness will escape execution of the sort experienced by Yeshua.

Some have argued that the *Yachad* literature's *Moreh haTzedeq* may have been identifiable as Yeshua. André Dupont-Sommer, professor of Semitic Studies at Sorbonne, was the first to do so. In the 1950s, he presented the following:

> Jesus appears in many respects as an astonishing reincarnation of the Teacher of Righteousness. Like the latter, he preached penitence, poverty, humility, love of one's neighbor, chastity…. Like him, he was the Elect and the Messiah of God…. Like him, he was the object of the hostility of the priests…. Like him, he was condemned and put to death. Like him he pronounced judgment on Jerusalem, which was

taken and destroyed by the Romans for having put him to death.... Like him, he founded a Church whose adherents fervently awaited his glorious return.[176]

The statement was met with uproarious criticism from all sides and opened the floodgates to alternative theories, including that the *Moreh haTzedeq* was possibly Yeshua's brother Ya'aqov (James)[177] or Yochanan the Immerser (John).[178]

Archaeologist Émile Puech, a recognized Dead Sea Scrolls scholar, insists that a *Yachad* text, by definition, cannot have as its subject Yeshua haNotzri.[179] The Damascus Covenant is the primary text presenting the *Moreh haTzedeq*, a text which has been dated to about 20 BCE[180] – well before Yeshua haNotzri's arrival. The *Moreh haTzedeq* was venerated

[176] André Dupont-Sommer, *The Essene Writings from Qumran* (transl. Geza Vermes; Oxford: B. Blackwell, 1961).

[177] Robert H. Eisenman, *James the Brother of Jesus: The Key to Unlocking the Secrets of Early Christianity and the Dead Sea Scrolls* (New York, N.Y.: Viking Press, 1997). This theory plays up the alleged tension between Ya'aqov and Sha'ul haTarsi, identifying the "Man of the Lie" prominent in this body of texts as the latter.

[178] Barbara E. Thiering, *Jesus and the Riddle of the Dead Sea Scrolls: Unlocking The Secrets of His Life Story* (New York, N.Y.: Doubleday, 1992). Her version controversially identifies Yeshua haNotzri as the "Man of the Lie" figure in the Qumran cache.

[179] Émile Puech, in Simcha Jacobovici, "Jesus Discovered in Dead Sea Scrolls," *Times of Israel* (25 Mar 2016).

[180] See pages 18-19 of the present work, footnote 40.

to the point that his name had come to be considered ineffable, while Yeshua was frequently addressed by name. The *Moreh* lived in Judea, but Yeshua's home was Galilee. The former was of the tribe of Levi, but the latter hailed from royal lineage, from the tribe of Yehudah. The scholarly consensus remains that the differences between the two figures are sufficient that the premise should be heartily rejected. It is much more feasible to deduce that the *Moreh haTzedeq* was Menachem, the former *Av Beit Din*.[181]

The theory that Yeshua was an Essene hinges, in part, upon the assumption that the Qumran community was representative of the mainstream Essene sect, but this has not been established. In fact, it has been thoroughly discredited. The Essene sect does not appear to be a monolithic one. Philo describes an element much more akin to the Qumran *Yachad* than to anything attributed to the Essenes in Josephus's works.[182] They seem to have had interaction with two very different sub-sects of Essenes. While Josephus's Essenes *did* participate in the sacrificial system in Jerusalem, those of whom Philo wrote, possibly the

---

[181] Godfrey Rolles Driver, *The Judaean Scrolls: The Problem and a Solution* (Oxford: B. Blackwell, 1965), 267ff.; Henri E. Del Medico, *The Riddle of the Scrolls* (London: Burke, 1958), 139-40; Cecil Roth, *Historical Background of the Dead Sea Scrolls* (Oxford: B. Blackwell, 1958), 12ff. This theory posits that the opponents of the *Moreh haTzedeq* are Shammai and his *talmidim*.

[182] Philo of Alexandria, *Quod Omnis Probus Liber Sit* (transl. Charles Duke Yonge), 12.75; *1QS (Community Rules Scroll)* (Ca. 100-75 BCE), 9:4-5.

Yachad community, did *not*. Hebrew University professor David Flusser concedes that on certain matters, e.g. poverty, Yeshua accepted some Essene views, but very few.[183]

The *Yachad* is understood by most scholars to be a "crisis cult," i.e. a fringe splinter group of the Essenes that emerged out of dissatisfaction with the ruling faction in Jerusalem.[184] There were two distinct communities at Qumran – one defined by the *Damascus Covenant* and presumably led by former *Av Beit Din* Menachem, and the other being the *Yachad*, defined to a large degree by the *Community Rules Scroll (1QS)*. What is interesting concerning these two is that neither is strictly Essene in its tenets. Neither honored the Essene practice of celibacy, though the *Yachad* did renounce marriage; and, though the *Yachad* kept property in common (in Essene fashion), the *Damascus Covenant* community did not.[185] Recent scholarship has been emerging that suggests the Qumran population may not have been Essenes at all. A few recent challenges to the assumption have

---

[183] David Flusser, *Jesus* (Jerusalem: Hebrew University Magnes Press, 2001; orig. 1997), 117.

[184] Roland de Vaux, *Archaeology and the Dead Sea Scrolls: The Schweich Lectures 1959* (London: Oxford University Press, 1973); Philip R. Davies, "The Prehistory of the Qumran Community," *The Dead Sea Scrolls: Fory. Years of Research* (ed. D. Dimant and U. Rappaport; Jerusalem: Magnes Press, 1992), 121-5.

[185] Eyal Regev, *Sectarianism in Qumran: A Cross-Cultural Perspective* (Berlin: Walter de Gruyter GmbH., 2007), 266.

emerged, proposing instead that the site was more likely associated with the Sicarii.[186]

Furthermore, Yeshua did not draw *talmidim* (disciples) exclusively from a single sect of Judaism, as would have been the expectation of an isolationist community like the *Yachad*. Depending on the translation, his *talmid* Shim'on was either a Zealot (*qa'ani*) or a Canaanite (Matthew 10:4; Mark 3:18),[187] and the *gens nomen* of Yehudah Skaryota (Judas Iscariot) most likely identifies him as a Sicarii (a segment of the Zealot faction).[188] Samaritans were not considered anathema to Yeshua either, as evidenced by His interactions with several in the record of Scripture (John 4:4-26; Luke 10:25-37; 17:11-19). Yochanan the Immerser could possibly have been an Essene, based on his more ascetic *halakha* and locust-rich diet,[189] though certainly not of the ulra-

---

[186] Robert H. Eisenman, "Sicarii Essenes, 'Those of the Circumcision,' and Qumran," *Journal of Higher Criticism* 12 (Spring 2006): 17-28; Yizhar Hirschman, *Qumran in Context: Reassessing the Archaeological Evidence* (Peabody, Mass.: Hendrickson, 2004).

[187] Reading from the Aramaic, the text indicates Canaanite, but from the Greek comes the rendering of Zealot. The present author contends that both readings are tenable. Yeshua is so inclusive that regardless of whether Shim'on were a Canaanite (Gentile) or a Zealot (revolutionary), he would have been welcomed either way.

[188] Andrew Gabriel-Yizkhak Roth bar Raphael, *Aramaic English New Testament* (5th Edition; Sedro-Woolley, Wash.: Netzari Press, 2012), 278fn177.

[189] James H. Charlesworth, "John the Baptizer and Qumran Barriers in Light of the Rule of the Community," in

isolationist *Yachad* community. If he were, perchance, an Essene, it would not dictate that Yeshua be thus affiliated. In fact, Yeshua's command to love one's enemy seems to be leveled *against* the Qumran doctrine of "sanctioned hatred."[190]

For a number of reasons, it is certain that Yeshua also could not possibly have been a Sadducee. That sect was the most hostile toward Him and His followers of any, as evidenced Luke's report:

> The High Priest and all who were with him who were of the doctrine of the Sadducees were filled with envy. And they placed hands on the Shlichim, and seized (and) bound them in prison. (Acts 5:17-18).

Despite finding agreement with them in the belief in Free Will (which at that time was rejected solely by the Essenes),[191] they, in contrast to the Pharisees, denied both the Resurrection and the existence of angels and spirits (Acts 23:8). Furthermore, there was never a Sadducean presence in the Galilee region (in

---

Donald W. Perry & Eugene Ulrich (eds.), *The Provo International Conference on the Dead Sea Scrolls: Technological Innovations, New Texts, and Reformulated Issues* (STDJ 30; Leiden: Brill, 1999), 366-8; cf. *Covenant of Damascus* 12:14-15.

[190] James H. Charlesworth, *Jesus and the Dead Sea Scrolls: The Controversy Resolved* (New Haven and London: Yale University Press, 1992), 24.

[191] Gary A. Rendsburg, "The Rise of the Jewish Sects," *The Dead Sea Scrolls* (Chantilly, Va.: The Great Courses, 2010), lecture 5 (DVD).

which Nazareth is located); that sect never took root there.[192]

Among those following Yeshua outside the Twelve were Sha'ul, Yosef of Arimathea,[193] and Naqdimon – all three of them Pharisees. In fact, within the first year after Yeshua's Resurrection, a number of Pharisees had come to faith in Him, and it seems that by the Jerusalem Council (49 CE) , many more had as well (Acts 15:5). As mentioned in chapter 4 of this work, Yosef of Arimathea, the man who offered his own tomb for Yeshua's burial (Mark 15:43-47; Luke 23:50-53), was a member of the Sanhedrin, as was Naqdimon (Nicodemus), whose testimony appears in John, chapters 3, 7, & 19.

Matthew 23 has often been cited as an example of "New Testament Anti-Semitism,"[194] but this

---

[192] The only sects in Galilee from 200 BCE to 100 CE were the Pharisees, the Zealots, and the *Netzarim*, per David A. Fiensy and James Riley Strange, eds., *Galilee in the Late Second Temple and Mishnaic Periods: Life Culture, and Society* (Minneapolis, Minn.: Fortress Press, 2014), 80.

[193] Emil Schürer, *Geschichte des jüdischen Volkes im Zeitalter Jesu Christi* (Leipzig, Germany: J. C. Hinrichs'sche Buchhandlung, 1898), II(1): 172.

[194] It has been erroneously depicted as such by hate-preachers throughout the ages, including John Chrysostom, Martin Luther, and countless others. Cf. David L. Turner (Ph.D., Hebrew Union College), *Israel's Last Prophet: Jesus and the Jewish Leaders in Matthew 23* (Minneapolis, Minn.: Fortress Press, 2015) for an excellent analysis presenting Matthew 23 as an "intramural" exchange taking place within Judaism.

understanding of the chapter's content comes from the Christian tendency to view Yeshua as an outsider to Judaism. It is significant, however, that the chapter begins with a command to be obedient to their teachings, even when they may not be backed up by an example of faithful orthopraxy (Matthew 23:1-2). He identifies the Pharisees as holding the Moshe seat, i.e. a continuation of his authority, which he had parted out to the seventy elders (Exodus 18:25; Numbers 11:16-30) and which passed thence to the Prophets and on to Ezra's *Anshei Knesset HaG'dolah*, and from that body to the Pharisees (*Pirqei Avot* 1:1). Yeshua selected the teachings of the Pharisees over those of every other sect as the model for His own *talmidim*, and apparently to their exclusion.

The old-guard (Reformationist) assumption that the hypocrites presented in Matthew 23 are representative of Pharisees in general was ill-informed. The Pharisaic movement was anything but monolithic. *Talmud Yerushalmi* identifies seven types of Pharisee (*y. Berakhot* 9), so disassociation from one type would not preclude Yeshua from one of the other six. Young observes that only one of the six "serves as a positive role model."[195] The positive type is likened to the patriarch Abraham (Genesis 15:6; James 2:23) and is classified as the "Pharisee of love." Yeshua's teaching in Matthew 25:31-46 would align Him with this type of Pharisee. He echoes the Prophet Yeshayahu's teachings (Isaiah 58:5-12) in His

---

[195] Brad H. Young, *Meet the Rabbis: Rabbinic Thought and the Teachings of Jesus* (Peabody, Mass.: Hendrickson Publishers, 2007), 36.

insistence upon feeding the hungry, visiting the sick and imprisoned, and welcoming the needy into one's home. That teaching is the core of *tiqun 'olam* (repairing the world).

In light of *Talmud Yerushalmi*, however, it can be seen that Yeshua's criticism is not aimed at all Pharisees of all seven types, but is directed only at those whose *halakha* betrays the hypocrisy of not living up to the standard's being taught. *Talmud Bavli* offers the same criticism with regard to Rabbi Ben Azzai. He is admonished, "You preach well, but put your message into poor practice!" (*b. Yebamot* 63b). In another tractate, it cautions, "Do not fear those who are Pharisees or those who are not Pharisees, but fear the painted ones [hypocrites] whose deeds are the deeds of Zimri, but who expect to receive the reward of Pinchas (Phinehas)"[196] (*b. Sotah* 22b). There is a striking similarity between the "painted ones" remark here and Yeshua's charge that certain hypocrites among the Pharisees were "whitewashed tombs" (Matthew 23:27-28).

It has been suggested that whatever tension existed between Yeshua and certain Pharisaic leaders is emphasized on account of vast similarities between the two, i.e. the "law of minimal differences."[197] This is to say that the perceived conflict between the two sects rises from their closeness of theology and ideology, i.e. their ideological "nearest neighbor"

---

[196] The Biblical account of the hypocritical Zimri and the righteous Pinchas can be found in Numbers 25:6-15.

[197] Rendsburg, loc. cit.

status. The evidence in support of this assertion is based on the "nearest neighbor" hypothesis, i.e. that in discussion with those who share the most in common with us, we tend to zero in on the points of difference or disagreement, while in communicating with those we share little common ground with, we are more likely to seek to find any sliver of commonality. Thus, one should expect two Pharisees to contend over fine points of the *Torah* more readily than a Pharisee and a Sadducee or Essene or member of the Damascus Covenant community. To hold a fellow Pharisee accountable to a certain standard of piety is, thus, a thoroughly Pharisaic thing to do. Indeed, the *B'rit Chadasha* even includes an account of Yeshua engaged in table fellowship with a Pharisee (Luke 7:36-50).

The most logical conclusion with regard to Yeshua's sect of Judaism was that He was furthest from the Sadducees, but also not belonging to the Essenes, the Therapeutae, the Zealots, or the Samaritans. Historically, there was much more hostility toward *HaDerekh* (Yeshua's movement) coming from the Sadducees than from the Pharisees, but Scripture underscores more strongly the discourse between *HaDerekh* and the Pharisees. This is likely intended to demonstrate the closeness between Yeshua and that sect. While it is true that correlation does not automatically equate to association, neither does the rule preclude it. The preponderance of evidence weighs overwhelmingly in support of Yeshua identifying with a Pharisaic *hashqafah*. His teachings "brought to fullness of understanding" the *Torah* and Prophets (Matt 5:17-18), most often in agreement with the understandings of the Pharisaic *Beit Hillel*.

Dr. Brad H. Young (Ph.D., Hebrew University) reminds us, "[Yeshua] offers heart-felt criticism of a movement with which he identifies…. Jesus' critique of the Pharisees reflects the self-critical tendencies of the Pharisaic movement itself."[198] His doctor-father (Ph.D. mentor) David Flusser asserts, "One point is certain, namely that sociologically Jesus belonged with them [the Pharisees]."[199] Second-Temple Judaism scholar Oskar Skarsaune concurs, offering the observation, "… when Jesus [Yeshua] debates with Pharisees, his own positions can be shown to agree with those of other Pharisaic authorities…. Jesus' debates with Pharisaic opponents is therefore an intra-Pharisaic debate."[200] Rabbis Abraham Geiger and M. H. Friedländer, et al. speculate that Yeshua was certainly a Pharisee and most probably aligned with *Beit Hillel*.[201] Yeshua's remarks against "the Pharisees" have been taught as being directed against all in the Pharisaic movement when only specific members of the leadership who were hypocritical in

---

[198] Young, *Meet the Rabbis*, 35.

[199] Flusser, *Jesus,* 117.

[200] Oskar Skarsaune, *In the Shadow of the Temple: Jewish Influences on Early Christianity* (Downers Grove, Ill.: IVP Academic, 2002), 106.

[201] Abraham Geiger, *Das Judenthum und seine Geschichte* (2nd ed.; Breslau, 1865), I: 117; M H. Friedländer, *Geschichtsbilder aus der Zeit der Tanaiten und Armoräer* (Brünn, Ger., 1879), 32.

their conduct were actually in view in the Gospel accounts.

Due to some unfortunate and enduring misconceptions regarding the character of the Pharisaic movement, the conflict between Yeshua and the certain hypocrites within that sect has been misconstrued and exaggerated, especially by those wishing to see and maintain a divorce between Yeshua's followers and Judaism. All of the charges levied against the Jews (especially of the Pharisaic sect) by anti-Semitic elements in the Church have been disproven by later scholarship – blood libel, identification as "the synagogue of satan," and perhaps the ugliest epithet of them all: "Christ-killer." Emil Schürer's observations regarding the Pharisaic sect are significant:

> "They had the bulk of the nation as their ally, and women especially were in their hands. They had the greatest influence upon the congregations, so that all acts of public worship, prayers, and sacrifices were performed according to their injunctions." [202]

Yeshua's ministry is characterized at every turn, however, as the embodiment of qualities which were exclusive to the Pharisaic movement. Young observes that Yeshua employed a *rabbi-talmid* mentoring model unique to the Pharisaic sect in His training of the *talmidim* and other *shlichim* (Matthew 4:19; 8:22; Mark 1:17; 2:4; Luke 5:27; and often), insisting on the same standard of conduct characteristic of a *talmid* of the

---

[202] Schürer, *Geschichte*, II (2): 28.

Pharisaic sect (Matthew 7:24; 16:24-28; Mark 8:34-39; Luke 6:47; 9:23-27).[203] The Sadducees did not engage such a model, as they rejected all writings and teachings except the *Torah* – especially the *Oral Torah*, and even the Prophets and Writings of the *Tanakh*. Additionally, Yeshua's teachings bear examples following the hermeneutics of *Beit Hillel*, such as the instances of *qal w'chomer* found in Matt 6:26-30, ‖ Luke 12:24, 28; Matthew 7:11 ‖ Luke 11:13; Matthew 10:25 & John 15:18-20; Matthew 12:12 & John 7:23. He even adopted the Pharisaic pedagogy of teaching via parables.[204]

In true Pharisaic fashion, Yeshua brought the rabbinical concept of building a "fence around *Torah*" (*Pirqei Avot* 1:1), i.e. a praxis of avoidance of not just the things *Torah* identifies as sin but also of anything that might lead one into those sins, to the heart of His teachings. The "Sermon on the Mount" (Matthew 5) is an apt example of this. *Talmud* scholar Jacob Neusner recognizes this pattern in Yeshua, commenting:

---

[203] Young, *Meet the Rabbis*, 36-7.

[204] The earliest known Jewish parable dates to about 180 BCE, a teaching from Antigonus of Socho preserved in *Pirqei Avot* 1:3. Other recorded parables hail predominantly from *Beit Hillel*, e.g. Hillel (*Wayyiqra Rabbah* 34.3), Gamli'el I (*Avot d'Rabbi Nathan* 40.10), and Yochanan ben Zakkai (*b. Shabbat* 153a). Consider this statement from David Flusser, "No Longer Hidden," in *Jerusalem Perspective Research* (vol. 2; Jerusalem: Synoptic Gospels in Jerusalem, Aug 1989), 11 – "Without knowing rabbinic parables, it is very difficult to learn what Jesus was teaching us with his Jewish parables."

[Yeshua] set forth as his demonstration of how not to abolish the *Torah* and the prophets but to fulfill them a set of teachings that, all together, point to a more profound demand – on the *Torah*'s part – than people have realized. Not only must I not kill; I must not even approach that threshold of anger that in the end leads to murder [Matthew 5:21-22]. Not only must I not commit adultery; I must not even approach the road that leads to adultery [Matthew 5:27-28].... These formulations represent an elaboration of... the Ten Commandments.[205]

Jewish historian Dr. Yosef Klausner concurs, stating, "throughout the Gospels there is not one item of ethical teaching which cannot be paralleled either in the Old Testament, the *Apocrypha*, or in the *Talmudic* and *Midrashic* literature of the period near to the time of Yeshua."[206] Note, for instance, how closely Yeshua's teaching on adultery mirrors that of the *Midrash Rabbah*: "Not merely one who sins with his body is called an adulterer, but he who sins with his eye is also so named" (*Wayyiqra Rabbah* 23.12). The same also do both *Talmuds* confess – in one: "He that looks upon the little finger of a woman is as if he gazed upon her genitals" (*b. Berakhot* 24a), and in the other, likewise: "He that looks upon a woman's belly as is if he had lain with her" (*y. Kallah* 58:3).

---

[205] Jacob Neusner, *Judaism When Christianity Began: A Survey of Belief and Practice* (Louisville, Ky.: Westminster John Knox Press, 2002), 24-5.

[206] Yosef Gedaliah Klausner, *Yeshu ha-Notzri: Zemanno, Chayyav ve-Torato* (Jerusalem: Shtibel, 1922), 384.

When Yeshua instructs his *talmidim* that if they have something against their brother, they are to leave their offering until they have reconciled with him (Matthew 5:24), an echo from the *Gemara* can be heard in it, as the latter gives similar counsel, in the names of several rabbis (*b. Yoma* 87a). Yeshua's advice that if one's hand stumbles him, better that he cut it off and cast it away than allow it to condemn him to *Gei-Hinnom* (Matthew 5:30) appears to be a euphemistic rephrasing of yet another *Talmudic* lesson: "Whosoever would bring his hand to his modest parts, his hand ought to be cut off to [not reach beyond] his navel" (*m. Niddah* 2:1). It is explained that "whosoever emits seed in vain deserves death, for it is written: And the thing which he [Onan] did displeased the Lord: wherefore he slew him also [Genesis 38:10]" (*b. Niddah* 13a).

Yeshua's ruling on divorce (Matthew 5:32) is nearly *verbatim* the ruling of Shammai (*m. Gittin* 9:10). Both of these are quoted in chapter 9 of the present work (On Divorce...). Likewise, His ban on swearing oaths, "you shall not say I swear..." (Matthew 5:34) is found also in the *Talmud*, albeit it not as exacting: "Be not profuse in vows" (*m. Demai* 2:3) and also in Ben Sira's maxim, "Do not accustom your mouth to oaths" (23:9). Yeshua's wording seems closest here to Philo's "To swear not at all is the best course and most profitable to life."[207] The pattern continues thus through the entirety of the sermon (Matthew 5-7).

---

[207] Philo, *De Decalogo*, 84. See also idem., *De Specialibus Legibus* 2:8 – "The more oath-taking, the more lying."

Were His connection with the ways and teachings of the Pharisees not strongly enough established thus far, it is compelling that Pharisaic stalwart Sha'ul haTarsi (Paul) joined with the "sect of the *Netzarim*" (Acts 9:1-22; 24:5, 14; 26:12-20) without ever relinquishing nor denouncing his identity as a Pharisee (Acts 23:6; 26:5). If Yeshua was also a Pharisee, as the evidence unabashedly suggests, there would be no perception of incompatibility, and in Sha'ul's mind, as a Pharisee in high standing, there was none. He testified, "But this indeed I acknowledge, that in the same doctrine of which they speak [i.e. *HaDerekh*], I do serve the Elohim of my fathers, believing all the things written in the *Torah* and in the Prophets" (Acts 24:14). He is found, roughly in the same timeframe, testifying to His faith in Yeshua and simultaneous strict adherence to Pharisaic Judaism (Galatians 1:11-14; Philippians 3:4-8).[208]

As much as Yeshua echoed the Sages, however, there were ways in which He was clearly

---

[208] The epistle to the Galatians is generally thought to have been composed either just before or just after the Jerusalem Council, which occurred in 49 CE. The date for Philippians is more difficult to pin down. It is one of the prison epistles, but which imprisonment? If Corinth, the date is 50 CE. If Ephesus, 54-57 CE. If Caesarea, 58-60 CE. If Rome, 60-63 CE. See Gerald F. Hawthorne, "Letter to the Philippians," in *Dictionary of Paul and His Letters* (Downers Grove, Ill.: IVP Academic, 1993), 709-711. The present author leans toward Caesarea, which would have Sha'ul still identifying as a Pharisee about two and a half decades after coming under Yeshua's teaching.

distinguishable from them. In Him, we encounter a figure who speaks and acts with a level of *samchut* (סַמְכוּת, i.e. authority) on par with Moshe and Ezra, and in some cases even exceeding theirs. Neusner recognizes this, writing:

> Jesus represents himself [in the Sermon on the Mount] not as a sage in a chain of tradition but as an 'I,' that is, a unique figure, a new Moses, standing on the mount as Moses stood on Sinai.[209]

It is undeniable that much harm has come to the Jewish people under the name of "Jesus" over the centuries. The blame for that, however, does not belong to Yeshua nor do such actions align with what He taught. What others have done with it does not at all reflect Yeshua's actual mission or teaching. The tension between the Pharisees and Yeshua was not of the character which later generations would depict it. The Christian or Messianic reader, and even the Jewish reader, would do well to recognize that there is no connection between the modern Jewish sects and the Jewish leaders who were responsible for arranging Yeshua's betrayal with Yehudah Skaryota (Judas Iscariot), conducting His "Sanhedrin" trial, ordering and setting guards at Yeshua's tomb, arresting *haDerekh/Netzari* talmidim, or authorizing Sha'ul to persecute them. Those leaders were Sadducees, not Pharisees. There was no sharp divide between the First-Century Pharisees, as a whole, and the *Netzarim*. With Sadducee Yehosef bar Qayafa (יְהוֹסֵף בַּר קָיָפָא; or *Caiaphas* in Greek) as the Roman appointee to the

---

[209] Neusner, *Judaism When Christianity Began*, 24.

office of High Priest, he was able to orchestrate all of these events. Nasi Gamli'el I (the subject of the present work's chapter 4) would not have had a hand in any of it.

The "Sanhedrin" convened for the trial was almost certainly a Sanhedrin Qatanah, i.e. a court of three rather than the full 71-judge body, and those three judges were likely bar Qayafa himself and two other Sadducees of his choosing. At the time of Yeshua's death, the Jewish Sanhedrin did not have authority to carry out capital punishment – according to Scriptural texts coming from all sides (John 18:31; *y. Sanhedrin* 1:1; 7:2). The hope for this chapter is that it has demonstrated that Yeshua was not an outsider passing judgment on Judaism. He aligned mostly with the *halakha* of *Beit Hillel*, occasionally with the *halakha* of *Beit Shammai,* and always within the *hashqafah* of Pharisaic *Torah*-obedient Judaism.

He was a faithful Jew engaged in the ongoing Jewish conversation about all things Jewish from a position unabashedly *within* Pharisaic Judaism. In fact, as late as 387 CE, there could be found at the Sabbath synagogue services and at the *moed* feasts a number of Yeshua's followers worshiping in community with their Jewish brethren and identifying as functioning within Judaism. This was happening on a grand enough scale in Antioch as to inspire anti-Semitic bishop John Chrysostom to compose, preach, and publish a series of eight homilies aimed at dissuading them from the practice.[210]

---

[210] John Chrysostom, *Adversus Judaeos* (Antioch, 387 CE).

Renowned *Talmud* scholar Jacob Neusner, under the heading of "Other Judaisms," includes the comment:

> The earliest Christians, Jesus and his family and Paul, all saw themselves as 'Israel' and called on Scripture to provide the framework of interpretation of the life and teachings, death and resurrection, of Jesus Christ. All of these groups [having previously discussed the *Yachad* and Alexandrian communities] fall into the category of 'Judaisms,' though each differs in fundamental ways from the others.[211]

The recommendation for Yeshua, though difficult to narrow to a single work, goes to:

> David Flusser, *Jesus* (3rd ed.; Jerusalem: Hebrew University Magnes Press, 2001).

Since its first edition emerged in 1968, the work (which has since been corrected and augmented) has quite properly become a classic. Flusser takes a Jewish approach to Yeshua marked by matchless erudition and historical integrity. This volume will challenge some of the presuppositions of Jew and Christian alike.

---

[211] Neusner, *Judaism When Christianity Began*, 9.

CHAPTER 8

JUDAISM'S MESSIAH

מָשִׁיחַ הַיְהוּדִי

This present chapter is, perhaps, a bit of an excursus from the teachings of the Sages, but to avoid the topics it addresses would be irresponsible, given their prominence in discussions of Yeshua – both in Jewish and Christian circles. Bear in mind, as Jewish scholar Pinchas Lapide reminds us: "'Messianitis' (i.e. the almost feverish expectation of the Redeemer) was and is a Jewish illness."[212] Judaism of the First-Century, as has herein been established, was a diverse proposition. The concept of its expected and awaited Messiah was an equally multi-faceted subject. Rabbi Itzhak Shapira reminds us that "rabbinic thought about the Messiah… is not systematic in nature and does not speak 'in one voice.'"[213] A Jewish person in Qumran had an image of Messiah very different than what would be met in a Pharisaic context.

Even within Pharisaism, there was more than one view to be found. The Pharisees, mostly of the School of Hillel, fully expected the coming of a literal Messiah, but also feared a climate where too much emphasis was placed on this expectation, so that a charismatic figure might force the eschaton.[214] A later

---

[212] Pinchas Lapide and Jurgen Moltmann, *Jüdischer Monotheismus, christliche Trinitätslehre: Ein Gespräche* (Munich: Chr. Kaiser Verlag, 1979), 68.

[213] Itzhak Shapira, *The Return of the Kosher Pig: The Divine Messiah in Jewish Thought* (Clarksville, Md.: Lederer Books, 2013), 77.

[214] Yosef Gedaliah Klausner, "The Rise of Christianity," in Michael Avi-Yonah, & Zvi Baras, eds., *The World History of the Jewish People: Society and Religion in the Second Temple Period* (Jerusalem: Massada Publishing Ltd., 1977), 258.

rabbinical voice, a student of *Beit Hillel*, would add to this conversation, "The Messiah – what is his name?... The Rabbis say, the leprous one, as it is said, 'Surely he hath borne our sicknesses'" (*b. Sanhedrin* 98b). The same tractate expresses the belief that, based on Jeremiah 30:9, the Messiah would be an heir to King David.

Centuries of catastrophe – from the Assyrian period through the Babylonian, Persian, and Roman conquests – was the likely catalyst for moving the Messianic Hope to the forefront of the Jewish mind. Karin Hedner-Zetterholm of the Swedish Research Council notes, "... we know messianism played a part in the uprisings against the Romans in 70 and 135 and that popular messianic and prophetic movements existed around the beginning of the common era."[215]

In fact, Messianic anticipation of the entire Second Temple era dominated not only the formal writings of Israel's prophets, but also the popular literature of the time period: *pseudepigrapha*, *apocrypha*, *midrash*, and even personal letters. There was never a time, however, when that hope was absent from Judaism. Cambridge University Jewish Studies professor Dr. William Horbury makes the point, "The messianic elements in this tradition were current in prosperity as well as adversity; they had the potential for startling empowerment in given political and

---

[215] Karin Hedner-Zetterholm, "Elijah and the Messiah as Spokesmen of Rabbinic Ideology;" pp. 57-78 in Magnus Zetterholm, ed., *The Messiah in Early Judaism and Christianity* (Minneapolis, Minn.: Fortress Press, 2007), 59.

social circumstances."[216] There are glimpses of Messiah in the Davidic psalms and even in the *Torah*, but the highest concentration of Messianic literature begins about 720 BCE.

The arrival of the Messiah was so anticipated and longed for that people who, in retrospect, were obviously not a fit with the Messianic prophecies were assigned (or were able to assume of their own volition) that title. Among the most prominent and widely accepted in the Second Temple era were Simon of Peraea, formerly a slave to Herod (ca. 4 BCE); Athronges, a shepherd-rebel (ca. 3 CE); Todah (also called Theudas), who had over 400 followers (see Acts 5:33-39); Yehuda haG'lili, founder of the Zealot faction;[217] Simon Magus, a Samaritan who claimed to be the "second coming" of Yeshua; Dositheos the Samaritan, the supposed founder of Mandaeanism; Rabbi Tzadok; and to a lesser extent Vespasian, self-declared but accepted to some degree (70 CE).

The title of "messiah" (the Hebrew word meaning "anointed") had even in Scripture been attributed to at least one Gentile figure in Koresh (Cyrus) of Persia (Isaiah 45:1), though never naming him as *the* Messiah (capital M) who would usher in the Messianic Kingdom. The fact that all of these came to be exposed as false Messiahs gives Judaism sufficient

---

[216] William Horbury, *Messianism among Jews and Christians: Twelve Biblical and Historical Studies* (London and New York: T & T Clark, 2003), 11.

[217] Flavius Josephus, *Bellum Judaicum* (75 CE), 6.312-13.

reason to test Yeshua's claims, but an honest investigation would be unable to legitimately refute them, at least as far as the "*Mashiach ben Yosef*" role (the "*Mashiach ben Dawid*" role being left to a yet-future fulfillment.[218] What is really most critical to the discussion of Yeshua is the fact that He came to be recognized by a number of Jews, including many Pharisees, as the Jewish Messiah.

Judaism would find no contradiction to its teachings in assigning that title of the ultimate Messiah to other figures contemporary or near-contemporary to Yeshua haNotzri. Indeed, others had been proclaimed to be manifesting in that role before Him, but their claims had proven false. In the next century, Shim'on bar Kokhba would find his way onto the list by declaration of Aqiva, as discussed in chapter 5. For the First-Century audience, there was no modern dilemma of how to fit all of the Messianic prophesies into a preterist timetable to serve as the stumbling block it has now become.[219]

---

[218] The case for this being so thoroughly and superlatively presented in Michael L. Brown's series *Answering Jewish Objections to Jesus* (5 vols.; Grand Rapids, Mich.: Baker Academic, 2000-2010), the present author refers the reader to that work, recognizing that his own efforts to address the matter in the space of this briefer work would only pale in comparison.

[219] The preterist view forces every prophecy to be understood as fulfilled at or before the destruction of the Jerusalem Temple in 70 CE. Preterism, principally espoused by Jesuits but with adaptations of the view found elsewhere as well, finds its genesis quite late, in the 17th Century CE with Alcassar, and thus was not a consideration of the First

It was not difficult to accept that *Mashiach ben Yosef* (i.e. the Suffering Servant)[220] and *Mashiach ben Dawid* (Delivering King)[221] could both be the same figure, and even that their functions might be accomplished at two different times. The dual-Messiah concept so prevalent in Modern Judaism was was just beginning to emerge in First-Century Israel, thus it was an even easier hurdle to clear for the thousands who came to follow Yeshua in those early years. Also in play is the fact that the pool of Biblical passages considered to be Messianic was not exactly as it is now. Some passages we now look at as such were not read that way in that time period, and some which were have come to be reinterpreted non-Messianically.[222] Swedish Bible scholar Magnus Zetterholm laments:

Century Jew, per Moses Stuart, *A Commentary on the Apocalypse* (Andover, N.Y.: Allen, Morrill, and Wardwell, 1845).

[220] H. L. Ginsberg, "The Oldest Interpretation of the Suffering Servant," *Vetus Testamentum* 3 (1953): 400-404.

[221] This Deliverer role of Mashiach emerges, in part, out of Daniel 7:13-14; and Isaiah 9:7; 16:5 – corresponding with Luke 1:32, "This one will be great and be called the Son of the Highest, and Master HASHEM (your) Elohim will give to him the throne of Dawid his father" (AENT).

[222] The passages which are still universally recognized as being Messianic are few, i.e. Isaiah 2, 11, 42; 59:20; Jeremiah 23, 30, 33; 48:47; 49:39; Ezekiel 38:16; Hosea 3:4-3:5; Micah 4; Zephaniah 3:9; Zechariah 14:9; Daniel 10:14. Notice that the list, borrowed from http://www.jewfaq.org/mashiach.htm, include neither Isaiah 53 nor any of the psalms generally classified as Messianic. See Appendix B.

... it is hard not to be astounded (and distressed) over the following development: a Jewish interpretation of Messiah eventually gave rise to a non-Jewish religion, Christianity, which used the concept to renounce its roots, resulting in a situation where contemporary Jewish messianic ideas lead to marginalization vis-à-vis mainstream Judaism.[223]

An example of this is the identity of the Suffering Servant in Isaiah 53, which has been hotly debated for over two centuries with mainstream Judaism and liberal Chritianity reading it as referring to national Israel and conservative Christianity insisting that it is a description of Messiah and appropriating it to Yeshua. This disagreement came about on the coattails of an emerging theory from the German school called the *Ebedlieder Hypothesis*, which insisted that all (deutero-)Isaiahic references to a servant must indicate the same servant, and since National Israel was the servant of Isaiah 40, that identification should carry through every reference to Isaiah 66.

Prior to the 19th Century, in fact, there was almost *universal* agreement among the Jewish Sages (the exception of note being Rashi[224]) that the Suffering Servant figured in Isaiah 52:13-53:12 was

---

[223] Magnus Zetterholm, *The Messiah in Early Judaism and Christianity* (Minneapolis, Minn.: Fortress Press, 2007), xxv.

[224] Nota bene: Though Rashi (Rabbi Shlomo Itzchaqi) insisted the Servant was National Israel in his commentary on Isaiah 53; in his *Talmudic* exposition, he contradicted himself and identified the passage as Messianic, per Shapira, *Return of the Kosher Pig,* 103.

the anticipated *Mashiach* (Messiah).[225] In order to harmonize with Jeremiah 31:35-6, Zechariah 12:9-13:9 (especially 12:10 and 13:7-9), and Daniel 11:33-35 and 12:2-3, it must be so interpreted. Alongside Delitzsch, the flood of "new interpretations" which filled the theological journals of the early 19th Century were littered with scholars (Jewish and Christian alike) trying to be the most innovative and novel interpreter of the passage. The submissions included monographs identifying the Servant figure as Jeremiah, Zerubbabel, Hezekiah, Job, and even Cyrus of Persia, among others – anyone but Yeshua was an option. None of these candidates passed the test of scholarly scrutiny, however, and the only two views left in contention at the close of the Twentieth Century were National Israel and Messiah… and it is hardly tenable that both of these Servants are present in tandem.

Nineteenth-Century Hebraist Franz Delitzsch rejected that hypothesis on the whole, though he did agree that National Israel was evident in the Servant of Isaiah 40. He suggested a narrowing of the

---

[225] Christopher R. North, *The Suffering Servant in Deutero-Isaiah: An Historical and Critical Study* (Oxford: Oxford University Press, 1956), 18-20, 192. Caveat: some cite Origin's *Contra Celsus* as confirming a non-Messianic interpretation among Jews in his time, but as an anti-Semite, he had good motive to misrepresent the Jewish view, rendering this non-Jewish source rather unconvincing as a witness to Jewish exegesis. *Nota bene:* Jewish law requires two witnesses testifying without deviation to an identical set of facts in order to establish those statements as fact (Deut 19:15; *b. Makkot* 2a-6b), and the allegation from Origin has no second witness contemporary with him.

identification down to A believing remnant in the second servant song (49:1-13) and Israel's anointed (prophets, priests, and kings) in the third servant song (50:4-11), culminating in 52:13-53:12 with a presentation of the Anointed (Messiah) as the ideal representative Israelite.[226] Beginning in chapter 54, Prof. David B. Kennedy observed, the identity fanned back out again to those who follow the figure presented in 52:13-53:12 (see the diagram below).[227]

Delitzsch-Kennedy Servant Analysis

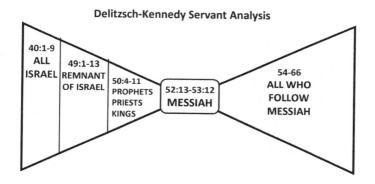

Qumran manuscript *1QIsaᵃ* (the "Great Isaiah Scroll") contains two variants which point the Isaiahic text even moreso in a Messianic direction. At 52:14, the usual מִשְׁחַת (as it is pointed in 𝔐) appears with a 1ˢᵗ person pronominal suffix, i.e. משחתי (read מָשַׁחְתִּי). It also adds a definite article to אָדָם (man) which is

---

[226] Franz Delitzsch. *Isaiah* (Keil-Delitzsch Old Testament Commentary 7; Edinburgh: T. & T. Clark, 1866).

[227] David B. Kennedy, Course lectures, *BBL-642: Old Testament Exegesis III – Prophets & Writings* (Grand Rapids, Mich.: Grand Rapids Theological Seminary, Fall 2009).

absent in 𝕸. With those variants present, Isaiah 52:14 would read, as Martin Hengel translates it: "*I have anointed* [מָשַׁחְתִּי] his appearance beyond that of any (other) man, and his form beyond that of the sons of humanity."[228] The other major variant is at 53:10, where 𝕸 contains the problematic *Hiphil* perfect form הֶחֱלִי ("he caused Him to become sick"). In 1QIsa[a], the alternate reading is ויחלל הו ("he pierced Him"), which forms an *inclusio*[229] with 53:5 and a more palpable intertextual connection with Zechariah 12:10.

Admittedly, Qumran documents are not the most reliable exemplars for Jewish thought outside of that closed community. Moving in a more mainstream direction, Yonathan ben Uzziel, author of *Targum Yonathan* (𝕿[J]), is a fairly early commentator on the passage. His Second-Century Jewish work inserts the title *Messiah* at the beginning of the passage, at Isaiah 52:13, thus: "Behold my servant *Messiah* [מְשִׁיחָא] shall prosper; he shall be high, and increase, and be exceedingly strong." In this, we see that the Messiah being identified with Isaiah's Suffering Servant it is

---

[228] Martin Hengel, "The Effective History of Isaiah 53 in the Pre-Christian Period," in *The Suffering Servant: Isaiah 53 in Jewish and Christian Sources* (ed. by Bernd Janowski & Peter Stuhlmacher; Grand Rapids, Mich.: Wm. B. Eerdmans, 2004), 75-146.

[229] An *inclusio* is a common Semitic literary device which identifies the start and end of a unit of thought be making almost identical statements on both ends of it, like bookends. Everything between the bookend statements is "included" in the unit of thought, thus the label *inclusio*.

not absent from Jewish expectations. The only way Moshe ben David was able to maneuver around this commentary was to democratize the title and role of Messiah so that "the [whole] Jewish people are the Messiah"[230] – an unconvincing proposition.

Isaiah presents the voice of HaShem saying of this Servant that He suffered "… for the transgression of my people to whom the stroke was due" (Isaiah 53:8). The "my people" (עַמִּי) is obviously Israel, so the Servant cannot also be Israel. Even if the speaker is Isaiah rather than HaShem, "my people" is still Israel. Rabbi Itzhak Shapira points out, "According to all the prophets, and Isaiah in particular, it is impossivle to see Israel as blameless,"[231] yet that is precisely how the Servant is presented in Isaiah 53. Verses 6-7 present Israel as the sheep, all of whom have gone astray, and the Servant as the lamb who is led to the slaugher on their behalf. A Third-Century Midrashic work joins its voice with that of ben Uzziel in affirming that the Servant is "King Messiah" (*Ruth Rabbah* 2.14). Several sources also cite the *Sifré* and *Midrash Tanchuma*, but specific citations are not given and the present author has been unable to find the passages quoted by these sources.[232] However, a voice from the *Talmud*, that of

---

[230] Moshe ben David, *At the Gate of Rome* (Las Vegas, Nev.: CreateSpace, 2012), 137-39.

[231] Shapira, *The Return of the Kosher Pig*, 101.

[232] These questionable quotations originated with Ramón Martí, *Pugio Fidei adversus Mauros et Judaeos* (Rome, 1280) and are repeated in Samuel Rolles Driver and Adolf D. Newbauer, *The Fifty-Third Chapter of Isaiah according to*

Rabbi Yanai, affirms, "We are to interpret Isaiah 53:4 as presenting Messiah whose name will be *Yinon* [Psalm 72] because his name was created before the sun" (*b. Sanhedrin* 98b). *Bereshit Rabbah* 44.8 also connects the Messiah to Isaiah 53 in proclaiming, "And when Israel is sinful, the Messiah seeks for mercy upon them, as it is written, 'By His stripes we were healed, and He carried the sins of many; and made intercession for the transgressors' (v. 5).

It was not foreign to the Jewish *hashqafah* to assign some semblance of Divinity to a person operating on HaShem's behalf via the alighting of His *Ruach* (רוּחַ, i.e. Spirit of Holiness) upon them. This is evident, to a degree, in the lives of Kings David and Sh'lomo (Solomon), and even Sha'ul (King Saul) for a time. Each of Judah's kings was considered a "son of G-d," for instance. Sha'ul opens his letter to the Romans with a recognition of Yeshua's Davidic lineage and a declaration that He "was made the Son of Elohim" (Romans 1:1-4). The Gospel accounts of Yeshua's *tevilah* (immersion) feature a *bat qol* declaring, "This is my beloved Son in whom I am pleased" (Matthew 3:17). A fair number of scholars see in this statement an allusion to Isaiah's presenation of the

Jewish Interpreters (New York, N.Y.: KTAV Publishing House, Inc., 1969) and Mark Eastman and Chuck Smith, *The Search for Messiah* (Fountain Valley, Calif.: Joy Publishing, 1996. It should be noted that Martí was appointed by the Pope to find and publish any and all *sugyot* (plural of *sugya*) of the *Talmud* which could be objectionable to Roman Catholics. It has been determined that a fair number of Martí's "*Talmud* passages" were fabricated.

Servant of HaShem: "Behold My servant, whom I uphold; Mine elect, in whom My soul delighteth; I have put My spirit upon him, he shall make the right to go forth to the nations" (Isaiah 42:1).[233]

Flusser interprets this event thus: "... at that time he was simply being addressed as the chosen servant. Not until the voice at the Transfiguration was he truly named 'Son.'"[234] It is said in the Apostolic writings (Luke 2:52) that Yeshua "grew in knowledge and stature" with regard to His role as Messiah. Perhaps that includes growing in degrees of Sonship. It can be effectively demonstrated that by the late First Century CE, "Son of Elohim" becomes democratized to refer to all Israel. This treatment resulted in prayers like the *Avinu Malkheinu* (attributed to Aqiva in *b. Ta'anit* 25b) and Aqiva's pronouncement that Israel is cleansed only through their sonship to their "Father in heaven" (*m. Yoma* 8:9).[235] This is based on Exodus 4:22,

---

[233] David Flusser, *Jesus* (The Hebrew University Magnes Press, 2001; orig. 1997), 40-41; Joachim Jeremias, in Gerhard Kittel, *Theologisches Wörterbuch zum Neuen Testament* V (Stuttgart: Verlag Von W. Kohlhammer, 1932), 699; Shlomo Pines, *The Jewish Christians of the Early Centuries of Christianity According to a New Source* (The Israel Academy of Sciences and Humanities Proceedings vol. II, no. 13; Jerusalem, 1966), 63; Krister Stendahl, *The School of St. Matthew and its Use of the Old Testament* (Uppsala: Almqvist & Wiksell, 1954), 110,144.

[234] Flusser, *Jesus*, 120.

[235] Alon Goshen-Gottstein, "God and Israel as Father and Son in Tannaitic Literature" (Ph.D. dissertation; Hebrew University of Jerusalem, 1986); James H. Charlesworth, *Jesus*

which records Moshe telling Pharaoh, "This is what the LORD says: Israel is my firstborn son," as well as Hosea 1:10; 11:1. Yochanan echoes this understanding as well, writing, "Everyone that is born of Elohim does not practice sin because His seed is in him and he cannot sin because he is born of Elohim. By this are the *children* [sons] *of Elohim* [Aramaic: בְּנוֹהִי דֵאלָהָא] discriminated from the children of Satan[236] [Aramaic: בְּנוֹהִי דְּסָטָנָא]" (1 John 3:9-10).

The term does, in First Century parlance, also carry a more specific connotation in some contexts. In the vernacular of the time, those two statements, i.e. "heir of David" and "Son of Elohim," can be used as equivalent terms. This is attested in the application of "Son of Elohim" to King David in the *Tanakh* (2 Samuel 7:12-14a; Psalm 2:7-8; & oft.). In Rabbinic literature, the moniker occurs as well – with both royal and Messianic connotations. It is found

---

within Judaism: New Light from Exciting Archaeological Discoveries (New York, N.Y.: Doubleday, 1988), 134.

[236] Roth's translation presents "Satan" as if a proper name, but in Hebrew, that is not what is being communicated. The word *haSatan* simply means "the adversary" or "the accuser." We are never told his name, lest some might call upon it. Some translations of Scripture mistranslate the word *heilel* (הֵילֵל; crescent moon) in Isaiah 14:12 as "Lucifer," but that is not drawn from the Hebrew text; it is a Latin (Vulgate) interpolation. See Brian Tice, "'Names' of False Deities in the Bible" (15 Nov 2011; online: https://www. facebook.com/notes/brian-tice/names-of-false-deities-in-the-bible/10150365099831825); Franz Delitzsch. *Isaiah* (Keil-Delitzsch Old Testament Commentary 7; Edinburgh: T. & T. Clark, 1866), 312.

referring to Messiah in a *Talmudic* passage referencing
Psalm 2:

> Our rabbis taught, The Holy One, blessed be He,
> will say to the Messiah, the son of David (May he
> reveal Himself speedily in our days), 'Ask of Me
> anything, and I will give it to You,' as it is said [in
> Psalm 2:7-8]: 'I will tell of the decree: the L-rd has
> said unto me, 'You are My son; this day I have be-
> gotten You. Ask it of Me and I will give the nations
> for Your inheritance.' (*b. Sukkah* 52a)

The juxtaposition of "Messiah" and "son of
David" found in *b. Sukkah* 52a can be seen employed
by Yeshua's *talmid* Matthew as well (Matthew 1:1). It
appears from the *p'shat* reading of that verse that the
soubriquet "son of David" is meant to serve
epexegetically in tandem with "Messiah" to crown
Yeshua with the an identification as the *Mashiach ben
Dawid* expected in much of the popular eschatological
literature of that time. *Bereshit Rabbah* 23 applies a
similar juxtaposition: "Chawwah had respect for that
seed which is coming from another place. And who is
this? This is the Messiah, the King." The psalm cited
in *b. Sukkah* 52a is the same one which inspired the
epithet "King Messiah" (מֶלֶךְ הַמָּשִׁיחַ) found in *Targum
Pseudo-Yonathan*'s treatment of Genesis 3:15. The text
of that *targum* makes it clear that the author un-
derstands Genesis 3:15 (called in evangelical Christian
thought the "proto-evangelium") is a Messianic passage: "For them [Adam and Chawwah's progeny]…
there will be a remedy, but for you [serpent] there will
be no remedy; and they are to make peace in the end,
in the days of King Messiah." That *targum* also
identifies King Messiah with the tribe of Yehudah in

its rendering of Genesis 49:12 – "How beautiful is King Messiah who is destined to arise from the house of Yehudah…. How beautiful are the eyes of King Messiah, as pure wine!"

There are two phrases in Hebrew which are generally translated identically, but their semantic domains, i.e. ranges of meaning, while enjoying some overlap, are not entirely interchangeable. Those terms are *ben enosh* (בֶּן אֱנוֹשׁ) and *ben adam* (בֶּן אָדָם), both of which are rendered "son of man." The former merely means "human," but the latter can be used in ways that give it a Messianic connotation, e.g. in Daniel 7. Yeshua may have been using the expression as a circumlocution in some cases (e.g. Matthew 8:20 and Luke 9:58), but a titular use is also apparent (e.g. Matthew 24:37-39; Luke 17:26-30). Horbury insists, "The phrase [son of man] necessarily had a wide semantic range; but it is likely that it included, within that range, established messianic associations, such that it could have been taken by Jewish hearers or readers as a reference to the messiah."[237] It was not even completely unconscionable to the Jewish mind, at least among some, that the phrase could even communicate heavenly origin in certain contexts.

Among those who understood Daniel's heavenly "Son of Man" figure as Messianic was First-Century Sage Aqiva, the subject of chapter 5 of this present work. Rabbi Aqiva even links the Danielic "Son of

---

[237] William Horbury, *Messianism among Jews and Christians: Twelve Biblical and Historical Studies* (London and New York: T & T Clark, 2003), 128.

Man" to David, teaching, "One passage says, 'His throne was fiery flames' [Daniel 7:9]; and another passage says, 'Til thrones were places, and One that was Ancient of Days did sit!' There is no contradiction: one [throne] for Him, and one for David... one is for justice, one for grace." (*b. Chagigah* 14a). By "David," it is understood that Aqiva was referring to *Mashiach ben Dawid* rather than imagining that King David was enthroned in heaven next to HaShem.[238] Though the date is uncertain,[239] 1 Enoch is another contemporary or near-contemporary witness to the "Son of Man" being a heavenly figure. The author of that *pseudepigraphon* presents the Son of Man as an angelic figure who had received his name before the creation of the sun and constellations (1 Enoch 48:2-3):

> In that hour was this Son of man invoked before the Lord of spirits, and his name in the presence of the Ancient of days. Before the sun and the signs were created, before the stars of heaven were

---

[238] For an alternative view: Daniel Boyarin, *The Jewish Gospels*, 41: "Rabbi Akiva perceives two divine figures in heaven, one God the father and one an apotheosized King David." The present author, however, maintains that, as stated above, "David" is a metonymy for the Messiah.

[239] In John J. Collins, "Pre-Christian Jewish Messianism: An Overview," in Magnus Zetterholm, ed., *The Messiah in Early Judaism and Christianity* (Minneapolis, Minn.: Fortress Press, 2007), 16, a probable date of early-to-mid First Century CE is suggested; but other proposals range from 200 BCE to 200 CE.

formed, his name was invoked in the presence of the Lord of spirits.[240]

This same figure is identified as the Messiah in 48:10 of that work.

The *Talmud*, possibly recalling 4 Ezra 13:3's depiction of Messiah descending on clouds, calls Messiah "Son of the Clouds" (*b. Sanhedrin* 96b). The rider of the clouds seems to be identified in Psalm 68:5 as HaShem: "extol Him that rideth upon the skies." Cambridge University Hebrew professor John Adney Emerton suggests, "The act of coming with clouds suggests a theophany…. If Daniel vii.13 does not refer to a divine being, then it is the only exception of about seventy passages [of the *Tanakh*]."[241]

There is a possible *Talmudic* foundation for asserting the concept of the preexistent *Mashiach* of the Enochian literature. Two separate *sugyot* declare, "Seven things were created before the world was created: the *Torah*, Repentance, the Garden of Eden,

---

[240] Ge'ez (Ethiopic) text: ወበይእቲ ሰዓት ተጸውዐ ዝኩ ወልደ ሰብእ በኀበ እግዚአ መናፍስት ወስሙ ቅድመ ርእሰ መዋዕል። ወዘንበለ ይትፈጠር ፀሐይ ወተአምር ዘእንበለ ይትገበሩ ከዋክብተ ሰማይ ወስሙ ተጸውዐ በቅድመ እግዚአ መናፍስት።; transl. Richard Laurence, *Enoch the Prophet* (Oxford: Parker, 1821). Aramaic fragments have been found in Qumran Cave 4, as well as a few Hebrew fragments in Qumran Cave 1; translations into Greek and Latin dating to the 6th, 8th, and 11th Centuries are also extant.

[241] John Adney Emerton, "The Origin of the Son of Man Imagery," *Journal of Theological Studies* 9 (1958):225-242 at 231-2.

Gei Hinnom, the Throne of Glory, and the Name of Messiah" (*b. Pesachim* 54a; *b. Nedarim* 39a). The wording is important to consider here: "the Name of Messiah." In Hebraic parlance, one must bear in mind, the word "name" most generally connotes the *character* of the one to whom it applies, i.e. the *p'shat* or natural way that this would come across to a Hebrew-speaker would be that *a* future Messiah's existence had been foreordained. The *midrashic* literature contributes: "God beheld the Messiah and his deeds before the Creation, but He hid him and his generation under His throne of glory" (*Pesiqta Rabbathi* 161b). Perhaps this passage provides more concretization to Messiah's preexistence, but it might also be understood as anthropomorphic language, such as is assigned to Lady Wisdom in the Proverbs.

This preexistence is explained by Hermas in a way which expresses the First-Century Jewish understanding of Divine Agency:

> The preexistent Holy Spirit, which created the whole creation, G-d caused to live in the flesh being that He wished. This flesh being, therefore, in which the Holy Spirit lived, served the Spirit well, living in holiness and purity, without defiling the Spirit in any way. (Shepherd of Hermas 59:5).[242]

This "flesh being" is called in 59:1 "the Son of G-d" and in 59:7 "the Son." The latter verse pronounces, "For all flesh in which the Holy Spirit has lived will, if it proves to be undefiled and spotless, receive a

---

[242] See page כ, footnote 13 re: the canonicity of this book.

reward." The next several pages (esp. pp. 164-172) will further unpack this concept.

Jewish scholar Daniel Boyarin opines that Yeshua "came in a form that many, many were expecting [in the Messiah]: a second divine figure incarnated as a human."[243] Horbury is correct, however, to reign in that claim a bit: "The expectation of a heavenly messiah, even if pre-Christian, was probably current only among the public for books like Enoch, a body not necessarily representative of Jews in general."[244] Important considerations with the Enoch literature include that the literature was understood by its audience to belong to a genre called *pseudepigrapha*, which was recognized as popular fiction. It was certainly religious in theme, but it was on par with the more recent works of J. R. R. Tolkien and C. S. Lewis, or on the Jewish side – Chaim Potok or Gene Roddenberry. Another difficulty with accepting 1 Enoch as authoritative or reliable is its contradictions to the text of Scripture.

---

[243] The present author concurs with the first part of that statement (with regard to Divine Agency), but questions the second part, as it seems to contradict the charges levied against Yeshua in Matthew 26:63-68, specifically the charges of blasphemy and self-exaltation. For Boyarin's argumentation, cf. Daniel Boyarin, *The Jewish Gospels: The Story of the Jewish Christ* (New York, N.Y.: The New Press, 2012).

[244] William Horbury, "The Messianic Associations of 'the Son of Man'," *Journal of Theological Studies* XXXII (1985): 34-55; repub. In William Horbury, *Messianism among Jews and Christians: Twelve Biblical and Historical Studies* (London and New York: T & T Clark, 2003), 126.

1 Enoch 7:3 imagines that angels bore giant human offspring, but the Biblical account it draws upon (Genesis 6:1-4) never mentions giants or angels. The surrounding context is a commentary on human depravity, not fallen angels and is better understood as describing children begotten of men of faith (sons of G-d) and pagan women (daughters of man). Such pairings are outside of the will of HaShem (Exodus 34:11-16). Reading the "fallen angel" motif into the text forced 1 Enoch to alter the text of Genesis 6:5 when it is referenced in 1 Enoch 7:3. The former states incontrovertibly that the Flood is brought on account of *man's* wickedness, but the Enochian text, in order to make it fit the storyline it presents, must corrupt the reading so that the destruction is the posited to be, instead, the result of the wickedness of *angels*.

"Sons of G-d" (in the plural; i.e. בְּנֵי הָאֱלֹהִים)[245] is consistently used of human beings throughout Scripture.[246] Even those instances of the phrase typically taught as referring to angels (Genesis 6; Job 1-2) might also be better understood by applying the persistent pattern established by all of the other occurrences – four in the *Tanakh* and six in the *B'rit Chadasha* (See *Appendix C*), as is done by Rabbi Shim'on bar Yochai, a first-generation *talmid* of Rabbi

---

[245] Note that the plural expression is used differently, i.e. in a more general way, than the singular "Son of Elohim" discussed earlier in the present chapter.

[246] Brian Tice, "Who or What were the Nephilim?" *Emunah BiY'shua* (2011; online: https://adiakrisis.files.wordpress.com/2014/10/imti-sons-of-g-d-study.pdf).

Aqiva. The rabbinic teaching on angels was that "angels were immortal and did not propagate their species (*Bereshit Rabbah* 8.11), neither were they susceptible to the *yetzer hara'* (*Bereshit Rabbah* 48.11). Other serious issues include Enoch speaking with Noach (1 Enoch 10:1) when there is a sixty-nine-year gap between Enoch's departure and Noach's birth and HaShem instructing Enoch to pray to angels (1 Enoch 12:4), a practice which HaShem prohibits and condemns elsewhere (Colossians 2:18-19).

What most *modern* adherents to Judaism are unable to accept about the Christian presentation is how to reconcile the idea of the "deity of Yeshua" with Jewish monotheism, however, is how to reconcile the idea of "the deity of Yeshua" with Jewish monotheism. There must be something in the First-Century Judaisms that is not being grasped – something that allows for those two concepts to marry in the ancient Jewish *hashqafah*. Hurtado has suggested that it has something to do with how the ancients understood *Divine Agency*.

One Jewish form of Divine Agency is the veneration of the patriarchs. Hurtado asserts that "the concept of the exalted Christ [Messiah] is not simply derived from the Greco-Roman idea of the *apotheosis* of heroes"[247] – an argument often made by opponents of Yeshua-centric faith. The idea of "hypostatic union," i.e. the concept of Messiah being simul-

---

[247] Larry W. Hurtado, *One God, One Lord: Early Christian Devotion and Ancient Jewish Monotheism* (2nd ed.; London and New York: T & T Clark, 1998), 98.

taneously fully human and fully divine,[248] was still centuries away in Yeshua's time. A rather convincing case has been made that the understanding of Yeshua's *qnume* (plural, i.e. the convergence of humanity and divinity) which undergirds the discussion was vastly different from what the controversial First Council of Ephesus (431 CE) imposed on the Eastern Church.[249]

---

[248] Robert P. Lightner, *Handbook of Evangelical Theology: A Historical, Biblical, and Contemporary Survey and Review* (Grand Rapids, Mich.: Kregel Publications, 1995), 82-83.

[249] The First Council of Ephesus conflated the ideas conveyed by the Aramaic words *partzupa* (פַּרְצוֹפֵה, i.e. the whole of the unique characteristics which make up and/or define the individual person) and *qnuma* (קְנוּמֵה, i.e. the set of traits common to all concrete occurrences of a given *khayana*) in their translation of the terms into Greek, sometimes covering both with the word *prósopon* (πρόσωπον, i.e. "person") or rendering *qnuma* with the ill-matched Greek word *hupóstasis* (ὑπόστασις, i.e. "underlying substance"). The problem with this is that they are vastly different in Semitic thought. The word *qnuma* is a term which has no counterpart in Greek, nor in Latin or English for that matter. It comes from the Aramaic shoresh or rootword *qᵉnam* (קְנַם), defined in Marcus Jastrow, *Dictionary of the Targumim, Talmud Babli and Yerushalmi, and the Midrashic Literature* (New York, N.Y.: Title Publishing, 1943; orig. 1903), 1393 as meaning "to make firm." In this usage, it might contribute to a working definition for *qnuma* as "the concreti-zation of something which, in its natural state, is abstract." Rendering *qnuma* as *hupóstasis*, however, is absolutely not an appropriate gloss for that concept as understood in a First-Century context, given the theological definition that it has come to embody, i.e. ignoring the distinctions between the concepts of *qnuma* and *khayana* and treating those terms (or rather their Greek glosses) as

Another facet of Divine Agency is the appointment of angels to certain tasks to be performed on behalf of the Almighty. This was certainly recognized in First-Century Pharisaic Judaism. Among some, an overfascination and even adoration/worship of angelic beings had developed (*Tos. Chullin* 2:18). Colossians warns against over-venerating angels, i.e. making them into objects of worship (2:18), indicating that this was an issue at that location. British Bible scholar Dr. James D. G. Dunn expresses that "worship of angels is something one would not expect in any of the forms of Judaism known to us

---

interchangeable. See Lightner, op. cit., 81-82. It is a particularly distasteful translation choice due tp its pagan usage in relation to deification of a human figure, i.e. the making of demigods. The Aramaic word *khayana* (כִּיָנָא) refers to the "ontological whole of the being," separate from the idea of the tangible *partzupa* – perhaps translatable as the "nature" (whether human or Divine), but *khayana* cannot refer to any actual occurrence or concretiza-tion of the abstract concept (*qnuma*), and certainly not to the whole of the specific characteristics which are unique to an embodiment of the concretization (*partzupa*). The common theological treatment of *khayana* as equating to *ousía* (οὐσία, i.e. "essence") is apt enough, though *phúsis* (φύσις, i.e. "nature"), which is also used in some instances, may be better.

Nota bene: The present author's understanding of these concepts is gleaned from discussions between three Aramaic scholars – i.e. Paul Younan, Andrew Gabriel Roth, and Glenn David Bauscher – on the forums at *peshitta.org*, as well as their respective written works (cited in the Works Consulted list). The reader is encouraged to study these terms more deeply via those sources.

for this period."[250] This phenomenon has been associated by others with First-Century Judaisms which were well outside the mainstream, e.g., the *Merkavah* cult (the Gnostic predecessor to *Qabbalah*)[251] or the *Yachad* community of Qumran (keepers of the Dead Sea Scrolls).[252]

The ultimate Divine Agent would not be an angel or even an archangel; this honor would belong to Israel's promised and long-awaited Messiah. As Messiah, Yeshua uniquely embodied the fullness of the Divine *qnuma*, i.e. the *Ruach Elohim*, as no one before Him or since ever could (Colossians 2:9; Romans 8:3). All of the *samchut* consigned to the various Divine Agents of every form of Judaism converged in a single Agent in the Person of Messiah, as embodied by Yeshua. Though anathema in modern Jewish thought, the idea of Messiah sharing in some way in the Divine *qnuma* was not always so unconscionable.

---

[250] James D. G. Dunn, *The Epistles to the Colossians and to Philemon: A Commentary on the Greek Text* (Grand Rapids, Mich.: Wm. B. Eerdmans, 1996), 179.

[251] F. F. Bruce, "Colossians Problems, Part 3: The Colossian Heresy"." *Bibliotheca Sacra* 141 (1984): 195-208.

[252] Ernest M Saunders, "The Colossian Heresy and Qumran Theology," *Studies in the History and Text of the New Testament in honor if Kenneth Willis Clark* (1967): 133-145; Lawrence H. Schiffman, "Merkavah Speculation at Qumran: the 4Q Serekh Shirot `Olat HaShabbat," *Mystics, Philosophers, and Politicians: Essays in Jewish Intellectual History in Honor of Alexander Altmann* (ed. J. Reinharz and D. Swetschinski; Duke University Press, 1982): 15-47.

Like Wisdom and Logos,[253] Yeshua is said to be a Divine Agent in the Creation and Ordering of the World (John 1:1-3; Hebrews 1:2, 10; 1 Corinthians 8:6). He is compared to Malki-Tzedeq,[254] to whom *11Q13* assigns a redemptive eschatological role (Hebrews 7:13-28) and said to have the same redemptive role (1 Corinthians 1:30; 15:20-28; Romans 3:23-26; 4:24-25; 1 Thessalonians 1:10). He was and is the ultimate Divine Agent, seated at the "right hand of Power" (Matthew 26:64), raised higher than *archangel* (ἀρχάγγελος, i.e. chief-angel) Micha'el, HaShem's *archistrategos* (ἀρχιστράτηγος, i.e. chief-general) as conveyed in *Testament of Abraham* (1:4; 2:1); *malakh* (מַלְאָךְ, i.e. angel) Yaho'el "in whom G-d's Name dwells" according to *Apocalypse of Abraham* (10:1-14), or Philo's version of Moshe, the *koinōnós* (κοινωνός, i.e. partner) of HaShem.[255] Even the pseudepigraphical Enoch literature only elevated its central figure to sit at the *left* of HaShem's throne, having been transformed from human to angel (2 Enoch 24:1-3).[256]

---

[253] Wisdom is given this role in Wisdom of Solomon 7:22, and Logos is so described in Philo of Alexandria, *Quæstiones et Solutiones: Genesis* (1st Century CE), 4.110-111.

[254] The reader is referred to the discussion of Malki-Tzedeq in the glossary following Chapter 7 for pertinent background on this figure.

[255] Philo, *De Vita Mosis*, 1:155-58.

[256] *Nota bene:* Most of the works listed in this paragraph are pseudepigraphical, i.e. belonging to a fiction genre popular primarily from about 200 BCE to 200 CE. Its original audience understood that these works were not actually penned by those to whose names they are ascribed. They

Though it has become *en vogue* in more liberal approaches to Yeshua to present His Divine *qnuma* as a late development in Christianity, i.e. a later concoction generally argued to make inception in the late Third or early Fourth Centuries, the historical record fails to support that presupposition. Dr. Amy-Jill Levine of the Vanderbilt University faculty declares, "First-century Judaism was sufficiently fluid to allow even the idea that an individual could embody divinity."[257] The *B'rit Chadasha* itself, every book of which dates to no more than sixty years following Yeshua's execution and some as soon as ten to fifteen years after,[258] presents Him as a figure whose redemptive role was defended by followers of *HaDerekh* immediately following His resurrection and forever after... even at the cost of martyrdom. Dr. Larry Hurtado of the University of Edinburgh's Bible faculty observes, "This reshaping of Jewish mono-

---

were enjoyed as Jewish-themed literature akin to the more modern works of J. R. R. Tolkien and C. S. Lewis. They did, however, represent Messianic hopes and expectations from the Jewish reality of the era.

[257] Amy-Jill Levine, "A Jewish take on Jesus: Jesus was smack in the middle of the Jewish tradition of his time. Remembering that can make you a better Christian, says this Jewish scholar of the New Testament," *U.S. Catholic* 77, no. 10 (Oct 2012): 18.

[258] Pantænas testifies to having been given an Aramaic copy of Matthew in India which had been carried there by Thomas and Bartholomew in 45 CE; and Revelation and Shepherd, the latest of the canonized books, were in place by 100 CE. (Eusebius Pamphilius, *Historia Ecclesiastica* (ca. 324 CE), 5.10.)

theistic devotion began among Jewish Christians[259] of the first few years after Jesus' execution and cannot be attributed simply to some later stage of the Christian movement"[260] Such thinking was not unique to the *Netzari* movement, though. *Shemot Rabbah* 8 confirms that "G-d will set His own crown on the head of King Messiah and clothe Him with honor."

Yeshua made claims during His brief ministry of being one (*echad*)[261] with the Father in Heaven (John 10:30; AENT – :אֲנָא וְאָבִי חַד נַחָן), and though such statements were seen as blasphemous by some (John 5:18; 10:31-33), the statement did not strike most as

---

[259] Though it was once commonplace to refer to First-Century followers of Yeshua as "Christians," it is now understood that it is anachronistic to use that term in reference to Bible-Era Believers outside of Antioch. The names *HaDerekh* and *Netzarim* were more common for that movement, which was still very much under the umbrella of Judaism at that time.

[260] Hurtado, op. cit., 100.

[261] There are two ways of expressing oneness in Hebrew – *echad* (*chad* in Aramaic), which is the word used in the Shema (Deuteronomy 6:4), and *yachid* (יָחִיד). The former conveys the idea of a composite unity, or unity of purpose, while the latter denotes absolute uniqueness, i.e. "the only exemplar of its kind." The word yachid is used of HaShem in Maimonides' *Shloshah Asar Ikkarim* ("Thirteen Fundamental Principles," first articulated in *Commentary on Mishna Sanhedrin 10:1* ca. 1168 CE), but never in the Tanakh. Its usage there is limited to "one and only child" (ten instances) and "lonely" (two instances). Its Aramaic equivalent (יְחִידָאִין) is used of Yeshua in the *Peshitta* (John 3:16) with the first definition: "only and unique Son."

deviating from their Jewish understanding of Divine Agency. Some of the Jewish religious leaders came to follow Yeshua. The Sha'ul haTarsi, once among His worst critics and a devoted persecutor of His followers, described Him as the One "in whom dwells all the fullness of *Elohim* bodily" (Colossians 2:9). It is worth noting that a solid definition of what "blasphemy" was considered to include had not been nailed down. Per *m. Sanhedrin* 7:5, the definition would be the public pronunciation of the ineffable Covenant Name of HaShem (the Tetragrammaton, called in Judaism the *Shem haMeforash*), but this definition may date closer to 200-220 CE. Juel suggests, "... the legal definition of blasphemy must have been considerably broader in the first century."[262] Roth adds, "The Pharisees, Sadducees, and most religions tend to make up religious traditions of what 'blasphemy' [גּוּדְפָּה] or 'unpardonable sin' [חֵטְא בִּלְתִּי נִסְלָח] is when their leadership authority is being challenged or questioned."[263]

This concentration of all accepted aspects of Divine Agency converging in a single *partzupa*, i.e. the Messiah, however novel, would certainly have been understood as within the bounds of Pharisaic Judaism and would also not be found by most to be incongruent with the First-Century Jewish perception

---

[262] Donald Juel, Messiah and the Temple: The Trial of Jesus in the Gospel of Mark (SBLDS 31; Missoula, Mont.: Scholars Press, 1977), 97–98.

[263] Andrew Gabriel-Yitzkhak Roth bar Raphael, *Aramaic English New Testament* (5th ed.; Sedro-Woolley, Wash.: Netzari Press, 2012), 82n280.

of monotheism.[264] The question was less one of Jewishness than of Messianic expectation. The *Talmud* makes mention of a title which is invoked by Jews and Christians alike, stating in *b. Sukkah* 52a: "*Messiah ben Yosef* was slain, as it is written, 'They shall look upon Me whom they have pierced, and they shall mourn for him as one mourns for his only son: (Zechariah 12:10).'"

Some of the Sages expected this to be a "War Messiah," who, according to their understanding of the figure, would die in battle. Whether their interpretation was correct or not is immaterial; the point is that it defined their expectations for the Messiah. What Yeshua brought to bear was a *Mashiach ben Yosef* who died... but not quite in the way expected. His martyrdom came upon a Roman execution stake like a common criminal – a death lacking the honor of a battlefield fatality. How ironic that the words emblazoned on the placard on His execution stake should be זֶה הוּא יֵשׁוּעַ מֶלֶךְ הַיְּהוּדִים (This is Yeshua: King of the Jews), given the manner in which He was killed.

Yeshua's battle was a war against sin and death... and His death was, thus, only temporary. Though apotheotic declarations eventually came to the forefront of Christian thought, such were not the norm prior to Yeshua's Resurrection.[265] His own

---

[264] Hurtado, op. cit., 20-21.

[265] The present author is not speaking to the veracity or lack thereof regarding claims of deity, but rather indicating that those developments in the topic cannot be adequately

talmidim apparently did not understand what was about to take place, as evidenced by their conversation with Him in the final hours leading up to His arrest (John 13:33-36) and their scattering after the event (Matthew 26:31 ‖ Mark 14:27).

After the Resurrection, however, those who followed Yeshua apparently made the same Messianic connection to Zechariah 12 as the *Talmudist*, as His *talmid* Matthew pulls text adjacent to it in the same passage into his gospel (Matthew 24:30, cit. Zechariah 12:10-14). Even those who did not noticed that something had changed in the atonement economy of the Temple's sacrificial system. It is important to bear in mind while reading these words from the *Talmud* that Yeshua's death occurred in 30 CE, i.e. forty years before the destruction of the Temple:

> Our rabbis taught: During the last forty years before the destruction of the Temple the lot [For the L-rd] did not come up in the right hand; nor did the crimson-colored strap become white; nor did the western most light shine; and the doors of the Temple would open by themselves. (*b. Yoma* 39b). For it is taught on *Tannaitic* authority: In olden times, they would tie a crimson thread to the outside of the door of the [Temple] entranceway. [If] it turned white, the people would rejoice; [if] it did not turn white, the people would be grieved.... And it is taught on *Tannaitic* authority: For forty years prior to the destruction of the Temple, the

demonstrated to have been a factor for the timeframe dealt with by this present work.

crimson thread did not turn white, but rather remained red. (*b. Rosh HaShanah* 31b-32a).

Talmud Bavli is not the sole witness to these phenomena. A similar report appears in *Talmud Yerushalmi:*

> It has been taught: Forty years before the destruction of the Temple, the western light went out, the crimson thread remained crimson, and the lot for the Lord always came up in the left hand. They would close the gates of the Temple by night and get up in the morning and find them wide open.... Said Rabban Yochanan ben Zakkai to the Temple, 'O Temple, why do you frighten us? We know that you will end up destroyed. For it has been said, 'Open your doors, O Lebanon, that the fire may devour your cedars' (*y. Yoma* 6:3-4).

The Sages' conclusion regarding these events at that time was that HaShem was no longer accepting Israel's sacrifices... beginning in the same year as Yeshua's death and resurrection.[266] The present author shall refrain from attempting to decide for the reader what to believe with regard to these matters. The aim here has been merely to contribute rabbinical data for the reader's consideration – some of which might reinforce what the beliefs already held and some of which might challenge them. Perhaps the

---

[266] Note that the Biblical year begins with the month of Abib/Nissan, the month of *Pesach* (Passover), so Yeshua's death occurred just 14 days into the year. The events described in *b. Yoma 39b* and *y. Sota 6:3* come about six months afterward, that same year, at *Yom Kippur*.

way to leave this chapter is with the questions asked by Rabbi Aharon Yaskil on this subject:

> Did we lose our way 2,000 years ago? ... Does this connection to a Tzaddik [Righteous One] represent a new Judaism? Or is this connection to the Tzaddik [the Messiah] the original Judaism?" [267]

While Flusser's work, recommended at the end of the previous chapter, does cover much on this subject as well, the reader very likely took notice of the great impact which Dr. Larry Hurtado had on the content of this chapter. The present author strongly encourages the reader to engage with his well-crafted tome:

Larry W. Hurtado, *One God, One Lord: Early Christian Devotion and Ancient Jewish Monotheism* (London and New York: T & T Clark, 1998; orig. 1988).

One God, One Lord is a work on the First-Century Jewish understanding of the concept of "Divine Agency." No available work on this subject does a better and more thorough job of presenting it than Dr. Hurtado's volume. Numerous others, including this present work, have presented it in part, but the reader will be blessed by going to the source and reading the full presentation in its original form.

---

[267] Aharon Yaskil, *Ish Peleh*, 9-10; transl. by Itzhak Shapira in *The Return of the Kosher Pig: The Divine Messiah in Jewish Thought* (Clarksville, Md.: Lederer Books, 2013), 100.

CHAPTER 9

SYNCHRONIZING THE SAGES

לְסַנְכְּרֵן הַחֲכָמִים

Though it might accurately be said that the Sages were all working in concert toward the common goal of defining *halakha*, the title of this chapter is not intended to suggest to the reader that they functioned like a synchronized swim team, in agreement on all the fine details of Jewish thought. Synchronic analysis is a study confined to a specific slice of time, in this case – the First Century CE. This final chapter aims to draw in the previous five and show these Sages' teachings side-by-side. Of course, not every rabbi spoke on every subject, so some will reflect a fuller panel of statements than others. Many of the topics important to Judaism which were debated and pondered in the First Century have dedicated categories in the *Talmudic* literature, making this task easier than it might be without such an ordered history of interpretation. The present work will also bring in a voice which is not present in mainstream Rabbinics, however, in its inclusion of Yeshua's teachings.

The structure of this present chapter is borrowed from the *Talmud*, i.e. it is divided by topic and presents a sort of hypothetical dialogue between the Sages on each subject presented. For ease of comparison, under each heading, the reader will find direct quotes (translated to English) from each of the Sages with published rulings on it, followed by analytical observations wherever such is deemed helpful. The topics are arranged according to the English alphabet, and the Sages are listed in the order in which their respective biographical sketches were previously presented in this work. These synopses are brief for the most part, though some are admittedly briefer than others, as availability of content has governed the length. Neusner observes, for instance, the sparcity of direct quotations from Rabban Gamli'el I: "All Gamaliel-materials in the *Mishnah* are in the form of stories or references, in indirect discourse, to his opinions and enactments. None supplies quotations of his words."[268]

Wherever cited by the Sages, the specific *Torah* verses being interpreted are designated under each topic, and also indexed at the end of this work. Inline citation of primary sources is used rather than footnotes in order to simplify the presentation, but secondary sources are footnoted. A list of abbreviations used for Biblical and Rabbinical works can be found in the front matter of the present work following the Preface (beginning on page ל).

On the Afterlife...

The *Torah* affirms an afterlife wherein the righteous are gathered unto their people (Genesis 25:8, 17; 35:29; 49:33; Deuteronomy 42:50) and the wicked are cut off from theirs (Genesis 17:14; Exod 31:14). The general belief is that all Israel has a share in the *'olam haBa* (World to Come), except "one who says there is no resurrection of the dead prescribed in the *Torah*" and Epicureans (*m. Sanhedrin* 10:1).

---

[268] Jacob Neusner, *The Rabbinic Traditions about the Pharisees before 70: Volume 1 — The Masters* (Eugene, Ore.: Wipf & Stock, 2005; orig. 1971), 345.

Shammai taught, "There are three classes: one of everlasting life, another of everlasting shame and contempt – who are accounted wholly wicked, and a third class who go down to *Gei-hinnom* [viewed as a sort of purgatory], where they scream and again come up and receive healing, as it is written, 'And I will bring the third part through the fire, and will refine them as silver is refined, and will try them as gold is tried; and they shall call on my name and I shall be their G-d.'" (*Tos. Sanhedrin* 13:3; cp. *b. Rosh HaShanah* 16b-17a).

Hillel saw the same three groups as did Shammai, but in his view the middle class does not go *Gehinnom*. In an act of Divine mercy, they go immediately to *Gan Eden* (lit. the Garden of Eden, i.e. Heaven/paradise) with the righteous. (*b. Baba Metzia* 58b). He insisted, "One who has acquired unto himself the words of *Torah* has acquired for himself the life of the world to come." (*Pirqei Avot* 2:7).

Though **Gamli'el**'s view on this topic is not cited in the literature, it is likely represented as aligning with that of his grandfather Hillel.

Ben Zakkai is represented by his final words as believing in a final judgment immediately upon death. It seems that he did not necessarily believe that salvation was certain for himself, and thus probably by extension, not for anyone – even though a devoted Jew (*Avot d'Rabbi Nathan* 40a, ch. 35). *See chapter 5* (page 85). As his death came so soon after the destruction of the Temple – 10-20 years at the most, it is easy to imagine that he may have had some doubts about the sweeping changes he had decreed in replacing the sacrificial system with the three Ts of *teshuva* (repentance), *tefillah* (prayer), and *tzedeqah* (righteousness/charitable acts).[269] This even after having had a dream wherein he and Rabbi Yosi haKohen were reclining on Mount Sinai when a *bat qol* resounded from heaven hearkening them, "Ascend hither!" At that moment, he was shown large banquet couches and was told by the *bat qol*, "This is all prepared for you, your disciples, and the disciples of your disciples – all of you invited to the Third Class of Paradise [reserved for great scholars]" (*b. Chagigah* 14b).

Aqiva taught, "The pious are punished in this life for their few sins, in order that in the next they may receive only reward; while the wicked obtain in this world all the recompense for the little good they have done, and in the next world will receive only punishment for their misdeeds" (*Bereshit Rabbah* 33; *Pesiqta Rabbathi* 9, 73*a*); but "He who at a banquet

---

[269] Rabbi Leazer would teach the same after him: "Three actions cancel out a harsh decree [of punishment from Heaven]. These are prayer, righteousness, and repentance. All three are mentioned in one verse [2 Chron. 7:14], 'if my people who are called by my name will humble themselves and pray....' This refers to prayer. 'And seek my face.' This refers to righteousness, which is further proven by Psalm 17:15, where it is said, 'As for me, I shall behold your face in righteousness.' Finally, the words, 'And turn from their wicked ways' refers to repentance. If an individual will do all three, the promise in Scripture is, 'then I will hear from heaven, and will forgive their sin and heal their land' [2 Chron 7:14]" (*y. Ta'anit* 2:1).

renders the Song of Songs in a sing-song way, turning it into a common ditty, has no share in the world to come" (*Tos. Sanhedrin* 10:1)., "Each person has two portions, one in *Gan Eden* and the other in *Gei-Hinnom*. If a person is meritorious and righteous, he takes his chair and that of his fellow in *Gan Eden*; and if he incurred guilt and is wicked, he takes his share and that of his fellow in *Gei-Hinnom*" (*b. Chagigah* 15a).

There is a fair amount of data on **Yeshua**'s view on this topic. Like Ben Zakkai, He confirmed that there was a judgment upon death. He taught, "All who loosen, therefore, from one (of) these small commandments [from the *Torah*] and teach thus to the sons of man, will be called little in the Kingdom of Heaven, but all who do and teach this will be called great in the Kingdom of Heaven." (Matthew 5:19). The least in the kingdom equate to the tares in Matthew 13 and the great correspond to the wheat/righteous, where Yeshua teaches, "Therefore, as the tares are plucked and burned in the fire, likewise it will be in the end of this world. The Son of man will send his Messengers out, and they will pluck from His Kingdom all stumbling blocks and all workers of iniquity [*Torah*-lessness]. And they will cast them into the furnace of fire, and there will be weeping and gnashing of teeth. Then, the righteous will shine like the sun in the Kingdom of their Father. He who has ears to hear, let him hear." (Matthew 13:40-43). "It will not be that just anyone who says to Me, 'My master, my master!' will enter the Kingdom of Heaven, but whoever does the will of My Father who is in Heaven. Many will say to Me in that day, 'My master, my master! By Your name, have we not prophesied? And by Your name, have we not cast out demons? And by Your name, have we not done miracles?' And then I will profess to them that from everlasting, I have not known you. Depart from Me, you workers of iniquity [*Torah*-lessness]!" (Matthew 7:21-23)

On Divorce...

The Sages vary wildly from one another – perhaps moreso than on any other subject. Of the five Sages herein examined, four views are to be found. Only Shammai and Yeshua agree on the matter, which is one of very few topics on which Yeshua aligns with Shammai or his *beit*. The key passage is Deuteronomy 24:1.

Shammai taught, "A man may not divorce his wife unless he has found unchastity in her, as it is said, ' ... because he has found in her indecency in a matter.'" (*m. Gittin* 9:10).

Hillel disagreed: "He may divorce her even if she [merely] burns his food, as it is said, '... because he has found in her indecency in a matter.'" (Ibid.). 'If a man vows he will not have intercourse with his wife... *Beit Hillel* [allows him] one week," after which if he does not return to her, he *must* divorce her and pay her the terms of the *kethubah*, i.e. marriage contract (*m. Kethubot* 5:6).

Gamli'el was what some would class as a proto-feminist with regard to divorce, reducing the *halakhic* hurdles a woman had to jump in order to be granted one. The ease with which the husband could divorce under Hillel was equaled in the wife's favor under this Sage (*b. Kethubot* 10b; *m. Sheqalim* 3:6; *m. Yebamot* 16:7).

By 70 CE, when **Ben Zakkai** was leading the Sanhedrin, Hillel's position on divorce was dominant. He was squarely within that "for any reason" camp.

As liberal as Hillel's position on divorce was, **Aqiva** might have actually been even laxer on the subject than he. Among Aqiva's teachings was this: "He may divorce her if he found another that is more beautiful than his wife, because it was said [Deuteronomy 24:1]. 'If it come to pass that she find no favour in his eyes'" (*m. Gittin* 1). Rabbi Aqiva is apparently the first Sage to advocate for the concept of *annulment*, as he saw fit to and did in his own praxis void every marriage which was in transgression of the prohibitions listed in Scripture (*b. Yebamot* 92a), even declaring any children born from an unbiblical marriage to be illegitimate (*b. Qiddushin* 68a). *Beit Aqiva* also allowed divorce to be initiated by the wife if her husband were to "contract a loathsome disease or engage in work which makes him repugnant to her... [e.g.] if he is a gatherer of dog dung, or a copper-smelter, or a tanner" (*m. Kethubot* 7:9). His student Rabbi Meïr added that even if he was already in that occupation or medical condition before they married, it could still be grounds for divorce if she testified, "I thought I could endure it, but now I see that I cannot" (ibid.).

Though **Yeshua** aligns with *Beit Hillel* on most subjects, He agreed with *Beit Shammai* on this matter, maintaining, "But I say to you that he who leaves his wife without a charge of adultery, and takes another, commits adultery. And he that takes a divorced woman commits adultery." (Matthew 19:9, emphasis added).

On Free Will/Agency...

It is said that where Genesis records the first man (Adam) being "formed" (Genesis 2:7), that specific verb occurs in the text because of its spelling. In Hebrew, it is spelled וַיִּיצֶר (*wayyitzer*), which the Rabbis took note of for the double yod (y). Since יֵצֶר (*yetzer*) also begins with a yod and derives from the same root, the observation was made that this was an indication that he was formed with two *yetzer*s – a *yetzer tov*, i.e. a good inclination, and a *yetzer ra'*, i.e. an evil inclination (*b. Berakhot* 61a). Jewish historian Josephus noted, "... man can [choose to] act virtuously or viciously,"[270] i.e. to choose to act in accord with the *yetzer hatov* or with the *yetzer hara'*.[271]

---

[270] Flavius Josephus, *Antiquitates Judaicae* (95 CE), xviii. i. 3.

[271] The use of two different spellings in this paragraph for "good inclination" and "evil inclination" is for grammatical reasons. The first occurrence is indefinite (a/an), so the definite article *ha* (the) is not used, but at the end of the paragraph, the instances are grammatically definite, so the *ha* on the second word is necessitated.

Judaism has always affirmed the existence of Free Will, but also acknowledges that G-d can and does bring some divine determinism into concert with that Free Will as well. Just as HaShem strengthened Pharaoh's resolve, so also does He do for every soul: "If one goes to defile himself, openings are made for him; and he who goes to purify himself, help is afforded him" (*b. Shabbat* 104a). "In the way in which a man wishes to walk, he is so guided" (*b. Makkot* 10b).

Ben Zakkai asked his inner circle for their views on how to live in alignment with the *yetzer hatov* as opposed to the *yetzer hara*. The responses were quite vaired, with Eliezer ben Hurqanus answering, "a good eye," Yosi advising being a good neighbor, Yehoshua insisting that keeping good company was integral, Shim'on suggesting that taking inventory of what is borne out of one's actions was the way, and Elazar opining that a good heart would keep one's path straight. Ben Zakkai agreed with all of these answers, but said that Elazar's response was the wisest, as it included all of the rest (*Pirqei Avot* 2:9). Note that in Ancient Near Eastern thought, the heart is the seat of rational thought rather than of emotion (those reside in and emanate from the "gut"), and it is rational thought that governs one's actions and decision-making.

Aqiva also believed that man is responsible for his actions, i.e. that each person acts out of free will, not according to a pre-written script or a grand Puppetmaster pulling his or her strings like a marionette. He taught, "Everything is foreseen; but freedom [of will] is given to every man, and the world is judged on its merits" (*Pirqei Avot* 3:15).

Yeshua was also in agreement with this, stating, "For anyone who does the will of my Father[272] who is in heaven, is my brother, and my sister, and my mother" (Matthew 12:50) and also, "He who desires to do His will can comprehend my teaching..." (John 7:17).[273] This implies that there is choice involved in following HaShem's will (*yetzer hatov*) or opting for a more carnal will (*yetzer hara*).

There is really no rational way to read Scripture as teaching the absence of Free Will. In the face of Joshua 24:15 – "Choose this day whom you will serve" – and Deuteronomy 11:26 – "I have set before you blessing and curse... choose life" – how can one possibly assert that we are not gifted with the ability to be obedient to those commands of HaShem? Every one of the Sages who influenced First Century Judaisms saw this... and it was not lost on any Jewish sect except the Essenes.[274] The Calvinistic/Islamic concept of salvific double-predestination does not exist in Pharisaic Judaism, the Sages of which declare,

---

[272] Often translated "whosoever will," this verse and its parallel at Mark 3:35 indicate free agency, i.e. it is up to the individual to decide whether to do the will of the Father or the will of the Adversary.

[273] This statement assumes that man can will to do HaShem's will, i.e. through his Free Will.

[274] Gary A. Rendsburg, "The Rise of the Jewish Sects," *The Dead Sea Scrolls* (Chantilly, Va.: The Great Courses, 2010), lecture 5 (DVD).

"All is given into the hands of heaven, except one's fear of heaven" (*b. Berakhot* 33b). The Pharisees, who absolutely believed in Free Will, are said to have "...rejected in themselves the will of Elohim..." (Luke 7:30) – obviously a Scriptural recognition of their ability to exercise Free Will to reject G-d's instruction. It is not HaShem's will for any to perish (so why would He predestine most to Hell?!), but for all to repent and live (Ezekiel 18:23; 33:11; 2 Peter 3:11). With all that these Sages disagreed with each other on, this matter constituted a point of harmony: man *is* endowed with Free Will.

On Humility...

On the creation of woman as naturally modest (in Hebrew, the word צָנַע means both modest and humble), there is, as the reader may by now have come to expect, a *midrash*. It is said that when she was created, Elohim contemplated from which part of Adam she should be formed. The head was ruled out, lest she be too prideful. The eye, as well, was decided against, as it might lead to over-curiosity. The same decision was made against the ear for fear of eavesdropping, the mouth for reason of loquatiousness, the heart to avoid jealousy. So too were the hand and foot eliminated from the running, as the former might cause her to be too acquisitive and the latter – prone to leave on a whim. Elohim's desire that she be modest led Him to form her from a rib, because it is a part which is hidden, and something hidden would find it difficult to be ostentatious (*Bereshit Rabbah* 18.2).

One might suppose that the least humble of the lot would be **Shammai**. While it is true that he was not particularly known for his humility, he is recalled as stating, "… one ought to teach [*Torah* to] only those who are talented and humble…" (*Avot d'Rabbi Nathan* 3). Rabbi Telushkin portrays him as "preaching to himself," i.e. acknowledging his shortcomings and speaking maxims which were at least as much intended to govern his own conduct as that of his *talmidim*.[275]

Hillel, who was renowed for his humility, is remembered for his dictum "My humiliation is my exaltation and my exaltation is my humiliation" (*Wayyiqra Rabbah* 1.5). He made another similar statement as well: "A name made great is a name destroyed" (*Avot d'Rabbi Nathan* 11). On one occasion, he was asked a question to which he could not recall the applicable *halakha*. It was a question regarding whether one could carry a knife to the Temple on *Pesach*. He had the humility to admit that he didn't know and suggested they go out and see what the people were doing, for those who aren't prophets themselves may be descended from them and would know the protocol. This provided Hillel with the answer, as he witnessed someone tucking the knife into the wool of his lamb, letting the lamb carry the instrument for him. He then declared, "Now I remember! I had learned this from Shemaiah and Avtalyon but had forgotten." (*b. Pesachim* 66a).

---

[275] Joseph Telushkin, *A Code of Jewish Ethics Volume 1: You Shall Be Holy* (New York, N.Y.: Bell Tower Books, 2006), 123.

Unable to find a direct quotation on the subject from **Gamli'el**, we look to his example. While in the role of *Nasi*, he hosted a feast for the rabbis and stood throughout the meal waiting on them. Some of the rabbis, speaking among themselves, voiced how inappropriate it was that the Nasi was acting the part of a servant. Rabbi Yehoshua, however, justified Rabban Gamli'el's conduct thus: "Avraham Avinu, who was a Prince of Elohim stood over the three nomads and served them (*Bereishit* [Genesis] 18:8). If it was legitimate for Avraham to serve the nomads, who appeared to be idol worshippers, this was certainly the case for Rabban Gamli'el, who served the Tanna'im out of humility" (*Mekh. Yitro Parsha* 1).

Yochanan ben Zakkai admitted that though he was a *Torah* scholar of the highest caliber, in prayer he was lacking. When his child was deathly ill, he called in Rabbi Chanina ben Dosa to pray for him. His wife, wondering why he called in another rabbi to pray, asked him, "Is Rabbi Chanina greater than you?" His reply was that whereas ben Zakkai was like a minister to HaShem, ben Dosa was as a servant at His feet. He was convinced that ben Dosa's prayers would be more effective than his own, as Chanina was devoted to that area of praxis, where he had dedicated himself more to study, i.e. orthodoxy, than to application, i.e. orthopraxy. (*b. Berakhot* 34b). The *sugya* ends with the child making a full recovery.

What first attracted Rachel to her husband **Aqiva** was his modesty (*b. Kethubot* 62b). This was a topic he spoke on often. At his son's funeral, he noticed the large number that was in attendance and greeted them. One of his many maxims was this: "He who esteems himself highly on account of his knowledge, is like a corpse lying on the wayside. The traveler turns his head away in disgust, and walks quickly by" (*Avot d'Rabbi Nathan* 11.46). Another of his *dicta* finds itself repeated in the Gospel of Luke (14:8-12): "Take your place a few seats below your rank until you are bidden to take a higher place; for it is better that they should say to you 'Come up higher' than that they should bid you 'Go down lower'" (*Wayyiqra Rabbah* 1.5).

Yeshua preached, "Whoever exalts himself will be humbled, and whoever humbles himself will be exalted." (Matthew 23:12 ‖ Luke 14:11); "Thus will the last be first and the first last. For many are those that are called, and few that are chosen" (Matt 20:16). Additionally, Yeshua was the very model of humility. His last night with His *talmidim* before His execution, He, whom they recognized as the Messiah of all Israel, insisted on washing their feet (John 13:4-14) – a great act of service.

On Love for One's Neighbor...

The *Torah* command is found in Leviticus 19:18b, in the midst of warnings not to curse the deaf, trip the blind, or engage in gossip. It is worth noting that the *p'shat* (plain) sense of Leviticus 19:18 limits the definition of "neighbor" contextually to mean fellow Israelites (בְּנֵי עַמֶּךָ, i.e. "the sons of your people"). Wisdom of Ben Sira 28:3-5 comments that it is sinful to withhold mercy from "a man like himself," a phrase which shares the same construction as the Leviticus 19:18 word/phrase כָּמוֹךָ (kamokha), which can be rendered "for he is like yourself."[276] Rabbi Joseph Telushkin observes, "The precise meaning of the Hebrew word *re-acha* is 'your fellow,' which, like neighbor, suggests someone with whom we routinely have contact (of course, we are alos obligated to act in a loving and helpful way even toward those with whom we have more casual interactions or perhaps none, such as victims of a natural catastrophe)."[277] Some Sages expand the definition by applying a hermeneutical rule from Hillel that allows for a principle from a verse found elsewhere in the canon to be applied to all verses involving that principle (*binyan ab mikathub echad*).

Shammai, who was perhaps one of the more abrasive of the Sages, taught the axiom, "Receive every man with a cheerful countenance" (*Pirqei Avot* 1:15).

The command to "Love your neighbor as yourself" (Leviticus 19:18b) was, in **Hillel**'s estimation, of utmost importance, as evidenced by his response to the request that he teach the *Torah* while standing on one foot: "That which is despicable to you do not do to your neighbor. This is the whole of the *Torah*. The rest is elaboration. Go forth and

---

[276] David Flusser, *Jesus* (Jerusalem: Hebrew University Magnes Press, 2001; orig. 1997), 87.

[277] Joseph Telushkin, *A Code of Jewish Ethics Volume 2: Love Your Neighbor as Yourself* (New York, N.Y.: Crown Publishing, 2009), 11n*.

study." (*b. Shabbat* 31a). In addition to that familiar *sugya*, he also encouraged adherence to the adage, "Be of the disciples of Aharon (Aaron), loving peace and pursuing peace, loving your fellow-creatures and drawing them near to *Torah*" (*Pirqei Avot* 1:12). Hillel is credited with originating the concept of *tiqun 'olam* (repairing the world), which is largely a formulation of "Love your neighbor as yourself" into tangible acts.

Gamli'el demonstrates love for neighbor in his attitude toward the sect of the *Netzarim*, which was known as *haDerekh* (The Way). Not only is he tolerant of a movement which is finding very little support among the Jewish leadership at the time, but he even takes a stand on their behalf, deterring those who wish to lash out against its adherents by raising the possibility that it might be a movement precipitated by HaShem, but assuring those hostile to it that if *haDerekh* were not so inspired, it would die out on its own just as several other movements had. It was perhaps a political soundbyte speech, but it spared those involved with *haDerekh* from what their opponents desired to do against them. The special allowances he made relaxing Sabbath regulations for midwives, firefighters, and the like certainly revealed a depth of compassion and love for his fellow (*b. Rosh HaShanah* 23b), as well as his easing the established standard for releasing a woman from her marriage when her husband was presumed lost in battle (*m. Yebamot* 16:7).

Aqiva recognizes as the chief and preeminent principle of Judaism the command, "Thou shalt love thy neighbor as thyself" (*y. Nedarim* 9:4; *Sifra Qiddoshin*

4). He does not maintain thereby that the execution of this command is equivalent to the performance of the whole *Torah*; and in one of his polemic interpretations of Scripture he protests strongly against the contrary opinion of the Christians, according to whom Judaism is "simply morality" (*Mekh. Shirah* 3:44*a*), Aqiva teaches that loving one's neighbor is the most important principle of Jewish life, but tenders the caveat: "If *Torah* had meant that a man must love his neighbor to the extent of sacrificing his life for him in all circumstances, it would have said, 'Thou shalt love thy neighbor *more than* thyself.'"[278] For Aqiva, the Samaritan was included in this command, even to the extent that he would, despite Jewish tradition against it, allow intermarriage between a Samaritan and a Jew.[279]

Yeshua: In agreement with Hillel haZaqen, Yeshua declared Leviticus 19:18b to be the second greatest command of the *Torah* behind the *Shema*, as recorded in Matthew 22:37-39; Mark 12:30-31. Some suggest that Yeshua's injunction to "love your

---

[278] J. H. Hertz, ed., *The Pentateuch and Haftorahs: Hebrew Text, English Translation, and Commentary* (2nd ed.; London: Soncino Press, 1971), 563-4.

[279] A wall inscription in Kuntillet 'Ajrūd from ca. 800 BCE ascribes to Samaria the same worship of "YHWH" practiced in Israel at that time. See Ziony Zevit, *The Religions of Ancient Israel: A Synthesis of Parallactic Approaches* (London and New York: Continuum, 2001), 650; Debra A. Chase, "A Note on an Inscription from Kuntillet 'Ajrūd," *Bulletin of the American Schools of Oriental Research* 246 (1982): 63-7. Perhaps a recognition of that common heritage was an influence on Rabbi Aqiva's rulings.

enemies" (Matthew 5:44a) was supererogatory, i.e. beyond the conduct required by Judaism, but it is more likely built upon the precedent set by King Sh'lomo (Solomon), who wrote, "If thine enemy be hungry, give him bread to eat, And if he be thirsty, give him water to drink" (Proverbs 25:21), which itself was an inspired *midrash* on a *Torah* command: "If thou see the ass of him that hateth thee lying under its burden, thou shalt forbear to pass by him; thou shalt surely release it with him" (Exodus 23:5).

On the Mo'adim (Biblical Feasts & Fasts)...

Shammai held to a strict observance of every detail of the *mo'adim*. He would have obligated his son at a very young age to observe the fast of Yom Kippur had his friends not succeeded in dissuading him from it (*b. Yoma* 77b, *Tos. Yoma* 4:2). When his grandson was just a newborn infant, Shammai took it upon himself to cut an opening in the roof over his daughter-in-law's bedroom so that his grandson's quarters would meet the definition of a *sukkah* for Sukkot (*m. Sukkah* 2:8), allowing him to look up at the stars. Shammai did not permit a sukkah to be reused in subsequent years; a new structure was to be built every *Sukkot* (*m. Sukkah* 1:1). He taught that in the *Pesach seder*, one should first pronounce the blessing over the day, and afterward over the wine (*m. Pesachim* 10:2).

Hillel contended that in the *seder*, the wine should be blessed first, and then the day (*m. Pesachim* 10:2). It is said that he also added an element to the

Pesach seder, namely, the *korech*, more commonly known by the moniker "Hillel sandwich." Where Hillel said to combine the *matzo* (unleavened bread), *maror* (bitter herbs), and lamb and eat them reclining, the *Chakhamim* before him insisted that they be eaten separately (*b. Pesachim* 115a). The *korech* is included in every *Pesach haggadah* and *seder* today, with the adjustment that in the absence of the Temple, *charoset* is now used for this element instead of lamb. With regard to *Sukkot*, Hillel ruled opposite Shammai, decreeing that a previously-used *sukkah* was to be considered valid (*m. Pesachim* 10:2).

Ben Zakkai made sure that the *mo'adim* could continue to be kept after the destruction of the Temple by enacting a series of edicts allowing for adjustments to be made to the rituals involved in the feasts and fasts. See Chapter 5 (esp. pp. 83-4). He decreed that some of the rituals which had been anchored to the Temple could be performed elsewhere in order to ensure that the traditions would not be lost in the absence of the Temple, applying the "guard" nuance of the verb *shamar* (to keep, guard, observe).

When Gamli'el II was head of the Sanhedrin, **Aqiva** affirmed the authority of the *Nasi* to declare the new moon, and by extension the dates on which the *mo'adim* would fall. He responded to one who disputed Gamli'el II's calendation saying, "Whether they [the *mo'adim*] are proclaimed in their time or not in their time, I have no holy days but these." Prior to Aqiva's time, it was not permissible to sell or give leaven to a Gentile when doing *Bedikat Chametz* (purging the leaven from one's home); it had to be destroyed. But, Aqiva not only ruled to allow dispensing it to Gentiles; he even encouraged it (*Tos. Pesachim* 1:7).

That **Yeshua haNotzri** honored the *mo'adim* of HaShem is well-established in the *B'rit Chadasha*. At the age of twelve, He is in Jerusalem with His family for *Pesach* (Passover), as it is written: "And every year his people [family] would go to Urishlim [Jerusalem] during the feast of Paskha [Passover]. Then when he was twelve years old they went up as they were accustomed to the feast" (Luke 2:41-42). That His "last supper" with the *talmidim* was a *Pesach seder* confirms that His obedience to the command to keep the annual feast of *Pesach* continued up to the very day of His death (Matthew 26:17-19 ‖ Mark 14:12-14 ‖ Luke 22:7-13).

In the "Mount of Transfiguraion" experience, it is clear that Yeshua and His *talmidim* honored the custom of observing *Sukkot* [Feast of Tabernacles] from the statement made by Keefa [Peter]: "And if you desire, let us make you here three tabernacles (*sukkot*), one for you, and one for Moshe, and one for Eliyahu" (Matthew 17:4b). When Messiah establishes His Kingdom, He will require that this feast be kept by all nations (Zechariah 14:16). In the Semitic world, referencing one component of a system is intended to call to mind the entire system, just as voicing the first line of a psalm (perhaps as a title for it) intends that the hearer recall the psalm in its entirety.[280] So, in

---

[280] This rhetorical device is called *synecdoche*.

validating even one feast, Yeshua was most likely validating them all. He also seems to have celebrated Chanukkah, called in John's Gospel "the Feast of Dedication" (10:22). During this holiday, the whole city of Jerusalem was illuminated by the light from the 40-foot menorahs in the Temple Court which formed the backdrop for at least one if not all three of the proclamations where Yeshua employed the "I am the Light of the world" motif, with the implied comparison that this was in contradistinction to these menorahs which only light up this one city (John 8:12; 9:5; 12:46).

On the *Oral Torah*[281]...

The *Oral Torah* is said to have been delivered to Moshe along with the Written at Mount Sinai – "if not in detail at least in principle." Dr. Abraham Cohen notes that forty-two "laws given to Moses on Sinai" with no counterpart in the Written *Torah* are extant in the *Talmud*.[282]

Shammai asserted the validity of the *Oral Torah* by stating that the number of *Torot* given to Israel was "Two - the written and the oral" (*b. Shabbat* 31a).

Hillel was asked about the number of *Torot* comprising Israel's Standard of Holiness, and his

---

[281] Also called תּוֹרָה שֶׁבְּעַל פֶּה (instruction by mouth), in contradistinction to the written *Torah* (תּוֹרָה שֶׁבִּכְתָב).

[282] Abraham Cohen, *Everyman's Talmud* (New York, N.Y.: E. P. Dutton & Co, 1949; orig. 1931), 146.

answer was not so straightforward. He told his questioner to recite the Hebrew *alef-bet*[283] and come back the next day. On the second day, Hillel told the student to recite the Hebrew *alef-bet* backwards. The student retorted, "Yesterday you taught it differently!" To this, Hillel replied, "Have you to depend on me for the letters of the *alef-bet*? So must you likewise depend on me for the interpretation of the *Torah*?" (*b. Shabbat* 31a).

When asked by Roman governor Quietus how many *Torot* had been given to Israel, **Gamli'el** replied, "Two – one in writing and the other orally" (*Sifré D'varim* §351; 145a).

It is said that "...a ruling came up for which Rabbi **Aqiva** could provide no source. A student asked of Rabbi Aqiva, 'Where do you learn this from?' Rabbi Aqiva responded, 'This is an oral tradition passed down from Moses.'" (*b. Menachot* 29b). As far as the *halakhic* tradition, Aqiva taught, "As a general principle, the halachah follows *Beit Hillel*. If one prefers, however, to adopt the rule of *Beit Shammai*, he may do so, and if he desires to adopt the rule of *Beit Hillel* he may do so. One, however, who adopts the more lenient rulings of both *Beit Shammai* and *Beit Hillel* [on the same subject] is a bad man, while to one who adopts the more stringent rulings of both *Beit Shammai* and *Beit Hillel* may be applied the verse, 'But the fool walketh in darkness.'

---

[283] Spelled *alef-bet* instead of *alphabet* because the first two letters are *alef* (א) and *bet* (ב); the more familiar spelling is based on the Greek first two letters: alpha (α) and beta (β).

No; either one must follow *Beit Shammai* both where they are more severe and more lenient or *Beit Hillel* both where they are more severe and more lenient" (*b. Rosh HaShanah* 14b).

After issuing a list of commands echoing dictums from the *Mishna* (see chapter 7, p. 132ff.), **Yeshua** commanded His followers, "You therefore be *perfect* as your Father in Heaven who is perfect" (Matthew 5:48 AENT, emphasis added). The Aramaic (*Peshitta*) words translated "perfect" in that verse are *g'mireh* (גְּמִירָא) in the command, and *g'mir* (גְּמִיר) in the comparison to the Father (HaShem).[284] Though the word גְּמִיר (without the final *alef*) does mean "perfec-tion," the word used in the command (גְּמִירָא) means "memorizing verbal teachings and traditions [*Oral Torah*]," sharing its *shoresh* (root) with the name of the *Amoraic* portion of the *Talmud*, i.e. *gemara* (גְּמָרָא). The Passover *seder* (highly symbolic meal), for example, is an *Oral Torah* tradition, and Yeshua observed that the night before his death. A few elements are commanded in *Torah* (the lamb, the bitter herbs, and the *matzo*), but the rest are rabbinic tradition. At that meal, it is recorded that "when it was evening, he [Yeshua] was *reclining* among his twelve disciples…. And while they were dining, Y'shua took bread, and *blessed it* and broke it and gave it to his disciples…."

---

[284] This is in contradistinction to the word *tamim* (perfect, unblemished; ritually clean) which the usual translation of "perfect" would suggest occurs in the *Urtext*, but as has been demonstrated, that is not the word. Most translations have relied on the Greek as their *Vorlage* in this instance, missing the nuance of the Aramaic *Urtext*.

(Matthew 26:20, 26 emphasis added). This reflects adherence to a teaching from *Oral Torah*, i.e. "If they sat down to eat, each one blesses for himself. If they reclined, one blesses for all" (*m. Berakhot* 6:6).

On Prayer...

Shammai taught that one should make certain that no other activity would interfere with the prescribed times of prayer. He said that since one had to stand for the *Amidah*, one should not sit in front of a barber or in front of a meal too near to the time appointed for *mincha* (afternoon) prayers, and also that once one began the *Shema* or the *Amidah*, it should not be interrupted or broken off short of completion (*m. Shabbat* 1:2).

Hillel, despite his name meaning "he has praised," is surprisingly silent on the topic of prayer – opining on it in only one regard: whether or not one must stand when reciting the *Shema* (he rejected Shammai's ruling that one must lie down when reciting it at night).[285] A modern parable is told of Hillel imagining that he had a student (named Maimon in the story) who had become more reliant on his own supposed wisdom than on prayer. This distressed Hillel, so when Maimon passed by his garden, he was inclined to speak with his student about it. He stopped Maimon and confided in him that he had a friend who was a successful farmer,

---

[285] Joseph Telushkin, *Hillel: In Not Now, When?* (New York, N.Y.: Schocken Books, 2010), 134.

enough so to feed himself and his family solely from the produce of his own fields. Hillel continued that recently, the man had disposed of his plough and his hoe and has determined to leave the field to nurture itself. Maimon exclaimed, "Has he gone mad? Has he fallen into despondency?" Hillel replied, "Neither. He is pious and well-learned." He proceeded to explain to Maimon that without prayer, he was a farmer with no implements. "Is prayer less noble than toil? O, my son: be humble, believe, and pray!"[286] It certainly sounds like advice the great Sage might have given, but this tale is, alas, a modern fiction based on Hillel's demonstrated and fabled quality character attributes.

Yochanan Ben Zakkai held in very high regard the importance of prayer. He even decreed it to be a valid substitute for sacrifice in the absence of the Temple, along with acts of righteousness (charitable giving) and repentance, with prayer now being the primary means of atonement between G-d and man (*Avot d'Rabbi Nathan* 4).

As discussed in chapter 6 of the present work, **Aqiva** promoted the praxis of exercising different prayer styles in different settings, i.e. something more reserved in public so as not to draw attention, but in private, his own prayers involved "genuflexions and prostrations" so spirited that he would invariably end in a spot some distance from where he began (*b. Berakhot* 31a). He also allowed those not yet fluent in

---

[286] Friedrich Adolphus Krummacher, „Hillel und Maimon," *Parabeln* (Essen und Duisburg: G. D. Badefer, 1817), 153-56 (present author's own translation and paraphrase).

prayer to employ the use of an abbreviated form of the *Amidah* (*m. Berakhot* 4:3).

Yeshua taught perhaps more directly on prayer than any of the other Sages herein represented, though not deviating from the traditional Pharisaic practice. The model He provided to His disciples at Matthew 6:9b-13 (commonly called the "Disciples' Prayer," the "L-rd's Prayer," or the "Our Father") was drawn from existing Jewish prayers. The present author has suggested elsewhere a connection to the Prayer of Agur located in Proverbs 30:7-9, i.e. that Yeshua's response to the request posed to Him by His *talmidim*, who should have known by this time, as Jews, how to pray: "Our Master (*Maran*), teach us to pray..." (Luke 11:1), He responded, in part, with a prayer crafted by a Gentile (Proverbs 30:7-9),[287] and also sees influence from the obligatory Jewish liturgical prayer known as the *Amidah* (*Shemoneh Esrei*), which dates back to the *Anshei Knesset HaG'dolah* of the early Second-Temple Period (*b. Berakhot* 33a, *b. Megillah* 17b).[288] The Matthean version of this prayer is preceded by specific instruction to be applied to spontaneous prayer, i.e. that it not be long-winded ("when you pray, you should not be chatterers like the pagans..."; Matthew 6:7a), that it not be ostentatious

---

[287] Brian Tice, "The Sayings and Prayer of Agur: The Possibility of Gentile Wisdom in Proverbs 30:1-14," (written for BBL-501 – Biblical Hermeneutics; Grand Rapids, Mich.: Grand Rapids Theological Seminary, 2008 unpublished).

[288] See Appendix D for a chart detailing the congruence between these two prayers and for the full text of Yeshua's prayer in Aramaic with transliteration.

("whenever you pray you should not be like the hypocrites that love to stand in assemblies and on the corners of the marketplaces to pray thaty they be visible ro the sons of men"; v. 5a), and that it be conducted in private ("But when you pray enter your inner room and close your door..."; v. 6). A unique feature of the Coptic translation of Matthew is that it presents, or possibly preserves, an image of the *Azazel* goat associated with *Yom Kippur* in a nowhere-else-extant "and our sins, send far away" (ⲔⲀⲚⲈⲚⲚⲞⲂⲈ ⲚⲀⲚ ⲈⲂⲞⲗ) in the place of "forgive us our offenses" (v. 12).[289]

On the Resurrection...

The Sadducees and the Samaritans both denied the Resurrection, but among the Pharisees, the belief was a litmus test of faith, a dogma. A later rabbi, R' Ishamel, reasoned, "Now, if glassware, which is the work of the breath of a mortal man, whn broken, can be repaired, a mortal man, who is made by the breath of the Holy One, blessed be He – how much moreso [that he can be repaired in the Resurrection]" (*b. Sanhedrin* 90b-91a; *Bereshit Rabbah* 14.7). Yair Lorberbaum of Bar-Ilan University asserts:

---

[289] Coptic text provided by Egyptologist Scott T. Carroll, Course Materials, *HIS-480: Coptic and Egyptian Christianity* (Grand Rapids, Mich.: Cornerstone University, Fall 2007). This reading is very unlikely to represent the original, but it does demonstrate a fairly early understanding of the Divine purpose the *Azazel* serves, in contradistinction to the oft-found idea that it was connected to a pagan goat-demon.

[Judaism's] monistic concept of mankind underlies the belief in resurrection (the return of the soul to the body): the separate existence of the soul apart from the body is ephemeral and partial, while bodily existence (psycho-physical reality) is human existence in its fullness.[290]

A Qumran text from the Second Century BCE, *4Q385 (Pseudo-Ezekiel)*, per professor C. D. Elledge of Gustavus Adolphus College, "reveals at a much earlier historical moment how Ezekiel 37, Isaiah 26:19, and Genesis 1 were already being studied together as precedents for hope in resurrection."[291]

Shammai taught, "Not like the formation of the human being in this world will be his formation in the World to Come. In this world, it begins with skin and flesh and ends with sinews and bones; but in the Hereafter it will begin with sinews and bones and end with skin and flesh. For it is so stated with regard to the dead in the vision of Ezekiel, 'And I beheld, and lo, there were sinews upon then, and flesh came up, and skin covered them above [Ezek 37:8]" (*Ber. R.* 14.5). Shammai believed that the resurrection body

---

[290] Yair Lorberbaum, *In God's Image: Myth, Theology, and Law in Classical Judaism* (New York, N.Y.: Cambridge University Press, 2015), 5n11.

[291] Casey D. Elledge, *Resurrection of the Dead in Early Judaism: 200 BCE – CE 200* (Oxford: Oxford University Press, 2017), 167. Note that this work was published 11 May 2017, just ten days prior to the present project, so it has not been studied thoroughly by the present author, but the initial reading proved fruitful.

would be of flesh and bone identical to the former body (*b. Sanhedrin* 92a).

Hillel, not surprisingly, disagreed with his colleague, believing that the resurrection body would be of a new and completely different quality than the old (*b. Sanhedrin* 92a). He also held an opposing view with regard to its creation process: "Similar to the formation in this world will be the formation in the World to Come. In this world, it begins with skin and flesh and ends with sinews and bones, and it will be the same in the Hereafter; for thus declared Job, 'Will You not pour me out as milk and curdle me like cheese?' [Job 10:10]. It is not written, 'Have You not poured me out?' but 'Will You not pour me out?' Nor is it written 'curdled me like cheese' but 'will curdle.' It is not written, 'You have clothed me with skin and flesh' [Job 10:11] but 'You will clothe;' nor is it written 'And you have knit me together with bones and sinews' but 'You will knit me together.' It is like a bowl of milk; until one places rennet therein the milk keeps fluid, but after the rennet is inserted the milk curdles and sets" (*Bereshit Rabbah* 14.5).

"The Sadducees asked R. **Gamli'el**, 'Whence is it known that the Holy One, blessed be He, revives the dead?' He answered, 'From the *Torah* [citing Deuteronomy 31:16], from the Prophets (*Nevi'im*) [citing 1 Samuel 26:19], and from the Holy Writings (*Kethuvim*) [citing Songs 7:9]'" The Sadducees accepting only the *Torah* as Scripture, Gamli'el quoted Deuteronomy 11:21 "'The land which the L-rd sware unto your father to give to them.' It is not stated 'unto you,' but 'unto them;' hence, the Resurrection is deducible from the *Torah*." (*b. Sanhedrin* 90b).

It is apparent that **Ben Zakkai** believed in an intermediate state which one entered into immediately upon death – a judgment involving consignment to *Gan Eden* or *Gei-Hinnom* (*Avot d'Rabbi Nathan* 40a, ch. 35).

The probable view of **Aqiva** is that reflected through the words of his student Rabbi Meïr: "Whence is the Resurrection derived from the *Torah*? As it is said: 'Then will Moshe and the children of Israel sing this song unto the L-rd' [Exodus 15:1]"[292] (*b. Sanhedrin* 91b).

Yeshua offered up this teaching: "For in the Resurrection of the dead, men do not marry women, nor are women given to husbands. Rather, they are as the Messengers of Elohim in Heaven" (Matthew 22:30), echoing the anonymous rabbi of *Talmud Bavli* tractate *Berakhot* who said, "Not like the *'olam haZeh* is the *'olam haBa*; in the World to Come there is neither eating nor drinking, nor procreation of children nor business transactions, nor envy or hatred or rivalry; but the righteous sit enthroned, their crowns on their heads, and enjoy the lustre of the *Shekhinah*" (*b. Berakhot* 17a). Arguing for the Resurrection against

---

[292] Abraham Cohen observes, "The verb in the Hebrew has the future form in accordance with the idiom that *az*, 'then,' is followed by the verb in the imperfect tense to denote a completed action;" Abraham Cohen, *Everyman's Talmud* (New York, N.Y.: E. P. Dutton & Co., 1949; orig. 1931), 359n1.

the Sadducees, Yeshua seems to be citing the second blessing of the *Amidah* (Matthew 22:29; Mark 12:24).[293]

Except as seen between Shammai and Hillel, there is reflected in the various teachings above not so much disagreement as, rather, the presentation of different nuances of the same event, held by all six to be an incontrovertible fact and expectation.

On Sabbathkeeping…

It was said of **Shammai haZaqen** that "remembrance of Shabbat was never far from his lips. When he bought a fine animal or a new vessel, he would say, 'This is for Shabbat'" (*Mekhiltha d'Shim'on on Shemot 20:8*). He maintained that one should do all in his power to avoid violation of the Sabbath, even that one should not begin a military action less than three days prior to *Shabbat*, but he did allow for a siege to continue through the Sabbath once it had begun, until the enemy had been subdued (*Tos. Eruvin* 3:7). He prohibited starting any activity on Friday unless one was certain that it would be completed before sunset, and so not carry over into *Shabbat* (*Tos. Shabbat* 1:19). Shammai viewed the *Shabbat* mandate as the second greatest command in *Torah* (behind the *Shema*) and, consequently, saw fit that one should spend the entire week preparing for *Shabbat*. He taught, "Remember it

---

[293] David Instone Brewer, "The Eighteen Benedictions and the *Minim* before 70 CE," *Journal of Theological Studies* (2003) 54 (1): 25-44.

before it comes, and keep it once it comes" (*Mekhiltha d'Shim'on on Shemot 20:8*). If he saw a fine animal, he would buy it and save it for the *Shabbat* meal, and if he later saw a better one, he would buy that one, eat the first, and save the better one for *Shabbat*. He believed every day should be a preparation for *Shabbat*. (*b. Beitzah* 16a).

Hillel opposed Shammai in his "week-long preparations," understanding the wilderness generation's collection of the double-portion of manna the day before *Shabbat* as advocating for Friday being alone in its designation as "preparation day" for the weekly *Shabbat* (*b. Beitzah* 16a). He held an uncharacteristically stricter view on Sabbath-keeping than Shammai in his insistence, in at least one case, that it extended to animals as well as humans, viz. "An egg which was laid on the Sabbath... Beit Hillel says may not be eaten." (*y. Beitzah* 1:1), but he insists that there are certain offerings that can be said to override the Sabbath, especially during Passover (*Tos. Chagigah* 2:11).

History records that "Rabban **Gamli'el** the Elder introduced a rule that... a midwife who has come [from a distance] to help in childbirth or one who comes to rescue from a fire or from bandits or from a river in flood or from a building that has fallen in – all these... may go two thousand cubits in any direction [on Shabbat]" (*m. Rosh haShanah* 2:5). He also allowed travel beyond the Sabbath limits in order to rescue a person, animal, or even certain inanimate objects, with the condition that it not be carried back after the rescue (*m. Eruvin* 4:3). If it is *tefillin* that are the object of rescue, they may not be carried back, but they may be worn, as wearing is different than carrying, even if that means wearing two sets at once, per Gamli'el. (*m. Shabbat* 6:1-4).

Ben Zakkai held the Sabbath in such high regard that as *Nasi*, he added restrictions to it which erewhile had not been in place. Prior to the destruction of the Temple in 70 CE, those tasked with the sighting of the new moon were permitted to violate the Sabbath prohibition in order to do so, but afterward, witnesses were no longer permitted to violate the Shabbat except for the months of Nisan (Aviv) and Tishrei (*b. Rosh HaShanah* 31b).

Aqiva advised, "Treat your Sabbath like a weekday rather than be dependent on any man" (*b. Pesachim* 112a). The meaning here is not that the Sabbath should not be honored, but rather that one should not borrow money from others, thus going into debt, in order to buy special foods for it.[294] He also maintained that saving a life merited violation of the Sabbath *malakhot* (prohibitions), reasoning, "On the basis of *qal w'chomer*, since [Temple] service overrides it [Shabbat], and doubt lives [i.e. live at risk] override the service, is it not logical that doubt lives override the Sabbath?" (*Tos. Shabbat* 15:16).

Yeshua observed *Shabbat* as the day for corporate worship, as Luke records, "And He came to Nasrath where He had been raised, and He entered

---

[294] Ronald L. Eisenberg, *Essential Figures in the Talmud* (Lanham, Md.: Jason Aronson, Inc., 2013), 18.

into the assembly [synagogue] as He was accustomed on the day of the Shabbat and stood up to read" (Luke 4:16). He also maintained, along with the Sages, that it was the day of rest, but that saving a life trumped the *malakhot* (Sabbath prohibitions): "And He said to them, 'Who among you men that if he has a certain sheep that falls into a pit on the day of the *Shabbat* would not grab and raise it out? Now how much more important is a man than a sheep? So then is it Lawful to do that which is good on the Shabbat?'" (Matthew 12:11-12 ‖ Mark 3:1-4); Opposite the dictum of Shammai, however, Yeshua taught, "For the *Shabbat* was created for man, and not man for the *Shabbat*. Thus the son of man[295] is also the Master of the Shabbat." (Mark 2:27-28), which parallels a very similar rabbinic teaching: "The Sabbath is given over unto you, but not you unto the Sabbath" (*Mekhiltha Ki Tissa* 1).

On Sin...

The *Talmud* and the *Bible* stand in agreement that "there is not a righteous man upon the earth that does good and sins not" (Eccl 7:20). Sin, however, refers to the conscious acts of each individual; the concept of

---

[295] The phrase "son of man" has been variously interpreted in this passage as meaning (most traditionally) the Danielic "Son of Man," i.e. Messiah; or alternatively, the common Aramaism "son of man" meaning human being, i.e. denoting the applicability of Shabbat to all humankind (not just Israel); see Exodus 20:10; 23:12; Deuteronomy 5:14 – "and the foreigner among you."

an "original sin" state inherited from Adam is not only virtually unknown to Jewish parlance, it is antithetical to the *hashqafah* of First-Century Judaism.[296] Universal descent from Adam is explained very differently in Judaism; it is said to have been planned out in that manner "because of the righteous and the wicked, that the righteous should not say, 'We are descendants of a righteous ancestor,' and the wicked say, 'We are the descendants of a wicked ancestor'" (*b. Sanhedrin* 38a). In other words, ancestry is not an excuse for one's behavioral choices.[297]

Talmud Yerushalmi does admit, however, "There is no generation in which there is not an ounce from the sin of the Golden Calf" (*y. Ta'anit* 68c), making that, rather than Adam's sin, the act of rebellion which impacted every generation thereafter. This is not to say that sinless perfection was the norm before that event. Even the Patriarchs of the faith are counted among those who have sinned: "If the Holy One, blessed be He, had entered into judgment with Avraham, Yitzchaq, and Ya'aqov, they would not have been able to stand against His reproof" (*b. Arakin* 17a).

Shammai taught that man was apt to sin, but concluded that although man is essentially a sinful creature, "it is better that he was created" (*b. Eruvin* 13b).

---

[296] Cohen, *Everyman's Talmud*, 96.

[297] See Adolph Büchler, *Studies in Sin and Atonement in the Rabbinic Literature of the First Century* (New York, N.Y.: KTAV Publishing House, 1967; orig. 1927) for fuller treatment.

Hillel agreed with him that man was sinful, but drew the opposite conclusion. He opined that because man is essentially a sinful creature, "it would have been better if man had never been created" (*b. Eruvin* 13b). The discussion closes with the pair agreeing that since man was created, he should strive to live in accordance with HaShem's *Torah* (ibid.).

Aqiva derides "those who find excuse for their sins in this supposed innate depravity" (*b. Qiddushin* 81a). He suggests that it is possible and expected that a Jewish person will act morally and rightly, even in the shadow of hurt or victimization.[298]

Yeshua commanded His followers, "Go and sin no more" (John 8:11), suggesting that abstinence from sin is attainable. Yet, He also recognized that Isaiahic truth, "All we like sheep did go astray, we turned every one to his own way" and believed that it was the duty of Messiah to take upon Himself the iniquity of the world (Isaiah 53:6). This He did willingly, submitting Himself to the Roman execution stake to become a substitutionary atonement.

On *Torah*-keeping...

Maimonides (known as the Rambam), the author of the *Mishneh Torah*, is frequently looked to for *halakhic* interpretation. He is well outside the scope of

---

[298] J. H. Hertz, ed., *The Pentateuch and Haftorahs: Hebrew Text, English Translation, and Commentary* (2nd ed.; London: Soncino Press, 1971), 563-4.

this work, about eleven centuries – but much of what he taught was merely an echo of what the Sages of this present work taught. He said of the *Torah*, "We disbelieve a prophet who comes to alter even one precept of the *Torah*, which Moshe told us was final and eternal."[299]

Shammai was a strict adherent to Torah as he interpreted it *halakhically*, i.e. literally and mostly conservatively. He insisted that even his young children and infant grandchild adhere to its precepts and commands, as presented in chapter 1 and here under "On the Mo'adim." He was indubitably seen by all who knew him as pious and devout to a fault. Shammai viewed *halakha* from the perspective of what man owed to HaShem, whereas Hillel approached it in terms of man's obligation to his fellow man.[300]

Hillel, like Shammai, believed in devoted adherence to Torah, but because of his more human-centered *hashqafah*, espoused a much more "spirit of the *Torah*" *halakha* than did his colleague. Rabbi Ishmael reflects the view of Hillel: "The *Torah* was given in public, openly in a free place. For had the *Torah* been given in the land of Israel, the Israelites could have said to the nations of the world: 'You have no share in it.' But now that it was given in the wilderness publicly and openly in a place that is free

---

[299] Moses Maimonides, *Al-Risala al-Yamaniyya* (1173 or 1174 CE).

[300] Yitzhak Buxbaum, *The Life and Teachings of Hillel* (Lanham, Md.: Jason Aronson, Inc., 2008), 198.

to all, everyone wishing to accept it could come and accept it." (*Mekh. BaChodesh* 1).

Aqiva taught that the *Torah* was HaShem's exclusive gift to the Jewish people and reserved for them only.[301] He believed that *Torah* was "the precious instrument by which the world was created," i.e. that it preexisted Creation (*Pirqei Avot* 3:14; cp. John 1:1).

Contrary to what is perhaps the commonest of Christian teachings, i.e. that **Yeshua**'s mission was to "nail *Torah* to the Cross,"[302] haNotzri declared in no uncertain terms, "Do not think that I have come to loosen *Torah* or the Prophets. I have not come to loosen but to fulfill them through proper meaning [i.e. bring them to fullness of understanding]. For truly I say to you that until Heaven and earth pass away not one yodh or one stroke will pass from *Torah* until everything happens. All who will loosen, therefore, from one (of) these small commandments and teach thus to the sons of man, will be called little in the Kingdom of Heaven, but all who do and teach this will be called great in the Kingdom of Heaven."

---

[301] Karin Hedner, Zetterholm, *Jewish Interpretation of the Bible: Ancient and Contemporary* (Minneapolis, Minn.: Fortress Press, 2012), 140.

[302] This doctrinal position is part of a larger theological understanding called supersessionism (or sometimes "replacement theology"). This is thoroughly discussed in Barry E. Horner, *Future Israel: Why Christian Anti-Judaism Must be Challenged* (NAC Studies in Bible & Theology; Nashville, Tenn.: B&H Academic, 2007).

(Matt 5:17-19).[303] His message to sinners is, "Go and sin no more!" (John 8:11),[304] and "If you love Me, keep My commandments [*mitzvot*]" (John 14:15). After healing a Jewish leper, Yeshua instructed him to fulfill the requirements of Leviticus 13:2, 49 and 14:2 (Matthew 8:1-4). He was circumcised in accordance with Leviticus 12:1-8 (Luke 2:21-24) and was obedient to *Torah* His entire life.[305] Orthodox Rabbi Pinchas Lapide says of Yeshua, "This Jesus [Yeshua] was utterly true to the *Torah*, as I myself hope to be. I even suspect that Jesus was more true to the *Torah* than I, an Orthodox Jew."[306]

---

[303] Compare to *y. Sanhedrin* 2:6 – "The Holy One, blessed be He, responded, "Behold! Solomon and a thousand like him will be abolished, but not one letter from you [O *Torah*] will ever be abolished."

[304] As what is numbered in most of the Greek versions as John 8:1-11 does not exist in the Aramaic nor in the four earliest extant Greek manuscripts, this verse is translated from a later Greek witness (UBS4), but may not actually be Scripture, thus the italicization is not for emphasis, but rather to convey the dubiousness concerning the originality of the passage.

[305] This is detailed in chapter 7 of the present work, and all the moreso in chapters 1-4 of David Friedman, *They Loved the Torah: What Yeshua's First Followers* Really *Thought About the Law* (Baltimore, Md.: Lederer Books, 2001).

[306] Pinchas Lapide, *The Resurrection of Jesus: A Jewish Perspective* (Eugene, Ore.: Wipf & Stock Publishers, 2002), 11; see also (Rabbi) Harvey Falk, *Jesus the Pharisee* (New York, N.Y.: Paulist Press, 1985), 21 – "Not one of our sages spoke out more emphatically [than Yeshua] concerning the immutability of the Torah."

On the Value of Human Life…

The reader may recall that **Shammai** held a view that was rejected by all other Sages of his time with regard to the hiring of merceneries to kill on one's behalf. The general consensus was that whoever did the actual act was responsible for it. Shammai contended, however, that the one who commissioned the act was also culpable – at least equally so if not moreso. He used as his Sciptural basis the account of David and Uriah the Hittite, and the judgment voiced by his prophet Nathan against King David rather than Joab, the actual assassin (*b. Qiddushin* 42b). It could be argued that his minority position in this matter communicates a greater respect for the sanctity of human life than that espoused by the rest of his fellow Sages. His unpopular view as articulated with reference to the military scenario from 2 Samuel 11-12 has been effectively extended to cases of Nazi commanders, without denying that soldiers "just following orders" still bear some share of the responsibility as well; and even to abortion, where a woman hires a mercenary practitioner to terminate her child.[307]

Hillel held the sanctity of human life to be among the highest of axiological truths. He opined, "Whosoever destroys a soul, it is considered as if he destroyed an entire world. And whosoever that saves a life, it is considered as if he saved an entire world."

---

[307] David Novak, *The Sanctity of Human Life* (Washington, D.C.: Georgetown University Press, 2009), 118-120.

(*y. Sanhedrin* 4:1)[308] He also upheld the *Torah* principle that blood demands blood (Genesis 9:5; Leviticus 17:11). When he happened upon a human skullbone floating in the river, he said to the skull, "You were drowned because you drowned others; and ultimately, those who drowned you will also drown" (*Pirqei Avot* 2:6). Buxbaum imagines that when Hillel saw the floating skull, he recalled the Pharaoh of the Exodus whose hatred of the Jews cost the lives of his entire army (Exodus 14:27-31).[309] It is worth noting that for Hillel, the value of human life was just as incumbent upon a Gentile as on a Jew. Joseph Telushkin observes, "The openness Christianity displays to Gentiles was already comfortably embraced by Hillel long before Jesus had preached his first sermon."[310]

There does not seem to be a word on this from **Gamli'el haZaqen**, but his son Shim'on ben Gamli'el defended the practice reasoning that without capital punishment, "they would have multiplied [the number of] murderers in Israel" (*m. Makkot* 1:10).

Ben Zakkai found himself in the unenviable position of having to weigh the lives of the Sages of Yavneh against the lives of all Jerusalem — a proto-Sophie's Choice. He chose to use his favor with Vespasian to save those he felt most confident he could bargain for, expecting that if he asked that larger group be spared, he would lose both Jerusalem

---

[308] "Soul" (*nefesh*) and "life" (*chai*) are used interchangeably here, as often in Scripture.

[309] Buxbaum, op. cit., 64.

[310] Telushkin, *Hillel*, 141.

and Yavneh (*Avot d'Rabbi Nathan* 4). He could not bare the possibility of not being able to save any of the Sages at all. It may seem that he valued the learned over the unlearned, but it is more likely that he feared if the Sages were lost, the whole Jewish faith would die with them, having no one to pass what were then yet oral traditions and *halakhot* on to the survivors of that generation. Thus, he valued his people having the opportunity to know and grow in HaShem over a scenario where they might all die as ignoramuses. Truly, love for another involves actions which open a window to the Father for them, and sparing the Sages of Yavneh was, in his estimation, the best way to accomplish that.

Aqiva once declared that every Jew should be regarded as a prince (*b. Baba Metzia* 113b), but this did not place the life of non-Jew in a diminished valuation. He believed that murder was the greatest insult to the *b'tzelem Elohim* (image of G-d) component of all and every human being (*Tos. Yebamot* 8:4). So great was his appraisal of the value of human life, he opposed capital punishment even in the worst of cases. Yair Lorberbaum, professor of Jewish Law and Thought, captures his heart with her avowal, "Executing a murderer – or any other trans-gressor deserving death according to *Bet-Din* – is an annulment (*mevatel*) or a diminution (*mema'et*) of the image of God."[311] Rabbis Aqiva and Tarfon famously declared, "If we had been in the Sanhedrin [before

---

[311] Yair Lorberbaum, "Imago Dei in Judaism: Early Rabbinic Literature, Philosophy, and Kabbalah;" in Peter Koslowski, ed., *The Concept of God, the Origin of the World, and the Image of the Human in the World Religions* (Dortrecht: Kluwer Academic, 2001), 65.

the fall of Jerusalem], no death sentence would ever have been passed" (*m. Makkot* 1:10).[312]

Yeshua, on the contrary, demanded capital punishment in cases which seem far less deserving of it than that of a murderer. He pronounced, for instance, "For Elohim said, 'Honor your father and mother, and anyone who reviles his father and his mother let him be put to death.'" (Matthew 15:4). If no sin warrants the death penalty, however, what sense would Yeshua's death make? It seems that Yeshua haNotzri believed that "the wages of sin is death" (Romans 6:23) and that it was a price which had to be paid by someone – whether the guilty party or a Substitute. On the other hand, He did effectively abrogate the death penalty associated with "the sins of the world" by voluntarily taking the punishment for them upon Himself. Though human sacrifice is against *Torah* (Deuteronomy 12:30-31; and also Jeremiah 19:4-6; Psalm 106:37-38; et al.), martyrdom is not.[313] As He put it, "There is no love that is greater than this – that a man lay down his life for the sake of his friends" (John 15:13).

---

[312] Note that at the time this statement was made, the Sanhedrin had not had the authority to exercise capital punishment in about a century, Rome having stripped that from them "40 years before the destruction of the Temple" (*y. Sanhedrin* 1:18; *b. Sanhedrin* 41a), so the discussion surrounding it was clearly hypothetical and idealistic.

[313] In Judaism, martyrdom is called *qiddush HaShem* (sanctification of G-d's Name) and martyrs are declared *qadosh* (holy, set apart).

CHAPTER 10

A PARTING BLESSING

בִּרְכַּת פְּרִידָה

To many followers of Yeshua, the Jewish writings invoke a sense of fear or reluctance. Centuries of anti-Jewish doctrine and misinformation are responsible for that. In discarding wholesale the *Oral Torah*, the ethical commentaries of Judaism, and the Midrashic literature; much of great value has been missed. It is not the intent of this work to draw a conclusion for the reader as much as to present the reader with portraits of First-Century Jewish thought through those who played the profoundest roles in defining and influencing it. Thus, the present chapter, in lieu of a conclusion, will serve as a parting blessing, expressing the hope that what has been presented herein has helped to open the reader up to a body of material which can aid in his or her engagement of the Scriptures as well as his or her pursuit of a Biblical *halakhic* praxis.

May the reader recognize that Yeshua haNotzri was much closer in thought to the Sages of the First-Century than Christendom has for far too long been willing to admit. For the Christian reader, may the derogatory imagery so long associated with the word "Pharisee" cease to be applied to the devout faith movement it historically represents, as anti-Judaic stereotypes are replaced with portraits of faithful figures such as those presented herein. May the name of Yeshua (or Jesus) cease to invoke in the Jewish reader images of the Crusades, the Inquisition, and the Holocaust; and may it instead be realized that the historical Yeshua haNotzri was a Jewish rabbi engaged in an intra-Judaic conversation on Jewish *halakha* and *hashqafah*.

After reflecting upon these teachers and the wisdom they offer, may the reader "become dusty in the dust of their feet and imbibe their words thirstily."[314]

---

[314] *Pirqei Avot* 1:4 (ca. 190 CE): וֶהֱוֵי מִתְאַבֵּק בַּעֲפַר רַגְלֵיהֶם
וֶהֱוֵי שׁוֹתֶה בְצָמָא אֶת דִּבְרֵיהֶם:

APPENDICES

נִסְפָּחִים

APPENDIX A: LETTERS FROM GAMLI'EL I

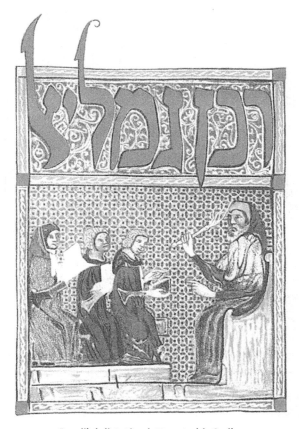

Gamli'el dictating letters to his Scribes

The two versions of each letter presented here are from the *Talmud Bavli* and the *Tosefta*, including the Aramaic of the former. It is unlikely that the entire letter is available, as some of the standard elements of First-Century epistolography are lacking, e.g. none of them has a closing salutation.

Galilee

לאחנא בני גלילאה עילאה ולאחנא בני גלילאה תתאה שלומכון
יסגא מהודעין אנחנא לכון דזמן ביעורא מטא לאפרושי מעשרא
ממעטנא דזיתא:

To our brothers, the people of the Upper Galilee and
to our brothers, the people of the Lower Galilee: May
your peace increase. We inform you that the time has
come for eradication, to separate the tithe from the
vat of olives. (*b. Sanhedrin* 11b).

To our brethren, men of Lower Galilee: May your
peace increase. We inform you that the time of the
burning has come, to bring out the tithe from the vats
of olives. (*Tos. Sanhedrin* 2:6).

Judea and Environs

לאחנא בני דרומא שלומכון יסגא מהודעין אנחנא לכון דזמן
ביעורא מטא לאפרושי מעשרא מעומרי שיבליא:

To our brothers, the people of the South: May your
peace increase. We inform you that the time has come
for eradication, to separate the tithe from the mounds
of stalks. (*b. Sanhedrin* 11b).

To our brethren, men of the Upper South and men of
the Lower South: May your peace increase. We
inform you that the time of burning has come, to
bring out the tithe from the sheaves of wheat. (*Tos.
Sanhedrin* 2:6).

Diaspora

לכון לאחנא בני גלוותא בבבל ולאחנא דבמדי ולשאר כל גלוותא
דישראל שלומכון יסגא לעלם מהודעין אנחנא דגוזליא רכיכין
ואימריא ערקין וזמנא דאביבא לא מטא ושפרא מילתא באנפאי
ובאנפי חביריי ואוסיפית על שתא דא יומין תלתין:

To our brothers, the people of the *Diaspora* in
Babylonia, and to our brothers who are in Medea, and
to the rest of the entire Jewish *Diaspora*: May your
peace increase forever. We inform you that the
fledglings are tender, and the lambs are thin, and time
for the spring has not come. And consequently, the
matter is good before me and before my colleagues,
i.e., in our estimation, and I have consequently added
thirty days to this year. (*b. Sanhedrin* 11b).[315]

To our brethren, men of the Exile of Babylonia and
men of the Exile of Medea and the rest of all the
Exiles of Israel: May your peace increase. We inform
you that the pigeons are tender and the lambs are
young, and the time of spring has not come, and it is
good in my view and in the view of my colleagues
that we have added to this year thirty days. (*Tos.
Sanhedrin* 2:6).

---

[315] In *b. Sanhedrin 11a*, this last line is attributed to
Shim'on ben Gamli'el rather than to Gamli'el I.

APPENDIX B: MESSIANIC *TANAKH* TEXTS

The passages of the *Tanakh* agreed upon by all Jewish and Christian exegetes as being Messianic make a rather short list. Those passages are listed below, followed by a second list of additional passages identified as Messianic by other early rabbinic sources. *Nota bene:* These lists are far from exhaustive, but are intended as a representative sample to demonstrate that the ancient domain of messianic passages is broader than opined in modern Jewish thought, and perhaps narrower than portrayed in modern Christian discourse.

Universally accepted texts: [316]

- Isaiah chapter 2, in full
- Isaiah chapter 11, in full
- Isaiah chapter 42, in full
- Isaiah chapter 59, verse 20 only
- Jeremiah chapter 23, in full (ref. Luke 1:32-33)
- Jeremiah chapter 30, in full
- Jeremiah chapter 33, in full (ref. Luke 1:32-33)
- Jeremiah chapter 48, verse 47 only
- Jeremiah chapter 49, verse 39 only
- Ezekiel chapter 38, verse 16 only
- Hosea chapter 3, verses 4-5 only

---

[316] This list comes from a Jewish contra-missionary site, http://www.jewfaq.org/mashiach.htm, so it may be shorter than what most mainstream Jewish scholars would compose. This particular list is used here in order to represent what passages are *universally* accepted as Messianic.

- Micah chapter 4, in full
- Zephaniah chapter 3, verse 9 only
- Zechariah chapter 14, verse 9 only
- Daniel chapter 10, verse 14 only

To these, the *Talmudic Sages* add:

- Genesis 49:10 (*b. Sanhedrin* 98b)
- Micah 5:2 (*y. Berakhot* 5a)
- Zechariah 9:9 (*b. Sanhedrin* 98-99)
- Zechariah 12:10 (*b. Sukkah* 52a)
- Malachi 3:1 (*m. Megillah*)
- Psalm 2:7-12 (*b. Sukkah*)
- Daniel 9:24-26 (*m. Megillah*)

And the *Targummim*[317] add:

- Genesis 3:15 ($\mathbb{T}^{J}$, $\mathbb{T}^{Yer}$)
- Genesis 49:10 ($\mathbb{T}^{Onq}$, $\mathbb{T}^{Yer}$)
- Numbers 24:17 ($\mathbb{T}^{Onq}$, $\mathbb{T}^{Yer}$)
- Isaiah 52:13-53:12 ($\mathbb{T}^{J}$)
- Micah 5:2 ($\mathbb{T}^{J}$)
- Psalm 2:7-12 ($\mathbb{T}^{J}$)

---

[317] $\mathbb{T}^{J}$ is the sigla for *Targum Yonathan*, $\mathbb{T}^{Yer}$ indicates *Targum Yerushalmi*, and *Targum Onqelos* is represented by the sigla $\mathbb{T}^{Onq}$.

And the *Midrashic Literature*[318] adds:

- Genesis 3:15 (*Bereshit R.*, *Pesiqta R.*; Matthew 1:18)
- Genesis 4:25 (*Bereshit R*)
- Number 24:17 (*Pesiqta R.*; Matthew 2:2, 9)
- Micah 5:2 (Matthew 2:1-5)
- Zechariah 9:9 (*Qoheleth R.* 1.9; Matthew 21:1-9)
- Psalm 2:7-12 (Matthew 1:21-22)
- Psalm 22 (*Pesiqta R.*)

---

[318] The *B'rit Chadasha* book of Matthew is included here as Midrashic Literature based on the style of writing, which Gundry categorizes as "*midrash* and *haggadah*" in Robert H. Gundry, *Matthew: A Commentary on His Literary and Theological Art* (Grand Rapids, Mich.: Wm. B. Eerdmans, 1982), though the present author is not in full agreement with the direction of exegesis Gundry applies to the content based on his own nuanced definition of *midrash*. See also M. D. Goulder, *Midrash and Lection in Matthew* (Eugene, Ore.: Wipf & Stock, 2004). The present work only lists those Matthean passages which have corroboration in accepted rabbinic works. Matthew identifies many more as Messianic.

APPENDIX C: "SONS OF G-D" IN THE BIBLE

בְּנֵי הָאֱלֹהִים	
Gen 6:2, 4	"sons of G-d" as human believers (Gen. 4:26 sets up the context: "then began **men** to call upon the name of the LORD," and 6:5 calls their offspring "men," not "demons" or even "giants")
Deut 32:8	"children/sons/people of Israel/G-d" (The fact that the terms בְּנֵי הָאֱלֹהִים (sons of G-d) בְּנֵי יִשְׂרָאֵל (sons of Israel) and are interchangeable between 𝔐 & DSS tells us human beings are in view.)
Job 1:6, 2:1	Since the fallen *haSatan* no longer has access to Heaven, this may be better understood as occurring on earth (at an altar perhaps), which would make this a **human congregation** infiltrated by *haSatan*.
Job 38:7	With a *waw-of-result* understanding, ongoing human rejoicing following creation may be in view.
בְּנֵי אֵל־חָי	
Hosea 2:1[319]	Used in parallel with the synonymous phrase בְּנֵי יִשְׂרָאֵל; "... it shall be said unto them: 'Ye are the **children of the living God**.'" (godly humans)
בְּנֵי אֵלִים	
Psalm 29:1	"godly people" (David addressing his human audience)

---

[319] In most English versions, this verse is numbered 1:10.

בְּנֵיָא דַאלָהָא	
Matt 5:9	AENT: "Blessed are they who make peace because they will be called sons of Elohim." (speaking of humans)
John 1:12	AENT: "But those who did receive Him He gave to them authority that they might be sons of Elohim, those who have believed in His name." (human worshipers)
Rom 8:14	AENT: "For they who are led by the Spirit of Elohim, they are the sons of Elohim." (human worshipers)
Rom 9:8	AENT: "That is, it is not the children of the flesh who are the children of Elohim; but the children of the promise are accounted for the seed. " (human Israelites, by "adoption as sons" from v. 4)
Gal 3:26	AENT: "For you are all children of Elohim by faith in Y'shua the Mashiyach." (writing to a human audience)
1 Jn 3:10	AENT: "By this are the children of Elohim discriminated from the children of Satan. Everyone that does not practice righteousness and that loves not his brother, is not of Elohim." (human beings)

Adapted from Brian Tice, "Who or What were the Nephilim?" *Emunah BiY'shua* (2011; online: https://adiakrisis.files. wordpress.com/2014/10/imti-sons-of-g-d-study.pdf).

APPENDIX D: THE DISCIPLES' PRAYER

The prayer presented in Matthew 6:9b-13 (and also partially presented in Luke 11:2-4), the present author contends, is a paraphrastic reworking of traditional Jewish prayers already in use at the time, principally the *Amidah*, but also the *Prayer of Agur* (Proverbs 30:7-9) and other common prayers. See chart below.

Matthew 6:9b-13 AENT	Jewish Parallel Texts
9b. Our Father in heaven.	Aqiva's *Avinu Malkheinu* prayer recited on *Yom Kippur* also begins with "Our Father."[320]
9c. Hallowed be thy name.[321]	The *Qedusha* (קְדֻשָׁה) portion (3rd Blessing) of the *Amidah*: "You are Holy, & Your Name is holy"[322]
10. Thy Kingdom come. Thy will be done. As in heaven, so on earth.	Rabbi Eliezer similarly prayed: "May Your Will be done in the heavens above... and [on earth] below do what is good in Your eyes" (*Tos. Berakhot* 3:7; b. *Berakhot* 29b)[323]

---

[320] There may also be correlation to the *Avot* (תאָבוֹ) portion (1st Blessing) of the *Amidah*, though somewhat tenuous, as the verbage there is "G-d of our fathers."

[321] Aram. נֶתְקַדֵּשׁ שְׁמָךְ. Alt: "May your name be sanctified" or "May your name be treated as holy."

[322] Heb. אַתָּה קָדוֹשׁ וְשִׁמְךָ קָדוֹשׁ. Also, the *Prayer of Agur* (Proverbs 30:7-9) – "Keep... *futility* far away from me" (v. 8). Futility is essentially worldliness, anything that does not contribute to advancing G-d's Kingdom. This would thus align with "May Your name be regarded as holy." The *Qaddish* aligns here as well.

[323] Heb. יעשה רצונך בשמים ממעל... בער"ז מתחת הטוב בעיניך עשה

11. Give us the bread of our need this day.	The *Prayer of Agur*: "But provide me with the bread I need for today" (Prov. 30:8). It may also reflect the *Birkhat HaShanim* (בִּרְכַּת הַשָּׁנִים) portion (9th Blessing) of the *Amidah*: "Bless this year unto us, O L-rd our G-d, together with every kind of the produce for our welfare."
12a. And forgive us our offenses	The *Selicha* (סְלִיחָה) portion (6th Blessing) of the *Amidah*: "Forgive us, O our Father, for we have sinned, and pardon us, O our King, for we have transgressed; for You do pardon and forgive."
12b. as we also have forgiven those who have offended us.	From the *Ma'ariv* Prayers: "Master of the universe, I hereby forgive anyone who angered or antagonized me or who sinned against me."
13a. And bring us not to trial, but deliver us from the evil one.	The *Ge'ulah* (גְּאוּלָה) portion (7th Blessing) or the *Amidah*: "Be our guardian and our advocate, and redeem us speedily from all evil, for in You do we trust as our mighty Redeemer."
13b. For Yours is the Kingdom and the power and the glory forever and ever.	The *Qedusha* (קְדֻשָּׁה) portion of the *Amidah*: "Your holy ones will praise you every day forever."[324]

---

[324] Heb. וּקְדוֹשִׁים בְּכָל יוֹם יְהַלְלוּךָ סֶּלָה. Also, the *Pesukei D'zimrah*, which is recited daily just before the *Shema*: "Blessed be Thou, O LORD, the God of Israel our father, for ever and ever." (1 Chronicles 29:10-13 JPS).

Aramaic Text of Yeshua's Prayer:[325]

אֲבוּן דְּבַשְׁמַיָּא נֶתְקַדַּשׁ שְׁמָךְ:

תֵּאתֵא מַלְכּתָךְ נֶהְוֵא צֶבְיָנָךְ אִיכַּנָא דְּבַשְׁמַיָּא אָף
בַּארעָא:

הַב לַן לַחמָא דְּסֻונקָנַן יַומָנָא:

וַשׁבֻוק לַן חַובַּין אִיכַּנָא דָּאף חנַן שׁבַקן לחַיָבַּין:

ולָא תַּעלַן לנֶסיֻונָא אֶלָא פַּצָּן מֶן בִּישָׁא מֶטֶל דְּדִילָךְ
הי מַלכֻּותָא וחַילָא ותֶשׁבֻּוחתָּא לעָלַם עָלמִין:

Transliteration:

Avun d'vashmaya nethqadash sh'makh.
Tiatheh malkuthakh nehweh tzevyanakh aikanah
d'vashmaya af ba'ar'a.
Hav lan lachmah d'sunqanan yawmanah.
Washvuq lan chawbayan aykanah da'af chanan
shavaqan lachayavayn.
W'lo ta'lan l'nesyunah elah patzan men biysha
metul d'thiylakh hai malkutha w'chaylah
w'theshbuch'tah l'olam 'olmiyn.

Audio available at https://youtu.be/MAEIrp4MFBE

---

[325] As found in the *Peshitta* (Khabouris Codex) with vowel pointing (*niqqudot*) as supplied in Andrew Gabriel-Yitzhak bar Raphael Roth, *Aramaic English New Testament* (5th Edition; Sedro-Woolley, Wash.: Netzari Press, 2012), 17.

GLOSSARY OF

JEWISH JARGON

זשַׁרגוֹן יְהוּדִי

The following list comprises the Jewish terms used in this work, and perhaps a few additional that were not used herein but which are common to the vernacular of Jewish parlance. Most are Hebrew in origin, but some are Aramaic and Yiddish, as well. Etymology will be listed in each entry where it is known, as the terms are listed alphabetically *en masse*, not separated out by source language.

Acharit Hayamim (Heb. אַחֲרִית הַיָּמִים): literally "end of times." This term is conceptually synonymous with *'olam haBa* (the world to come) in referring to the Messianic Kingdom.

Adonai: (Heb. אֲדֹנָי or אֲדֹ-נָי) literally "my L-rd." The Hebrew Bible uses this title to refer to G-d, sometimes in all capital letters (when standing in for the tetragrammaton, i.e. Covenant Name of HaShem consisting of the four letters yod, hey, waw, hey) but spelled "Adonai" (only the first letter capitalized) when not representing the Covenant Name. Note that in the Ashkenazi dialect, this is pronounced "Adonai" in general, but "Adonoi" when used as a circumlocution for the *Shem haMeforash*.

Aggadah: (Aram. אַגָּדָה) literally "tale, lore." The body of non-legal teachings of the Sages which do not concern *halakhic* matters. Etymologically related to the Aramaic word הַגָּדָה (*haggadah*), which means "telling" and is the name given to the Passover reading recounting the Exodus. The latter is a good example of aggadic literature. The aggadic literature tends more toward moral or ethical content.

alef-bet (Heb. אָלֶף־בֵּית): literally "A B" as a synecdoche for the whole 22-letter character set of the Hebrew language, i.e. the Hebrew "alpha-bet." Spelled *alef-bet* instead of *alphabet* because the first two letters are *alef* (א) and *bet* (ב); the more familiar English spelling is based on the Greek first two letters: *alpha* (α) and *beta* (β).

am haAretz (Heb. עַם הָאָרֶץ): literally "people of the land." This term was used to describe "marginal Jews," i.e. those who had Jewish ancestry, but did not tithe, were ritually impure, and were willfully *Torah*-illiterate; or also, depending on context, unconverted Gentiles residing in *Eretz-Yisrael*.

am seghulah (Heb. עַם סְגֻלָּה): literally "treasured people." The Bible uses this term, often translated "chosen people," as a euphemism for Israel. See Deuteronomy 7:6; 14:2; 26:18.

Amora'im (Aram. אֲמוֹרָאִים): literally "sayers, recounters." In differentiation from the *Tanna'im* who devised *halakha* and are credited with the content of the *Mishna*, the *Amora'im* were the next generation of Sages, i.e. those who wrote commentary on the *Mishna* and composed what is referred to as the *Gemara* (defined later in this glossary). No *Amora* (אֲמוֹרָא; singular of *Amora'im*) could disagree with a *Tanna* (singular of *Tanna'im*) without the support of another *Tanna*, and disagreement with the *Mishna* was also prohibited for an *Amora*.

Amidah (Aram. עֲמִידָה): literally "standing [prayer];" synonymous with the Eighteen Benedictions. *See Shemoneh Esrei.*

Anshei Knesset haG'dolah (Heb. אַנְשֵׁי כְּנֶסֶת הַגְּדוֹלָה): The council convened by the Scribe Ezra in Babylonian captivity with the purpose of unifying the scattered synagogues through the development of a common organized liturgy. This included the original *Shemoneh Esrei* (*b. Berakhot* 33a), the division of *Torah* into its 54 parashot (portions) and the synching of those to specific weeks on the Biblical calendar, and certain synagogue traditions including providing seats for worshipers (prior to this, all worshipers stood). Members of this council also authored the Biblical books of Ezra, Nehemiah, Ezekiel, Daniel, Esther, and the Book of the Twelve (*b. Baba Bathra* 15a). This body was the predecessor to the Sanhedrin, being replaced by it in 270 BCE.

Apocrypha (Grk. ἀπόκρυφα): literally "hidden things." This term refers to a body of Second-Temple Jewish literature viewed by most as non-canonical (though Catholics assign it deutero-canonical status). This collection includes the four books of Maccabees, Additions to Daniel, Bel and the Dragon, the Wisdom of Solomon, and several other works which contribute to Jewish Studies in various ways, e.g. providing historical insight or opening a window into the Jewish frame of reference of the time period. An individual exemplar from the collection is called in the singular an *apocryphon* (ἀπόκρυφον).

Aramaic (Aram. אֲרָמִית): The ancient Semitic language originally spoken by the Aramaeans, but also spoken by the Babylonians and Persians of the Exile Period. Aramaic became the *lingua franca* of the Israelite exiles in the 6th Century BCE and thereafter.

Av Beit Din (Heb. אָב בֵּית דִּין): literally "father of the house of justice." During the Second Temple Period, this was the title used for the head of the Sanhedrin Gedolah (the highest *halakhic* and civil court in Israel). This office ranked second in Israel to the *Nasi* (president of the Sanhedrin).

bat qol (Heb. בַּת קוֹל): literally "daughter of a voice," equivalent in meaning to "a still, small voice," or a Divine whisper. This idiom refers to an audible manifestation or occurrence of the voice of HaShem. It is said that the *bat qol* pronounced the priority of the rulings of Hillel over those of Shammai (*b. Eruvin* 13a-b), the approval of Rabbi Aqiva at his execution (*b. Berakhot* 61b), and the approval of Yeshua HaNotzri at his baptism (Matthew 3:17). This is to be distinguished from the voice of G-d heard by all from Mount Sinai.

Beit haMidrash (Heb. בֵּית הַמִּדְרָשׁ): house of study. In First-Century Israel, this was the term for any setting where the *Torot* (Written *Torah* and *Oral*

Torah) were being taught by a *Madrikh* (*Torah* teacher) or *Chakham* (Sage).

Beit Hillel (Heb. בֵּית הָלֵּל): House of Hillel. The proto-yeshiva (school) founded by *tanna* Hillel haZaqen.

Beit Shammai (Heb. בֵּית שַׁמַּאי): House of Shammai. The proto-yeshiva (school) founded by *tanna* Shammai haZaqen.

bimah (Heb. בִּימָה): literally "elevated place, high place." This term is used in synagogue architecture to designate the raised platform from which the *Torah* is read and expounded. Frequently, the *chazzan* (cantor) and *nasi* (congregational president) also present from the *bimah*.

biqur cholim (Heb. בִּיקוּר חוֹלִים): literally "examination of the sick." In Judaism, "visiting the sick," as the term is generally translated, encompasses much more than keeping the patient company, though that is certainly included. It also means surveying his or her room and doing all that one can to make it as conducive to recovery as possible – both physically and spiritually.[326]

Birkhat HaMinim (Heb. בִּרְכַּת הַמִּינִים): literally "blessing of the heretics," but more accurately a

---

[326] Joseph Telushkin, *A Code of Jewish Ethics Volume 2: Love Your Neighbor as Yourself* (New York, N.Y.: Bell Tower, 2009), 68-71 (6.1-6.6).

curse. This daily liturgical element has long been understood to be directed at First-Century followers of Yeshua haNotzri, but more likely was intended to target Sadducees or Samaritans. See chapter 6 for further discussion.

Boethusians (from Heb. בַּיְיתוֹסִים): literally "followers of Boethus." A late Second-Temple era politico-religious party originally a Sadducean sub-sect. Like the Sadducees, they denied the existence of an afterlife or a future resurrection. They lived a very hedonistic *"carpe diem"* lifestyle, making everyday use of extravagant silver and golden vessels for even the commonest of meals due to their belief that this life was all there was.

B'rit Chadasha (Heb. בְּרִית חֲדָשָׁה): literally "renewed covenant."[327] Also called the "Apostolic Scriptures," this term denotes the same collections of books which comprise the Christian "New Testament." This name is a preferred alternative to the anti-Semitically-motivated term common to Christian parlance which wrongly implies that the *Tanakh* ("Old Testament" in the post-Nicene jargon) and, indeed, everything "Jewish" about the faith is obsolete, no longer relevant.

chesed (Heb. חֶסֶד): literally "lovingkindness." The word has frequently been translated as "mercy" and "grace" as well, and these meanings are

---

[327] See Ronald Wayne Moseley, *Yeshua: A Guide to the Real Jesus and the Original Church* (Clarksville, Md.: Lederer Books, 1996), chapter 4 (53-65).

certainly not foreign to the word's semantic domain (range of meaning).

Chakhamim (Heb. חֲכָמִים; plural of חָכָם): literally "wise, shrewd, skilled person." The Hebrew word for Sages. Both the *Tanna'im* (תַּנָּאִים: Sages of the *Mishna*) and the *Amora'im* (אָמוֹרָאִים: Sages of the *Gemara*) are referred to as *Chakhamim*. They are frequently referred to by the acronym *Chazal* (חז״ל), which stands for ***Ch****akhameinu* ***Z****ikhronam* ***LiV****'rakhah* (חֲכָמֵינוּ זִכְרוֹנָם לִבְרָכָה; i.e. "Our Sages, may their memory be blessed").

Decalogue (Grk. δέκα λόγια or δεκάλογος): literally "ten words." A scholarly designation for what is commonly called the "Ten Commandments," used in recognition of Exodus 34:28 and Deuteronomy 10:4 referring to them as "words" rather than "commandments." A Septuagintal translation of the biblical term *Aseret haD'varim* (עֲשֶׂרֶת הַדְּבָרִים). Rabbinic literature used the similar but slightly different term *Aseret haDiv'rot* (עֲשֶׂרֶת הַדִּבְּרוֹת). "Word" (דָּבָר) in Hebrew signifies a complete thought.[328]

deoccidentation (English): synonymous with "de-Westernization" or "orientation," where *orient* meant "east" and *occident* means "west." This term was coined by the present author to

---

[328] Bruce K. Waltke, "Agur's Hebrew Words for 'Words'," in Milton Eng and Lee M. Fields, eds., *Devotions on the Hebrew Bible: 54 Reflections to Inspire and Instruct* (Grand Rapids, Mich.: Zondervan, 2015), 137.

emphasize the need to detach oneself from Western world thought paradigms when engaging an (Ancient Near) Eastern world text, such as the *Bible*, the *Talmuds*, the *Targums*, and *Midrashic* literature.

Diaspora (Grk. διασπορά): literally "dispersion" or "scattering." The Hebrew equivalents to this term are *galut* (גָּלוּת) and *tfutza* (תְּפוּצָה), both meaning "exile." *Diaspora* refers to the Jewish (or Israelite) people living outside of *Eretz-Yisrael* (the holy land).

echad (Heb. אֶחָד): literally "one." The word *echad*, however is not a singular one (the word for that is *yachid*; Heb. יָחִיד, used 12 times in the *Tanakh*); *echad* represents a composite unity.[329]

Eloqeinu (Heb. אֱלֹקֵינוּ): a circumlocution for *Eloheinu* (our G-d) often used in written works to avoid using a term traditionally reserved for use in Scripture, prayer, or worship in any lesser (mundane) context.

Eretz-Yisrael (Heb. אֶרֶץ־יִשְׂרָאֵל): literally "Land of Israel" or "Land of the prince of G-d." The term designates the geographical land given by

---

[329] See Itzhak Shapira, *The Return of the Kosher Pig: The Divine Messiah in Jewish Thought* (Clarksville, Md.: Lederer Books, 2013), 56, 72; Francis Brown, Samuel Rolles Driver, and Charles A. Briggs, *The Brown-Driver-Briggs Hebrew and English Lexicon* (Boston, Mass.: Houghton, Mifflin, and Company, 1906), 402.

HaShem to His people Israel, or whatever portion of it they are in possession of at any given time.

Essenes (Heb. אָסִיִּים): Not as much is known about this sect as was previously thought, as it is now in question whether the *Yachad* community of Qumran was Essene or, alternatively, Zealot. What is known is that this sect is that they held to a practice of celibacy and lived in *kibbutz*-style communities where they shared property in common. They were dedicated to asceticism, voluntary poverty, daily baptisms, and abstinence from worldly pleasures, including marriage.[330] The name was possibly truncated from עֹשֵׂה הַתּוֹרָה (Doers of the *Torah*).[331] They were comparatively few in number and apparently had died out by the close of the First Century CE.

Gan Eden (Heb. גַּן־עֵדֶן): literally "Garden of Delight." Both the site of the garden temple into which Adam and Chawwah (Eve) were installed as priests in Genesis 2 and the Jewish metaphor for Heaven.[332]

---

[330] Flavius Josephus, *Bellum Judaicum* (Ca. 75 CE); Pliny the Elder, *Historia Naturalis* (First Century CE), V, XV.

[331] Raymond Apple, *New Testament People: A Rabbi's Notes* (Bloomington, Ind.: AuthorHouse, 2016).

[332] Brian Tice, "Eden as a Garden Temple," *Emunat BiY'shua* (online: https://adiakrisis.files.wordpress.com/2014/10/eden-as-a-garden-temple.pdf; 2011).

Gei-Hinnom (Aram. גֵּיא־הִנֹּם): literally "valley of lusts." Explained in *Talmud* as "a deep valley into which all descend on account of lusts" (*b. Eruvin* 19a); one of the seven biblical (*Tanakh*) names for hell.[333]

Gemara (Aram. גְּמָרָא): literally "completion, study." The component of the *Talmud* comprising rabbinical analysis and commentary on the *Mishna* portion. The *Gemara* was composed by the *Amora'im* (אָמוֹרָאִים, i.e. later rabbis), whereas the *Mishna* was composed by the Tanna'im (תַּנָּאִים, including the first four subjects of this work). Also called the הֲלָכָה (*halakha*).

ger tzedeq (Heb. גֵּר־צֶדֶק): literally "righteous sojourner." Refers to a righteous convert to Judaism from among the Gentiles, in contradistinction to the גֵּר־תּוֹשָׁב (*ger toshav*, i.e. "resident alien"), a term which indicates a non-Jewish inhabitant of *Eretz-Yisrael* who observes the "Seven Laws of Noah" and has repudiated all links with idolatry, but has not made a full conversion to Judaism via *b'rit milah* (בְּרִית מִילָה,

---

[333] The other names are Sheol (Jonah 2:2), Abaddon (Psalm 88:11), Shachat (Psalm 16:10), Mibbor Sha'on (Psalm 40:2), Mittit Hayawen (Psalm 40:2), Shadow of Death (Psalm 107:10), and Topheth (Isaiah 30:33). Also in Jewish tradition (non-Scriptural) is the name "Nether World." Some Jewishmysticism literature connected with *Merkavah* and *Qabbalah* also records 7 heavens, i.e. Vilon, Rakia, Shechakim, Zebul, Maon, Machon, and Araboth. These, however are unattested in Scripture.

i.e. circumcision) and *tevilah* (טְבִילָה, i.e. immersion).

gnostic (Grk. γνωστικός): literally "knowledgeable," but by usage, referring to cults which actively sought to attain "secret" knowledge of G-d through interaction with the spirit world, astral ascent to the heavenly plane, or other biblically-deprecated practices.

haggadah (Heb. הַגָּדָה): literally "telling." The homiletic portions of the *Talmud*; also used of the Passover *siddur*, i.e. the book used to present the Biblical account of the exodus and the order of the *seder* meal.

halakha (Heb. הֲלָכָה): literally "walk," but with the idea of how one walks out one's faith. The term also refers, sometimes synonymous with *Mishna*, to the rulings of the *Tanna'im* (*Mishnaic* Sages), as those rulings inform our *halakha* and interpret how to give practical application to *Torah* mandates and prohibitions.

HaShem: (Heb. הַשֵּׁם): literally "the Name." This is frequently used in Jewish contexts as a circumlocution for the *Shem haMephorash* of Israel's G-d (represented by the *tetragrammaton*, i.e. the four Hebrew letters *yod, hey, waw, hey*).[334] The *Torah* itself is the origin of this

---

[334] Christina Oakes, *God: Getting to Know Him – Experiencing God through His Names and Titles* (BookBaby, 2016), 13.

circumlocution, being used therein at Leviticus 24:11 and Deuteronomy 28:58.

hashqafah (Heb. הַשְׁקָפָה): literally "observation," but more practically translated "worldview." The term finds its origin in *Tosefta Ma'aser Sheni* 5:25. For further discussion, see *Weltanschauung*.

HaZaqen (Heb. הַזָּקֵן): literally "the elder." In the Tannaitic Age which lasted from the death of the last member of the *Anshei Knesset HaG'dolah* until the fall of Jerusalem in 70 CE (immediately preceding the Rabbinic Age), this was the title given to the *zughot* (ruling pair) of *Tanna'im* (chief religious leaders, or Sages) in *Eretz-Yisrael*. The plural form is הַזְּקֵנִים (*haZeqenim*).

Hellenism (Grk. Ἑλληνισμός): literally "Greek culture; Grecanization." The spread of Greek culture and ideals throughout the ancient world orchestrated by Alexander the Great and his successors to the throne of the Greek Empire.

khayana (Aram. כְּיָנָא): literally "nature" (whether humanity, Divinity, *flora*, *fauna*, etc.) The "ontological whole of the being," separate from the idea of the tangible *partzupa* or *qnuma*. The common theological treatment of *khayana* as equating to the Greek term *phúsis* (φύσις, i.e. "nature") is preferable to translation as *ousía* (οὐσία, i.e. "essence").

kosher (Yid. כּשר; fr. Heb. כָּשֵׁר): literally "straight, right, upright." This word is typically used in reference to the biblical definitions for what is to be considered food in Leviticus 11 and Deuteronomy 14; equivalent to the word כַּשְׁרוּת (*kashrut*). The root word also has uses that go beyond the concept of *kashrut*, however, including moral uprightness.

machaloqet (Aram. לוֹמַחֲקֵת): literally "division, separation, difference, dissension, strife, or faction."[335] In the rabbinic literature, it is often used of any open discussion or dialogue about halakhic matters, which it speaks of as a positive engagement, or מַחֲלוֹקֵת לְשֵׁם שָׁמַיִם, i.e. "debate for the sake of Heaven" (*Pirqei Avot* 5:17).

Malki-Tzedeq (Heb. מַלְכִּי־צָדָק): literally "my king is righteous" or (if treated as being in the construct state) "king of righteousness." This theophoric name or epithet is applied to an enigmatic figure (or perhaps multiple figures of the same priestly order) who seems to appear and reappear over a span of thousands of years. The first appearance is at Genesis 14:18-20 and reappears in the Psalter (Psalm 110:4). He is also prominently figured in the Christian Book of Hebrews (5:6, 10; 6:20, and throughout ch. 7). Malki-Tzedeq is identified in some of the rabbinic literature as designating Shem ben Noach (𝕿ᴶ *Bereshit* 14:18–20; *b. Nedarim* 32b; Bem. R. 4.8), the son of Noach (Noah) from whom the Jewish Patriarchs

---

[335] Marcus Jastrow, *Dictionary of the Targumim, Talmud Babli and Yerushalmi, and the Midrashic Literature* (New York, N.Y.: Title Publishing, 1943; orig. 1903), 762.

descend. He is midrashically described as being so perfect that he was born already circumcised and is credited with instructing Avraham in the *Torah* (*Bereshit Rabbah* 43.6). Qumran text *11Q13* presents him as the eschatological judge[336] who salvifically atones for the sins of HaShem's "elect" (cp. Matthew 1:21). *Eikhah Rabbathi* seems to portray him in Messianic terms: "The proper name of Messiah is Adonai-Tzidqeinu" (tr. "HaShem is our righteousness), a term which also bears a Messianic connotation in Jeremiah 23:5-6. Some Christian sources identify Malki-Tzedeq as being the pre-incarnational form of Yeshua haNotzri, viewing his appearances as "Yeshuophanies" (e.g., the Coptic "Melchizedek" text from the *Nag Hammadi* cache, 4th Century CE[337]), though most see Yeshua as being "a priest after the Order of Malki-Tzedeq" rather than the self-same figure.

malakh (Hebrew מַלְאָךְ): literally "messenger." A *malakh* can be either a heavenly messenger (angel) or a human one (e.g. a prophet). The Greek word *angelos* (ἄγγελος) has the same dual meaning. The root word can also mean "to work," so "worker" is sometimes an appropriate gloss as well.

---

[336] He may also described as having this role in *b. Sukkah* 52b, if "Kohentzedeq" (כֹּהֵן צֶדֶק) in that text is intended to indicate Malki-Tzedeq.

[337] *MsCopt Melchizedek* (online: *Nag Hammadi Library*; http://www.gnosis.org/naghamm/melchiz.html; 4th Century CE).

melakhot (Heb. מְלָאכוֹת): literally "works, tasks, or vocations." The word in the previous entry derives from the same Hebrew *shoresh* (root), but the derived noun meaning "angeldom" or "function of a messenger/angel/prophet" is spelled slightly differently – *malakhut* (מַלְאָכוּת).[338] The spelling *melakhot* is uniquely applied to the thirty-nine Sabbath work prohibitions derived from Torah and delineated in tractate Shabbat in both of the Talmuds (*b. Shabbat* 75b; *y. Shabbat* 7:1-2).

masechet (Aram. מַסֶּכֶת; pl. *masechetot*, מַסֶּכְתוֹת): literally "tractate." The *Talmud* is divided into 63 *masechetot*, each covering a different subject. These are classified into six סְדָרִים (*sedarim*, i.e. orders), making up the organization of the *Talmud*. These divisions are what give the *Talmud* value as a halakhic reference library, i.e. the ease with which one can zero in on a specific topic.

Mashiach (Heb. מָשִׁיחַ): literally "anointed." Equates to the Aramaic מְשִׁיחָא (*Meshicha*), the Greek Χρίστος (*Christos*), and the English "Messiah." The Rabbinic literature speaks of the coming *Mashiach* both as *Mashiach ben Yosef* and as *Mashiach ben Dawid. See* next two entries.

Mashiach ben Dawid (Heb. מָשִׁיחַ בֶּן־דָּוִד): literally "Messiah son of David." This personage is referred to in some of the Rabbinic literature as

---

[338] Jastrow, *Dictionary of the Targumim*, 786.

"King Messiah," in contrast to the "War Messiah" of the next entry. This role includes building of the Temple (whether 3rd or 4th is debated), the ingathering of the Exiles (though some texts suggest this happen before He is revealed), and reigning over the Messianic Kingdom, characterized by a time of freedom and peace (*b. Sanh.* 98a–99a). In Christian thought, the *Mashiach ben Dawid* role is to be fulfilled in the Messiah's second *Parousia*, having accomplished the aims of the *Mashiach ben Yosef* in His original advent.

Mashiach ben Yosef (Heb. מָשִׁיחַ בֶּן־יוֹסֵף): literally "Messiah son of Joseph." The *Mashiach ben Yosef* is referred to in the literature as a craftsman who would be martyred at the hand of the enemies of G-d and Israel. The Yehoshua who is the subject of the fourth testimonium of poly-messianic Qumran text *4Q175* could be a reference to this same figure.[339] It was understood that this Messiah would be killed based on Zechariah 12:10 (cited in *b. Sukkah* 52a). *Mashiach ben Yosef* comes in advance of *Mashiach ben Dawid* (*Ber. R.* 70:15). Judaism interprets this title as indicating descent from the Tribe of Yosef (specifically Ephraim).

Mekhiltha (Aram. מְכִילְתָא): an ancient halakhic midrash on Shemot (Exodus) reflecting the

---

[339] Alan J. Avery-Peck, ed., *The Review of Rabbinic Judaism: Ancient, Medieval, and Modern* (Martinus Nijhoff Publishers, 2005).

Aqiva tradition. Two versions exist, one compiled by his student Rabbi Shim'on bar Yochai and the other by Rabbi Ishmael. This work dates to ca. 250 CE. It is sometimes also referred to by its Hebrew name *Middah*. Both titles translate to English as "measure, rule."

Merkavah (Heb. מֶרְכָּבָה): literally "chariot" or "throne of Elohim" (drawing the name from the vision described in Ezekiel 1:4-26). The *Merkavah* was a Jewish mysticism cult chastised by Sha'ul haTarsi (Paul) in his letter to the Colossians for their hyper-veneration of angels. Some scholars see a direct line of development between First-Century *Merkavah* mysticism and *Qabbalah*, which emerged in the Fourteenth Century.[340]

metonymy (Latin): a rhetorical device whereby an alternative wording is used to denote a person, place, thing, or idea – such as a descriptive title or pseudonym.

Midrash (Aram. מִדְרָשׁ): literally "study." The term refers in Rabbinic literature to the allegorical or homiletical application of a text. In Jewish hermeneutics, this is shortened to "drash" and

---

[340] F. F. Bruce, "Colossians Problems, Part 3: The Colossian Heresy"." *Bibliotheca Sacra* 141 (1984): 195-208; Lawrence H. Schiffman, "Merkavah Speculation at Qumran: the 4Q Serekh Shirot `Olat HaShabbat," *Mystics, Philosophers, and Politicians: Essays in Jewish Intellectual History in Honor of Alexander Altmann* (ed. J. Reinharz and D. Swetschinski; Duke University Press, 1982): 15-47.

connotes a deeper level of analysis than the simple *p'shat* (פְּשָׁט, plain reading).[341] The Midrashic works include *Avot d'Rabbi Nathan*, *Mekhiltha*, *Midrash Rabbah*, *Sifra*, *Sifré*, and *Tanchuma*.

minhag (Heb. מִנְהָג): literally "driving (a chariot)," but by rabbinic usage "custom." It is sometimes used in tandem with *Israel*, i.e. מִנְהַג יִשְׂרָאֵל (custom of Israel) and either form (the full of the truncated) connotes the collective accepted traditions and customs of Judaism.

minim (Heb. מִינִים; singular מִין): literally "kind, species." In First-Century usage, the term meant "heretic," as it does today, but without the Christian implication it now carries. In its original usage, it was only used in reference to apostate Jews, especially Sadducees and Samaritans.

Mishna (Heb. מִשְׁנָה): literally "study by repetition." The component of the *Talmud* composed by the Tanna'im (the rabbis featured in this work, et al.). Due to the organization of its 63 *masekhetot* (מַסֶּכְתוֹת, tractates) into 6 *sedarim* (סְדָרִים, orders), it

---

[341] In Jewish hermeneutics, there are four levels of meaning to a passage, the first letters of their names forming the acronym PaRDeS: *p'shat* (פְּשָׁט, plain reading), *remez* (רֶמֶז, "hint," or allegorical reading), *'drash* (דְּרַשׁ, "inquiry," or homiletical reading), and *sod* (סוֹד, "mystery," or the meaning received by Divine inspiration).

is often referred to by an acronym for שִׁשָּׁה סְדָרִים ("six orders"), i.e. שַׁ״ס (*shas*).[342]

mitzwah (Heb. מִצְוָה): literally "commandment," frequently transliterated *mitzvah*. The Hebrew word *mitzwah* derives from the *shoresh* (root) צָוָה (*tzawwah*) – to command. The plural form is *mitzwot* (וּמְצָוֹת), frequently *mitzvot*. The *mitzwot* are the 613 commands of the *Torah* in Jewish parlance, though the 1050 commands of the *B'rit Chadashah* would also meet the definition.

mo'adim (Heb. מוֹעֲדִים; plural of מוֹעֵד): literally "seasons" or "appointments." The *mo'adim* of HaShem, i.e. the feasts and fasts of Israel, are laid out, among other places, in Leviticus 23. Purim and Chanukah, being post-Mosaic, are not included under this designation, as it applies to those *mo'adim* given in *Torah* only.

Nasi (Heb. נָשִׂיא): literally "prince," but more at president in First-Century and Modern usage. This was the title for the president of the Sanhedrin Gedolah (the highest *halakhic* and civil court in Israel). This office was held by Hillel until his death, and thereafter by Shammai, Shim'on ben Hillel, Rabban Gamli'el haZaqen, and a line of Gamli'el's descendants thereafter (plus Yochanan ben Zakkai) until its abolishment in 426 CE.

---

[342] For a more detailed introduction to the Mishnaic material, see Jacob Neusner, *The Mishnah: An Introduction* (Lanham, Md.: Jason Aronson, Inc., 1994).

Netzarim (Heb. נְצָרִים): literally "Nazarethites." This was one of the earliest designations for followers of Yeshua haNotzri. Other monikers included *HaDerekh* (The Way), and χριστιανοί (Chrisitans), but this last label was originally used only in Antioch (Acts 11:26), probably in a derogatory sense initially.

'Olam haBa (Heb. עוֹלָם הַבָּא): literally "the world to come." In the Rabbinic literature, this generally refers to the Messianic Kingdom (also called *Acharit Hayamim*, i.e. אַחֲרִית הַיָּמִים), but in some instances can also refer to heaven (the temporary stopping grounds before Resurrection and subsequent Messianic Kingdom.

'Olam haZeh (Heb. עוֹלָם הַזֶּה): literally "this world." The use of this term in Jewish thought for life in our present bodies implies that there is another life to follow, i.e. the *'olam haBa*.

partzupa (Aram. פַּרְצוּפָּה): literally "person." In Semitic thought, the whole of the unique characteristics which make up and/or define the individual person, making their *qnuma* distinguishable from that of another.

Pentateuch (Grk. πεντάτευχος): literally "five scrolls." See *Torah* and/or *Samaritan Pentateuch*.

Pharisees (Heb. פְּרוּשִׁים): A political party in *Eretz-Yisrael* first appearing in the time of John Hurqanus (135-105 BCE) in hostile opposition to the Maccabeeans, whose chief concern by this time was no longer the carrying out of *Torah*, but rather on expanding their own political power.[343] They originally called themselves *Chasidim* ("pious ones"), but were derogatorily called *P'rushim* (Pharisees, i.e. "separated ones") by their Sadducean opponents.[344] Note that there is no strict correlation between the *Chasidim* (Pharisees) of the First Century and the later movement of the same name founded in Eighteenth-Century Russia.[345] The basic First-Century definition of a Pharisee was anyone who professed a belief in the Resurrection and the validity of the *Oral Torah*, though there were actually four degrees of Pharisaism.[346] This sect was subdivided into at least two "mental directions" – that of *Beit Hillel* being *halakhically* dominant over that of *Beit Shammai*.

Pirqei Avot (Aram. פִּרְקֵי אָבוֹת): literally "Chapters of the Fathers," but generally translated "Ethics of Our Fathers." A compilation of the ethical teachings and maxims of *Mishnaic*-period Rabbis. Though included as one of the 63 tractates

---

[343] Emil Schürer, *Geschichte des jüdischen Volkes im Zeitalter Jesu Christi* (Leipzig, Germany: J. C. Hinrichs'sche Buchhandlung, 1898), II (2): 28.

[344] Alfred Edersheim, *The Life and Times of Jesus the Messiah* (Oxford: Longmans, Green, and Company, 1883), I:323.

[345] Aaron J. Hahn Tapper, *Judaisms: A Twenty-First Century Introduction to Jews and Jewish Identities* (Oakland, Calif.: University of California Press, 2016), 107.

[346] Moseley, op. cit., 113.

(מַסֶּכְתּוֹת) of the *Mishna*, it is really a separate work dated about a generation later.[347] It is found in *Seder Nezikim* (Damages) of the *Mishna*, second-to-last *masekhet* (מַסֶּכְת, singular form of מַסֶּכְתּוֹת).

pruzbul (Heb. פְּרוּזְבּוּל; orig. from Grk. προσβολή): literally "application." A rabbinic exception to a rabbinic enactment or *Torah* command.

Pseudepigrapha (Grk. ψευδεπίγραφα): literally "falsely-attributed writings." This was a popular genre of literature from about 200 BCE to 200 CE characterized by its pseudeponymous authorship, i.e. that the works written under this genre were attributed to important Jewish figures who were not actually the authors. This was not done in order to deceive the audience; the audience understood the genre and was entertained by this "what if" style of writing – "What if Enoch had interacted with Noah?" (1 Enoch) or "What if Yeshua was a shapeshifter?" (*MsCoptPseudo-Cyril*).[348] What would these situations have looked like? A singular exemplar of the genre is called a *pseudepigraphon* (ψευδεπίγραφων).

---

[347] Jacob Neusner, *Rabbinic Literature: An Essential Guide* (Nashville, Tenn.: Abingdon Press, 2005), 8.

[348] English translation published in Roelof van den Broek, *Pseudo-Cyril of Jerusalem on the Life and the Passion of Christ* (Leiden: Brill, 2013). This work was likely an embellishment on an earlier statement made by Origen (early 3rd Century CE): "To those who saw him [Yeshua] he did not appear alike to all."

Qabbalah (Heb. קַבָּלָה): literally "that which has been received." It can alternatively be spelled *Kabbalah*, *Kabbala*, *Qabbala*, or (less frequently) *Cabala*. This is the name of a mysticism approach to Scripture which emerged in 12th or 13th Century Spain and Southern France. It is more embraced in the Chasidic sect of Judaism than in any other, though it does also have a foothold in Orthodox Judaism. There are variations of *Qabbalah*, ranging from the celebrity version popularized by Madonna to the precipice of gnosticism (i.e. the less popular *Prophetic-Ecstatic* and *Magico-Theurgical* versions), though the average *mekubbal* (מְקוּבָּל, i.e. student of the *Qabbalah*) falls some-where between those two extremes in what is called *Theoretical Qabbalah*. The principle text besides the *Tanakh* is the *Zohar*. Qabbalah's contributions to modern Jewish thought include *gematria* (the study of the significance of numbers in Scripture) and most elements of the Friday evening *Qabbalat Shabbat* liturgy.

qnuma (Aram. קְנוּמָה): *no literal English equivalent exists.* In Semitic thought, the set of traits which is common to all occurrences of a particular *khayana* (e.g. humanity, Divinity, *fauna*, *flora*, etc.); the concrete representation of a given *khayana* through the definition thereof by the identification of such traits. The term, as used in First-Century thought, does *not* correlate with the Greek concept of *hupóstasis* (ὑπόστασις, i.e. "underlying substance"). See pp. 165ff., esp. footnote 248.

Qumran (Arab. قمران ‎; spelled קוּמְרָאן in Heb.):
literally "two moons;"often referenced as Chirbet
Qumran (חִירְבַּת קוּמְרָאן / خرب ة ق مران), i.e. "ruins
of Qumran." An ancient settlement on the
northwest bank of the Dead Sea in Israel, "but
out of range of the noxious exhalations of the
coast,"[349] inhabited by the *Yachad* and *Damascus
Covenant* communities from the latter third of the
2nd Century BCE until its destruction by the
Romans in 68 CE. The "Dead Sea Scrolls" were
discovered at this site in 1947. The Dead Sea
Scrolls and Scraps consist mainly of Bible scrolls,
though community standards and common items
such as recipes and grocery receits have also been
found there. Its original (Second Temple Era)
name is believed to have been *S[ᵉ]khakhah* (Heb.
סְכָכָה, Aram. סְכָכָא),[350] which means "enclosed" or
"covered."[351]

Rabban (Aram. רַבָּן): literally "our great one." The
title of *Rabban* ranks above that of *Rabbi*. The
first to be awarded this title was Gamli'el I, the
grandson of Hillel. The equivalent form בַּרוֹן
(*Rabon*) is also found in the *Targumim* (early
Aramaic commentary-translations of the *Tanakh*).

---

[349] Pliny the Elder, *Historia Naturalis* V (1st Century CE), 17,
4.

[350] The Hebrew spelling appears in Joshua 15:61, and the
Aramaic is attested in *3Q15* (the Copper Scroll).

[351] Ludwig Köhler, and Walter Baumgartner, *The Hebrew
and Aramaic Lexicon of the Old Testament: Study Edition* (vol.
1; New York: Brill, 2001), 754, s.v. סכך I and III.

The latter also occurs in *m. Ta'anit* 3:8, Mark 10:51, and John 20:16.

Rabbi (Aram. רַבִּי): literally "my great one." This honorific title took on a more formal meaning after 70 CE than prior, but was in use as the designation for a teacher of the *Torot* (both *Torahs*) from the generation following Hillel and Shammai to the close of the Second Temple era. Prior to 70 CE, the title "Rabbi" was reserved for use by those teaching the *Torot* within *Eretz-Yisrael*, the *Diaspora* Sages, then serving primarily in the Babylonian Academy, using the similar title רַב (*Rab*). Among the Ashkenaz, the related Yiddish title of רִבִּי (*Rebbe*) is common. The plural or *Rabbi* is an irregular form, i.e. רַבָּנִים (*Rabbanim*), rather than the expected רַבָּי (*Rabbai*).

Ruach (Heb. רוּחַ): literally "spirit, breath, wind." This Hebrew word shares its semantic domain with the Greek word *pneuma* (πνεῦμα). When followed by *haQodesh* (הַקֹּדֶשׁ) or *Elohim* (אֱלֹהִים), it represents HaShem's Spirit of Holiness (Holy Spirit).

Sadducees (Heb. צְדוּקִים): literally "righteous ones." A political party in *Eretz-Yisrael* which rejected the writings of the Prophets (*Nevi'im*), Hagiographa (*Kethuvim*), and Oral Torah (*Torah shebe'al Peh*), accepting as Scripture only the *Torah*. They also rejected belief in the Resurrection. This party was founded by Zadok and Boethus, students of Antigonus of Sokho, in the early Second Century BCE.[352]

Samaritans (Heb. שַׁמְרִים): literally "guardians." They took this name as they saw themselves as the guardians or keepers of the "true" *Torah*, their version of it (*Samaritan Pentateuch*) differing significantly from the standard Masoretic Text (see next entry). They established their temple at Mount Gerazim, in the north of Israel, instead of Jerusalem and still practice the sacrificial system at their temple site today. Like the Sadducees, they reject the books of the Prophets and Writings as non-inspired and accept no other prophet but Moshe (Moses).

Samaritan Pentateuch (הַתּוֹרָה הַשּׁוֹמְרוֹנִית): The Samaritan Pentateuch (often abbreviated by the siglum 𝖆𝖆) is more often in line with the Dead Sea Scrolls (DSS) than is the Hebrew Masoretic Text (𝔐) and is likely the primary source text for the Qumran (ℚ) version of the *Torah*. The differences between 𝖆𝖆 and 𝔐 number around 6000, about half of which are merely orthographical, i.e. variations in the spelling of words or the embellishment of the text by the addition of extra words for clarification. The remaining 3000 are more significant, including the replacement of Jerusalem as the Temple site with Mount Gerazim in the former. The

---

[352] Daniel Cohn-Sherbok, *Dictionary of Jewish Biography* (London: Continuum, 2005), 13.

Septuagint (𝕲 or LXX) favors **ᴌᴌ** in 1900 of the passages where **ᴌᴌ** differs from **𝕸**.[353]

samkhut (Heb. סָמְכוּת): literally "authority." This word applies to any authority, whether civil, religious, or Divine (i.e. a Divine agent functioning as a representative of HaShem).

Sanhedrin (Aramaized סַנְהֶדְרִין; but orig. Grk. Συνέδριον): literally "sitting together."[354] Josephus affirms the continued existence of this Court from the days of Moshe (Moses) to the 426 CE, though not always by this name. It succeeded the authority of the *Anshei Knesset HaG'dolah*, which was successor to Moshe's Elders. There were two levels of Sanhedrin court – the *Sanhedrin Gedolah* (Great Sanhedrin) was the highest court in *Eretz-Yisrael*, comprised of 70 ruling rabbis overseen by the *Nasi*. The lower Sanhedrin, or *Sanhedrin Qatanah* (Small Sanhedrin) was the name for localized courts of 23 members convened to arbitrate on non-*halakhic* matters.[355]

---

[353] Emanuel Tov, *Textual Criticism of the Hebrew Bible* (Grand Rapids, Mich.: Wm. B. Eerdmans, 1992), 159-60.

[354] Marcus Jastrow, *Dictionary of the Targumim, Talmud Babli and Yerushalmi, and the Midrashic Literature* (New York, N.Y.: Title Publishing, 1943; orig. 1903), 1005; Walter Bauer, F. W. Danker, W. F. Arndt, & F. W. Gingrich, *A Greek-English Lexicon of the New Testament and other Early Christian Literature* (3rd ed.; Chicago, Ill." University of Chicago Press, 2000; orig. 1957), 967.

[355] J. H. Hertz, *Pentateuch and Haftorahs* (London: Soncino Press, 1985; orig. 1971), 823; Marcus Jastrow, *Dictionary of*

The Sanhedrim.

A depiction of the Sanhedrin Gedolah in session from *People's Cyclopedia of Universal Knowledge* (1883)

savlanut (Heb. סַבְלָנוּת): literally "patience." This quality character attribute is lauded and applauded in the rabbinic literature.

seder (Heb. סֵדֶר): literally "order." The Passover meal is called by this name, as it is an orderly presentation of the Exodus account.

Septuagint (Latin *septuaginta*): literally "seventy." Properly, the Koine (common) Greek translation

---

the Targumim, Talmud Babli and Yerushalmi, and the Midrashic Literature (New York, N.Y.: Title Publishing, 1943; orig. 1903), 1005.

of *only* the five books of Moshe (*Torah/Pentateuch*), originally translated beginning in about 250 BCE and concluding in 132 BCE. The work was commissioned by King Ptolomy II, but he died in 246 BCE, before seeing the work come to completion. The tale of the original translation process by seventy (or seventy-two, depending on the version of the story) Jewish elders in seventy days, as recounted in the pseudepigraphical *Letter of Aristeas*, is not considered reliable, understood by current scholarship to have been written as advertising propaganda. The term has come to be widely used, incorrectly, of the whole corpus of Greek Jewish Scriptures.[356] By the close of the First Century CE, there was more than one Greek translation of the *Torah*, all of them generically called *septuagints*, some more "Christianized" than others. These several variants have since been amalgamated into a "scholarly edition" including the contents of the full *Tanakh* and referred to, somewhat misleadingly, as *the Septuagint*.

Shabbat (Heb. שַׁבָּת): Sabbath. In this work, *Shabbat* is used to indicate the seventh-day (Saturday) Sabbath exclusively (though it can also be used of the high holy days as well). The present author does not subscribe to the "floating Sabbath" or "moveable Sabbath" movements. This is also the

---

[356] George W. E. Nickelsburg, *Jewish Literature between the Bible and the Mishnah* (2nd ed.; Minneapolis, Minn.: Fortress, 2005), 192-3.

title of tractates in both *Talmuds* relating to the subject of Sabbath-keeping.

shalom (Heb. שָׁלוֹם): literally "completeness, wholeness." The word commonly translated "peace" has a far deeper connotation to the Hebrew mind. It represents not just "absence of war," though that is within the realm of meaning, but also a restoration of the world to Edenic conditions and every thought, word, and action that contributes to realizing that vision. It might seem ironic to the non-Hebraic mind that the ideographic meaning of the Hebrew word can be read as "destruction (ᴡ) of rule (ᴜ) connected with (ᵞ) chaos (ᴍ)," but that action would indeed render the result of peaceful existence.[357]

Shema (Heb. שְׁמַע): literally "listen with intent to obey." This is the central statement of faith of Judaism, located in the *Torah* at Deuteronomy 6:4-9. At some point, the *minhag* (custom) expanded from the recitation of that single block of text to a "string of pearls" consisting of three passages: Deuteronomy 6:4-9; 11:13-21; and Numbers 15:37-41, in that order. The first and arguably most important line reads, "Hear, O Israel, HaShem is our G-d, HaShem is one (*echad*)." In modern liturgical practice, Leviticus 19:18b ("and you shall love your neighbor as yourself") is often recited immediately afterward.

---

[357] Early Semitic font courtesy of Ancient Hebrew Research Center (online: http://www.ancient-hebrew.org/hebrew_type.html).

Shem haMeforash (Heb. שֵׁם הַמְּפוֹרָשׁ): literally "the exclusive Name." This is the Hebrew appellation for the "Tetragrammaton" – a label for the ineffable Name of HaShem, i.e. *yod – hey – waw – hey*. The root פָּרַשׁ means "to divide, to separate."[358] The rabbinic literature also uses the designation *Shem haMeyuchad* (שֵׁם הַמְּיֻחָד), which is a synonymous term, interchangeable with *Shem haMeforash*. These are generally truncated to *haShem* (הַשֵּׁם), "the Name," in liturgy and prayer.

Shemoneh Esrei (Heb. שְׁמוֹנֶה עֶשְׂרֵה): literally "eighteen." This selection of benedictions is commonly called the "*Amidah*" (עֲמִידָה; standing prayer) and is the core of the Jewish prayer service. Its authorship is traditionally attributed to the *Anshei Knesset HaG'dolah* (*b. Berakhot* 33b). During the First Century CE, a nineteenth blessing (curse) was added to it calling for the destruction and/or punishment of the "heretics." It was most likely originally aimed at the Sadducees, but in the Middle Ages, *haMotzerim* (sic.) was added to it, which has been interpreted as intending to include Christians (*Notzerim*) in the malediction.

Shisha Sedarim (Heb. שִׁשָּׁה סְדָרִים): literally "six orders;" frequently abbreviated ש"ס (*shas*). The 63 *masechetot* (tractates) of the *Mishna* are organized into 6 themed, chapter-like units called *sedarim*

---

[358] Marcus Jastrow, *Dictionary of the Targumim, Talmud Babli and Yerushalmi, and the Midrashic Literature* (New York, N.Y.: Title Publishing, 1943; orig. 1903), 1241-2.

(orders). They are titled: *Zeraim* (Seeds), *Moedim* (Appointments/Seasons), *Nashim* (Women), *Nezikim* (Damages), *Kodshim* (Holinesses), and *Taharot* (Purities).

shiva (Heb. שִׁבְעָה): literally "seven." "Sitting *shiva*" refers to the initial mourning period observed in Judaism after the death of a close relative. For seven days, the mourner sits at home or in the home of the deceased receiving visitors and processing the loss.[359]

shlichim (Heb. שְׁלִיחִים; plural form of שָׁלִיחַ, i.e. *shaliach*): literally "those sent out" or "emissaries," i.e. the Hebrew equivalent to the Greek word ἀπόστολοι (*apostoloi*, i.e. "apostles"). In First-Century context, when Judaism was more of a "missionary religion" than it is now, it was used to refer to those who were sent out to promulgate Judaism in various locations around the world (Numbers 28:18). The term was not exclusive to the *HaDerekh/Netzarim* movement.

shoresh (Aram. שׁוֹרֶשׁ): literally "root."[360] This comes from the verb "to take root" and is used in

---

[359] **Publisher's Note:** MJR offers a free self-paced, 6-lesson mini-course on Jewish mourning and grieving customs. The interested reader is welcome to participate: https://mjrabbinate.teachable.com/p/imj-093.

[360] Marcus Jastrow, *Dictionary of the Targumim, Talmud Babli and Yerushalmi, and the Midrashic Literature* (New York, N.Y.: Title Publishing, 1943; orig. 1903), 1635.

grammar to indicate the base form of a Semitic word, usually a tri-radical (three-consonant) root.

Shulchan Arukh (Aram שֻׁלְחָן עָרוּךְ): literally "the set table." The most influential work on Jewish *halakha*, *Shulchan Arukh* was written by Joseph Caro (1488-1575), a Sephardic Jew who had been expelled from Spain during the Spanish Inquisition (1492).

Sicarii (Latin; from Heb. סִיקָרִיים): literally "dagger men." A slinter group from the Zealot faction so called due to the daggers (*sicae* in Latin) concealed in their cloaks. This "cloak and dagger" squad predated the Islamic *hashishin* and Asian *ninjas* by centuries.

siddur (Heb. סִידּוּר): literally "order" (related to the word *seder*). The order of worship is called by this name; any Jewish prayer book would also be a *siddur*.

Sifra (Aram. סִפְרָא): the companion to *Mekhiltha* covering Leviticus. This works date to about 250 CE.

Sifré (Aram. סִפְרֵי): Companion volumes to *Mekhiltha* and *Sifra* corresponding to Numbers and Deuteronomy. Unfortunately, save a few portions, these volumes are no longer extant.

Sitz im Leben (Ger.): literally "situation in life." In the *Formesgeschichte* (Form-Critical) approach to biblical theology, the term refers more to the way the story is presented than to the historical setting, i.e. the *Sitz im Leben*[361] of the Bible is the Jewish Tradition through which the message is transmitted.

Soferim (Heb. סוֹפְרִים): literally "scribes," i.e. those who copy [holy] books. A class of Pharisees who were learned in *Torah*. Ezra was among the most prominent to be assigned the title of *sofer* (singular form of *soferim*).

sugya (Aram. סוּגְיָא): literally "category, topic." "A distinct matter for consideration in discussion, thought, or study, particularly in reference to an informal division of the Gemara."[362]

s'yag l'Torah (Heb. סְיָג לַתּוֹרָה): literally "fence for *Torah*." The origin of this phrase is *Pirqei Avot* 1:1, which advocates the development of a super-erogatory lawcode to help keep adherents of the faith from transgressing the *Torah*. It includes precautions such as, "Not merely one who sins with his body is called an adulterer, but he who sins with his eye is also so named" (*Wayyiqra Rabbah* 23.12).

synecdoche (Latin): a rhetorical device common in Semitic literature and parlance whereby

---

[361] In German, all nouns are capitalized, regardless of their position within a sentence, thus both *Sitz* and *Leben* should always be spelled with a capital initial letter.

[362] Chaim M. Weiser, *Frumspeak: The First Dictionary of Yeshivish* (Lanham, Md.: Jason Aronson, 2004; orig. 1995).

referencing one component of a system is intended to call to mind the entire system, e.g. voicing the first line of a psalm when the entire content of the psalm is intended.

talmidim (Heb. תַּלְמִידִים; plural form of תַּלְמִיד, i.e. *talmid*): literally "disciples" or "scholars" from the verb לָמַד (*lamad*), "to learn." In all forms of Pharisaic Judaism, a *talmid* was one who was apprenticed to a rabbi for his study of the *Torot*.

Talmud (Aram. תַּלְמוּד): Either or both of the two works which contain the codification of Jewish *halakha* by the Sages of Judaism's Tannaitic and Amoraic periods. See next two entries. Like the entry above, this word also derives from the root verb לָמַד (*lamad*), "to learn."

Talmud Bavli (Aram. תַּלְמוּד בַּבְלִי): aka the *Babylonian Talmud*, more of a history of interpretation than what a modern scholar would consider a commentary, but useful in its cataloging of rabbinical teachings from some of Judaism's most renowned Sages. Comprised of the *Mishna* (compiled by Yehudah the Prince ca. 200 – 220 CE and divided into six orders of seven to twelve tractates each) and the *Gemara* (named from the Aramaic verb "to study," codified ca. 600 CE). Levine observes, "The *Talmud* happily puts into conversation teachers who lived centuries and hundreds of miles apart."[363]

---

[363] Levine, op. cit., 27.

Talmud Yerushalmi (Aram. תַּלְמוּד יְרוּשַׁלְמִי): aka *Jerusalem Talmud*, the "shorter" *Talmud*; produced in *Eretz-Yisrael*, but for whatever reason, never as popular as its Babylonian counterpart. It does, however, contain some data which the *Talmud Bavli* does not, and thus finds its value for this present project. Dating for this *Talmud* slightly predates that of the *Gemara* of its Babylonian counterpart, set at about the 375-425 CE.

Tanakh (Heb. abbr. תַּנַ"ךְ): acronym for *Torah, Nevi'im, and Kethuvim* (Instruction, Prophets, and Writings), a common moniker for the Hebreo-Aramaic text of the Jewish Bible (OT) or any translation thereof.

Tanna'im (Aram. תַּנָּאִים; plural form of תַּנָּא, i.e. *tanna*): literally "repeaters." These Pharisaic Sages were the authors of the *halakha* contained in the *Mishna*. Note that the terms *Tanna'im* and *Mishna* are linguistically connected. The root verb for each is the word meaning "to repeat" in the respective source language. In Hebrew, it is שׁנה,[364] the Aramaic cognate of which is תנא.[365]

---

[364] Francis Brown, Samuel Rolles Driver, and Charles A. Briggs, *The Brown-Driver-Briggs Hebrew and English Lexicon* (Boston, Mass.: Houghton, Mifflin, and Company, 1906), 1040-41.

[365] Marcus Jastrow, *Dictionary of the Targumim, Talmud Babli and Yerushalmi, and the Midrashic Literature* (New York, N.Y.: Title Publishing, 1943; orig. 1903), 1679.

The differing initial and final letters is due to a phenomenon called "Canaanite shift."[366]

Targum (Aram. תַּרְגּוּם): literally "translation, paraphrase, interpretation, or explanation." The term derives from the use of a form of the *shoresh* (root) in Ezra 4:7. In the rabbinic literature, it refers to a specific body of works, i.e. early Common Era paraphrases of books of the *Tanakh* into Aramaic by Onqelos, Yonathan ben Uzziel, Pseudo-Yonathan, et al. The fullest *Targum* is Neofiti. A Western version also exists called *Targum Yerushalmi*. The *Talmud* instructs that a *Torah* reader should read from the Hebrew text twice and the associated *Targum* once in public readings (b. *Berakhot* 8a–b).

tevilah (Heb. טְבִילָה): literally "immersion, bath." A full body immersion ritual. In antiquity, this was done, generally, in a natural water source such as a river or lake, though in later times, a miqweh (מִקְוֶה; i.e. man-made immersion pool) was/is often used.

tiqun 'olam (Heb. תִּיקוּן עוֹלָם): literally "repairing/ improving the world." This is seen as the obligation of the Jewish community, a charge that goes along with being chosen by HaShem to be His light to the world. It can take many forms, and includes anything aimed at bringing *Torah*

---

[366] Miles V. Van Pelt, *Basics of Biblical Aramaic* (Grand Rapids, Mich.: Zondervan, 2011), 10-11.

standards to fruition and healing physical and spiritual brokenness wherever it is found to exist.

Torah (Heb. תּוֹרָה): literally "instruction." The term has three basic meanings in Judaism: (1) the first five books of the Jewish Bible, frequently referred to in the literature as *Torah shebiKhtav* (Written *Torah*); (2) the whole *Tanakh*, i.e. *Torah*, Prophets, and Writings of the Hebrew Bible; and (3) the whole instruction of HaShem, i.e. the Written Word and the *Oral Torah* in tandem.[367]

Torah shebe'al Peh (Heb. תּוֹרָה שֶׁבְּעַל פֶּה): literally "*Torah*/instruction by mouth," i.e. the *Oral Torah* handed down to Moshe at the same time he received the written. The term has come to include both the *Mishna* and the *Gemara* portions of *Talmud* (except content which is clearly opinion-oriented), including the history of interpretation reflected in the *halakhic* rulings of the Sages. Judaism holds that these have been handed down orally since the time of Moshe until concern that they might become lost in time of persecution led to their being written down.

Torah shebiKhtav (Heb. תּוֹרָה שֶׁבִּכְתָב): literally "*Torah*/instruction by writing." This term refers to the first five books of the Jewish Bible, i.e. the "*Torah* of Moshe."

---

[367] Magnus Zetterholm, ed., *The Messiah in Early Judaism and Christianity* (Minneapolis, Minn.: Fortress Press, 2007), 124.

Tosefta (Heb. תּוֹסָפְתָּא): literally "supplements." Additions to the *Mishna* compiled by Rabbi Nehemiah, a student to Rabbi Aqiva, in the late Second Century CE (*Mishnaic* Period), reportedly in 189 CE. Tosefta often attributes laws that are anonymous in the *Mishna* to specific Tanna'im (Mishnaic Sages). This is considered "commentary" on the *Mishna*, thus not enjoying the same authoritative status, though it is the standard reference work on the *Mishna* and might be classed "deuterocanonical" in the *Talmudic* corpus. It is written in *Mishnaic* Hebrew, with some Aramaic.

treif or treyf (Yid. טרייף; fr. Heb. טְרֵפָה): literally "torn." This term can refer to either (1) animals which do not fit the biblical definition of food per Leviticus 11 and Deuteronomy 14, or (2) anything that does fit the biblical definition of food but has been defiled so that it can no longer be considered edible, generally by coming into contact with something else *treif*.

Urtext (Ger. compound word formed from *Ur* and *text*): literally "original text" or "primitive text." *Ur* is an archaeological referent to the earliest known developed city of that name in Sumer of the Mesopotamian region (in the Bible, Ur of the Chaldees), located where the modern city of Tell el-Muqayyar, Iraq is today. An Urtext is the earliest known form of a text, in the original language and without emendation. Subsequent products deriving from the *Urtext* are often called *hypertexts*.

Vorlage (Ger.): literally "prototype or template." A prior version of a text under consideration, and usually the immediately prior, i.e. the text from which the exemplar under review was created; the underlying template text. E.g. the Vorlage behind the KJV was the Erasmian compilation resulting from the amalgamation of six very late, very flawed, partial Greek texts with the remaining *lacunae* (textual gaps caused by holes in the documents) filled in by back-translating the Latin *Vulgate* into Greek; the resulting product, completed in 1516 and called by scholars "the most poorly edited volume in all of literature"[368] (and rebranded in the royal propaganda as *Textus Receptus*), being what was used by the KJV translators to construct the original *1611 King James Version* of the Bible.

Weltanschauung (Ger. compound word formed from *welt* and *anschauung*): literally "worldview;" synonymous with the Hebrew word *hashqafah*. This loanword has come into the jargon of philosophical theology, often untranslated, to refer to one's ideological outlook. Judaism, being anything but monolithic, is a meta-*Weltanschauung* comprised of several micro-*Weltanschauungen* (the plural form). In the First-Century context, these included Essene, Sadduceic, Damascus Coven-

---

[368] Daniel B. Wallace, "Why I Do Not Think the King James Bible Is the Best Translation Available Today," *Bible.org* (online: https://bible.org/article/why-i-do-not-think-king-james-bible-best-translation-available-today; 2 Jun 2004).

ant, Yachad, Hillelite Pharisaic, Shammaite Pharisaic, and *Netzari* Pharisaic (*HaDerekh*).

Yachad (יַחַד): This is the scholarly moniker, derived from *1QS*, for the Jewish community identified with the Dead Sea Scrolls at Qumran. This sect had severed its ties with Jerusalem and the Sanhedrin, opting for self-governance as an independent Jewish community. Their Messianic hope was in a figure they called the *Moreh haTzedeq* (Teacher of Righteousness), as opposed to the Prophet-Priest-King Messiah expected by the Pharisaic sect.

yeshiva (Heb. יְשִׁיבָה): literally "sitting," an academy of intensive higher learning in the *Torot* in *Talmudic-Era* Israel and Babylon; in modern usage, used to refer to an Orthodox Jewish college or seminary.

Yeshuophany (Hebronics: Aram. יֵשׁוּעַ, i.e. the Aramaic name Yeshua + Grk. φάνεια, appearance, manifestation): literally "appearance of Yeshua." This amalgamation was coined by the present author as shorthand for discussing the assertions that Yeshua made appearances to HaShem's people before His emergence in First-Century Israel, e.g. in the furnace with Shadrach, Mesach, and Abed-Nego; as Malki-Tzedeq meeting with Avraham; walking in *Gan Eden* with Adam and Chawwah; or participating in Creation. Plural: *Yeshuophanies.*

yetzer hara' (Heb. יֵצֶר הָרַע) **w'yetzer hatov** (Heb. יֵצֶר הַטּוֹב): literally "the evil inclination" and "the good inclination." Judaism teaches that every person has both of these within him/her, and along with them, the capability (by virtue of our innate free will/agency) of choosing one or the other in any given cirucumstance (Genesis 6:5; 8:21; *b. Berakhot* 32a; *ARN* 16). There is a *Talmudic midrash* about the *yetzer hara* being locked away, and the result was that the world came to a productive hault, so it had to be released back out into the world (*b. Yoma* 69b). The point was that it is not a matter of good versus evil, but more of altruism and assertiveness needing to be held in proper balance, of choosing to temper the one with the right amount of the other.

Zealot (Grk. ζηλωτής; equivalent to Heb. קַנָּאִי): literally "one burning with zeal." The Zealots of the First Century CE were the opposition party in re: the Romans, militarily defeating the Romans to wrest control of the fortress at Masada. They also targeted Jews whom they deemed to have assimilated too far into Greco-Romanism.

zughot (Aram. זוּגוֹת): plural of זוּגָא (*zogha*, meaning couple, spouse), literally "couples." The term applies to the five pairs of Sanhedrin leaders (the *Nasi* and the *Av Beit Din*) culminating with Hillel and Shammai. They were:
- Yosi ben Yo'ezer & Yosi ben Yochanam
- Yehoshua ben Perachyah & Nittai of Arbela
- Yehudah ben Tabbai & Shim'on ben Shetach
- Shemaiah & Avtalyon
- Hillel & Menachem/Shammai

BIBLIOGRAPHY OF

WORKS CONSULTED

בִּיבְּלִיוֹגְרָפְיָה

PRIMARY SOURCES

1Enoch. Ca. early-to-mid 1ˢᵗ Century CE.[369] Online: http://enoksbok.se/. Cited 1 Nov 2014.

1QHᵃ (Hodayot or הוֹדָיוֹת, i.e. Thanksgiving Psalms*).* Qumran, 1ˢᵗ Century CE.[370] As published in Eileen Schuller and Carol A. Newsom. *The Hodayot (Thanksgiving Psalms): A Study Edition of 1QHa.* Early Judaism and its Literature 36. Atlanta, Ga.: Society of Biblical Literature, 2012.

1QIsᵃ (The "Great Isaiah Scroll"). Qumran, ca. 150-125 BCE.[371] Online: http://dss.collections. imj.org.il/isaiah. Cited 19 Apr 2017.

---

[369] A date in the 1ˢᵗ Century CE is preferred, based on the occurrence of allusions to events leading up to Herod's 4 BCE death in 1 Enoch 67:8-13, per Darrell D. Hannah, "The Book of Noah, the Death of Herod the Great, and the Date of the Parables of Enoch," pp. 469-77 in Gabriele Boccaccini, ed., *Enoch and the Messiah Son of Man: Revisiting the Book of Parables* (Grand Rapids, Mich.: Wm. B. Eerdmans, 2007).

[370] Émile Puech, "Hodayot," in Lawrence H. Schiffman and James C. VanderKam, eds., *The Encyclopedia of the Dead Sea Scrolls* (tr. Robert E. Shillenn; Oxford: Oxford University Press, 2000), 366.

[371] The dating presented here is based on paleographic analysis, which coincides with the later part of the range established by radiocarbon dating methods. See Armin Lange, Emanuel Tov, and Matthias Weigold, *The Dead Sea Scrolls in Context: Integrating the Dead Sea Scrolls in the Study of Ancient Texts, Languages, and Cultures* (Leiden: E. J. Brill, 2011), 485.

1QM (Milchama or *War Scroll).* Qumran, ca. 2nd Century BCE.[372]

1QS (Serek haYachad or *Community Rules Scroll).* Qumran, ca. 100-75 BCE. Online: http://dss.collections.imj.org.il/community. Cited 19 Apr 2017.

2 Enoch. Egypt, ca. 1st Century CE.

3Q15 (Copper Scroll). Qumran, ca. 50-68 CE.[373] In the holdings of the Jordan Museum, Amman.

4Q174 (Florilegium). Qumran, late 1st Century BCE.

4Q175 (Testimonia). Qumran, mid-1st Century BCE.

4Q 213-214 (Testament of Levi). Qumran, ca. 100-200 BCE.

4Q246 (Apocryphon of Daniel or *Aramaic Apocalypse).* Qumran, late 1st Century BCE. As published in Cook, Edward M. "4Q246." *Bulletin for Biblical Research* 5 (1995): 43-66.

4Q252 (Pesher on Bereshit). Qumran, late 1st Century CE.

---

[372] Russell Gmirkin, "The War Scroll and Roman Weaponry Reconsidered," *Dead Sea Discoveries* 3, no. 2 (1996): 89-129.

[373] Émile Puech, "Some Results of the Restoration of the Copper Scroll by EDF Mecenat;" in Lawrence H. Schiffman, Emanuel Tov, and James C. VanderKam, eds., *The Dead Sea Scrolls Fifty Years After Their Discovery* (Jerusalem: Israel Exploration Society, 2000), 893.

4Q285 (Pierced Messiah or *War Rule fragment)*. Qumran, ca. 2nd Century BCE.

4Q385 (Pseudo-Ezekiel). Qumran, ca. 2nd Century BCE.

4Q451 (4Q Prayer C). Qumran, ca. 142-63 BCE. Online: http://www.deadseascrolls.org.il/ explore-the-archive/manuscript/4Q451- 1?locale=en_US

4Q521 (Messianic Apocalypse fragment*)*. Qumran, ca. 142-63 BCE. Online: http://www.deadseascrolls. org.il/explore-the-archive/manuscript/4Q521- 1?locale=en_US. Cited 26 Apr 2017.

4Q541 (Apocryphon of Levi fragment*)*. Qumran, ca. 142- 63 BCE. Online: http://www.deadseascrolls.org. il/explore-the-archive/manuscript/4Q541- 1?locale=en_US. Cited 25 Apr 2017.

11Q13 (11QMelchizedek). Qumran, ca. 100 BCE. Online: http://tovresearch.com/ deadseascrolls/11q13.html. Cited 21 Apr 2017.

Aland, Kurt; Black, Matthew; Martini, Carlo M; Metzger, Bruce M; & Wikgren, Allen (Editors). *The Greek New Testament.* 4th Revised Edition. Stuttgart, Germany: Deutschebibelgesellschaft, 2001.

Avot d'Rabbi Nathan. As published in Schechter, Solomon. אֲבוֹת דְּרַבִּי נָתָן. Frankfurt am Main: D. Kauffmann, 1887.[374]

Damascus Covenant (4Q266-271, 5QD, 6QD). Qumran, ca. 20 BCE. Online: http://www.deadseascrolls. org.il/explore-the-archive/manuscript/4Q266-1. Cited 19 Apr 2017.

Gospel of Gamli'el (Coptic). 300-600 CE.[375]

Gospel of Thomas (Coptic). Egypt, Mid-2nd Century CE.

Josephus, Flavius. *Antiquitates Judaicae.* 94 CE.

_____. *Bellum Judaicum.* 75 CE.

Maimonides, Moses. *Al-Risala al-Yamaniyya.* 1173 or 1174 CE.

Masoretic Text. As published in Biblia *Hebraica Stuttgartensia.* Stuttgart, Germany: Deutschebibelgesellschaft, 1997.

Mekhiltha. Venice Edition, 1545.

---

[374] *Avot d'Rabbi Nathan* is extant in two rescensions, making fixing the date of the *Urtext* difficult, though a date within a few generations of *Pirqei Avot* may be tenable.

[375] *Nota Bene:* The fragments given this name may belong instead to a work known as *Gospel of the Twelve Disciples*, per J. K. Elliot, *The Apocryphal New Testament* (Oxford: Clarendon Press, 2005; orig. 1993), 159.

Mekhiltha. As published in Hoffman, David Zvi. 1900-04. "Mechilta des R. Simon b. Jochai." *HaPeles I-IV.*

Midrash Tannaim. As published by Hoffman, David Zvi. 1908.

MsCopt Melchizedek. Nag Hammadi, 4th Century CE. Online: *Nag Hammadi Library.* http://www. gnosis.org/naghamm/melchiz.html. Cited 21 Mar 2017.

MsCoptPseudo-Cyril. Monastery of St. Michael, ca. 9th Century CE. English translation published in Roelof van den Broek, *Pseudo-Cyril of Jerusalem on the Life and the Passion of Christ* (Leiden: E. J. Brill, 2013).

Ms. Rome Biblioteca Casanatense 3085. Ca. 14th-15th Century CE.

Pamphilius, Eusebius. *Historia Ecclesiastica.* Ca. 324 CE. Cited 31 May 2014. Online: http://www. perseus.tufts.edu/hopper/text?doc=urn:cts:greek Lit:tlg2018.tlg002.perseus-grc1.

Peshitta. As published in Roth bar Raphael, Andrew Gabriel-Yizkhak. *Aramaic English New Testament.* 5th Edition. Sedro-Woolley, Wash.: Netzari Press, 2012.

Philo of Alexandria. *De Decalogo.* Early 1st Century CE.

_____. *De Specialibus Legibus.* Early 1st Century CE.

_____. *De Vita Mosis.* Early 1st Century CE.

_____. *Quæstiones et Solutiones: Genesis.* Early 1st Century CE.[376]

_____. *Quod Omnis Probus Liber Sit.* Early 1st Century CE.

Photius, *Bibliotheca (Myriobiblos).* 9th Century CE.

Pliny the Elder. *Historia Naturalis.* 1st Century CE.

Psalms of Solomon. Bet. 48 BCE and 70 CE.[377]

Pseudo-Clement. *Recognitions of Clement.* 2nd – 4th Century CE.

Samaritan Pentateuch. Ca. 122 BCE. Online: https://www.stepbible.org/?q=version=SPMT|reference=Gen.1&options=VUNHG.

Shemoneh Esrei (Amidah). Yavneh: Council of Yavneh, 90 CE.

Shepherd of Hermas. 70-90 CE. As published in J. B. Lightfoot and J. R. Harmer, eds. *The Apostolic Fathers: Greek Texts and English Translations of their Writings.* 2nd Edition. Grand Rapids, Mich.: Baker Book House, 1992; orig. 1891. Pages 329-527.

---

[376] Though all that remains extant of this work is in Latin and Armenian, based on portions of the Exodus counterpart in Greek, it is supposed that this was the language of the original, likely titled *Ζητήματα καὶ Λύσεις.*

[377] Marinus DeJonge, ed., *Outside the Old Testament* (Cambridge: Cambridge University Press, 1985), 160-61.

Sifra. Ca. 250 CE. Online:
http://he.wikisource.org/wiki/ספרא. Cited 21 Mar 2014.

Sifré D'varim. Ca. 250 CE.

Sibylline Oracles. Ca. 115-132 CE.[378]

Talmud Bavli. Koren Edition. Commentary by Adin Even-Israel. Jerusalem: Koren Publishers, 2012.

Talmud Bavli. Vilna Edition. 1880.

Talmud Yerushalmi. Leiden Ms. Oriental 4720. 1289.

Tanakh. Translation of *Masoretic Text.* Jerusalem Publication Society, 1917.

Testament of Abraham. Late 1st Century CE.[379] As published in James, Montague Rhodes. *The Testament of Abraham: The Greek Text Now First Edited with an Introduction and Notes.* Cambridge: Cambridge University Press, 1892. Greek text on pages 77-119.

Testament of Judah. 1st Century BCE.

---

[378] Larry R. Helyer, *Exploring Jewish Literature of the Second Temple Period* (Downers Grove, Ill.: InterVarsity Press, 2002), 443.

[379] Dating estimate from E. P. Sanders, "The Testament of Abraham," in Marinus DeJonge, ed., *Outside the Old Testament* (Cambridge: Cambridge University Press, 1985),56.

Tobit. [380]

Tosefta based on Erfurt Manuscript with Variant Texts. Compiled by Moshe Shmuel Tzuckermandel. Jerusalem, 1963.

Translation of 1 Enoch. Ca. early-to-mid 1st Century CE. As published in Laurence, Richard. *Enoch the Prophet.* Oxford: Parker, 1821.

Translation of *Apocalypse of Abraham.* Ca. 70–150 CE. Online: http://www.pseudepigrapha.com/ pseudepigraphp/Apocalypse_of_Abraham.html. Cited 20 Apr 2017.

Translation of Philo of Alexandria. *Quod Omnis Probus Liber Sit* (Every Good Man is Free). In *The Complete Works of Philo: Complete & Unabridged.* Translated by Charles Duke Yonge. 1854-5.

Translation of *Talmud Bavli.* Translated by Isadore Epstein. Brooklyn, N.Y.: Soncino Press, 1935-1948. Partially online: http://halakhah.com/. Cited 28 Mar 2014.

---

[380] Per George W. E. Nickelsburg, *Jewish Literature between the Bible and the Mishnah: A Historical and Literary Introduction* (2nd ed.; Minneapolis, Minn.: Fortress Press, 2005), 35: "The date of Tobit is uncertain. The last historical event mentioned is the rebuilding of the Jerusalem Temple (515 B.C.E.). We may posit a date before the persecution of the Jews by Antiochus Epiphanes (168 B.C.E.) since the historical summary in chapter 14 makes no reference to it – a glaring omission in a book so concerned with sin, punishment, and Israel's suffering."

Translation of *Talmud Yerushalmi*. Translated by Yosef Gavriel Bechhofer. Online: http://www. yerushalmionline.org/. Cited 24 Mar 2014.

Translation of *Tosefta*. Compiled by Yosef Gavriel Bechhofer. Online: http://www. toseftaonline.org/. Cited 24 Mar 2014.

Wisdom of Ben Sira (Sirach or *Ecclesiasticus).* 196-175 BCE.[381]

Wisdom of Solomon. 100 BCE – 40 CE.[382] Online: http://www.ellopos.net/elpenor/greek-texts/septuagint/chapter.asp?book=29. Cited 19 Apr 2017.

---

[381] Nickelsburg, op. cit., 62-63.

[382] As the author is pseudonymous, dating is difficult. This range is taken from Larry R. Helyer, *Exploring Jewish Literature of the Second Temple Period* (Downers Grove, Ill.: InterVarsity Press, 2002), 290.

SECONDARY SOURCES

Adayemo, Tokunboh (Editor). *Africa Bible Commentary.* Nairobi, Kenya: WordAlive, 2006.

Apple, Raymond. *New Testament People: A Rabbi's Notes.* Bloomington, Ind.: AuthorHouse, 2016.

Auerbach, Leo. *The Babylonian Talmud in Selection.* New York, N.Y.: Philosophical Library, 1944.

Aus, Roger David. *'Caught in the Act', Walking on the Sea, and the Release of Barabbas Revisited.* South Florida Studies in the History of Judaism 157. Atlanta, Ga.: Scholars Press, 1997.

Avery-Peck, Alan J., Editor. *The Review of Rabbinic Judaism: Ancient, Medieval, and Modern.* Martinus Nijhoff Publishers, 2005.

Avi-Yonah, Michael. „Geschichte der Juden im Zeitalter des Talmud." 2nd Edition. *Den Tagen von Rom und Byzanz* XVI (890), 1962.

Avi-Yonah, Michael, &, Zvi Baras, Editors. *The World History of the Jewish People: Sociey. and Religion in the Second Temple Period.* Jerusalem: Massada Publishing Ltd., 1977.

Bacher, Wilhelm. „Die Jüdische Bibelexegese vom Anfange des Zehnten bis zum Ende des Fünfzehnten Jahrhunderts." In Jakob Winter and August Wünsche. *Die Jüdische Literatur seit Abschluss des Kanons: Eine prosaische und poetische Anthologie mit biographischen und litteraturgeschicht-lichen Einleitungen.* Trier: n.p., 1894.

Bailey, Kenneth E. *Jesus through Middle Eastern Eyes.* Downers Grove, Ill.: IVP Academic, 2008.

Bateman, Herbert W., IV. "Early Jewish Hermeneutics and Hebrews 1:5-13." *American University Studies.* Peter Lang Publishers, 1997.

Begg, Christopher T. "Josephus's Portrayal of the Disappearances of Enoch, Elijah and Moses: Some Observations." *Journal of Biblical Literature* 109 (1990): 691-93.

Ben David, Abraham. *Seder haQabbalah L'haRavad.* Jerusalem: 1971.

Ben David, Moshe. *At the Gate of Rome.* Las Vegas, Nev.: CreateSpace, 2012.

Ben Maimon, Moshe (Maimonides, Rambam). "Shloshah Asar Ikkarim." In *Commentary on Mishna Sanhedrin 10:1.* Ca. 1168 CE.

Ben-Shalom, Israel. *The School of Shammai and the Zealots' Struggle against Rome.* Jerusalem: Ben Gurion University of the Negev Press, 1993.

Biale, Rachel. *Women and Jewish Law: The Essential Texts, Their History, and Their Relevance for Today.* New York, N.Y.: Schocken Books, 2011; orig. 1984.

Bildersee, Adele. *Jewish Post-Biblical History through Great Personalities: From Jochanan ben Zakkai to Moses Mendelssohn.* Cincinnati, Oh.: Union of American Hebrew Congregations, 1918.

Black, Matthew. *An Aramaic Approach to the Gospels and Acts.* Oxford: Clarendon Press, 1946.

Boccaccini, Gabriele, Editor. *Enoch and the Messiah Son of Man: Revisiting the Book of Parables.* Grand Rapids, Mich.: Wm. B. Eerdmans, 2007.

Bock, Darrell L. *Blasphemy and Exaltation in Judaism: The Charge against Jesus in Mark 14:53-65.* Eugene, Ore.: Wipf & Stock, 2016; orig. 1998.

_____. "Blasphemy and the Jewish Examination of Jesus." *Bulletin for Biblical Research* 17.1 (2007): 53–114.

Boman, Thorleif. *Das Hebräische Denken im Vergleich mit dem Griechischen.* 2nd Edition. Göttingen: Vandenhoeck & Ruprecht, 1960; orig. 1954.

Bonchek, Avigdor. *Studying the Torah: A Guide to In-Depth Interpretation.* Oxford: Jason Aronson, 1997.

Bousset, Wilhelm. *Die Religion des Judentums im Spät-hellenistischen Zeitalter.* 3rd Edition. Tübingen: Mohr Siebeck, 1926.

Boyarin, Daniel. *A Radical Jew: Paul and the Politics of Identity.* Berkeley, Calif.: University of California Press, 1994.

_____. *The Jewish Gospels: The Story of the Jewish Christ.* New York, N.Y.: The New Press, 2012.

Brewer, David Instone. *Divorce and Remarriage in the Bible: The Social and Literary Context.* Grand Rapids, Mich.: Wm. B. Eerdmans, 2002.

_____. "The Eighteen Benedictions and the Minim before 70 CE." *Journal of Theological Studies* 54 (2003): 25-44.

_____. *Techniques and Assumptions in Jewish Exegesis before 70 CE.* Texte und Studien zum antiken Judentum 30. Tübingen: Mohr-Siebeck, 1992.

_____. *Traditions of the Rabbis from the Era of the New Testament, Volume I: Prayer and Agriculture.* Grand Rapids, Mich.: Wm. B. Eerdmans, 2004.

_____. "The Use of Rabbinic Sources in Gospel Studies." *Tyndale Bulletin* 50.2 (1999): 281-98.

Bromberg, Irv. 30 Sep 2016. "Hebrew Calendar Studies: Why Divide Hours into 1080 Parts?" *University of Toronto website.* Online: http://individual.utoronto.ca/kalendis/hebrew/chelek.htm.

Brown, Michael L. *Answering Jewish Objections to Jesus: Volume 4 – New Testament Objections.* Grand Rapids, Mich: Baker Academic, 2007.

Bruce, Frederick Fyvie (F. F.). Jul-Sep 1984. "Colossians Problems, Part 3: The Colossian Heresy." *Bibliotheca Sacra* 141(563): 195-208.

Büchler, Adolph. *Das Synhedrion in Jerusalem.* Vienna, 1902.

_____. *Studies in Sin and Atonement in the Rabbinic Literature of the First Century.* New York, N.Y.: KTAV Publishing House, 1967; orig. 1927.

Buxbaum, Yitzhak. *The Life and Teachings of Hillel.* Lanham, Md.: Jason Aronson, Inc., 2008.

Carroll, Scott T. *Biblical Backgrounds – Ad Fontes: Back to the Original Sources.* Version 2.1 (DVD). Grand Rapids, Mich.: Cornerstone University, 2007.

_____. Course Materials, *HIS-480: Coptic and Egyptian Christianity.* Grand Rapids, Mich.: Cornerstone University, Fall 2007.

Chancey, Mark A. *The Myth of a Gentile Galilee.* Cambridge: Cambridge University Press, 2002.

Charlesworth, James H. *Jesus and the Dead Sea Scrolls: The Controversy Resolved.* New Haven and London: Yale University Press, 1992.

_____. *Jesus within Judaism:New Light from Exciting Archaeological Discoveries.* New York, N.Y.: Doubleday, 1988.

_____. *Jesus' Jewishness: Exploring the Place of Jesus within Early Judaism.* New York, N.Y.: Crossroad Herder, 1996; orig. 1991.

_____. "John the Baptizer and Qumran Barriers in Light of the Rule of the Community," in Perry, Donald W., & Ulrich, Eugene (Editors). *The Provo International Conference on the Dead Sea Scrolls: Technological Innovations, New Texts, and Reformulated Issues.* Studies on the Texts of the Desert of Judah 30; Leiden: E. J. Brill, 1999.

Charlesworth, James H. & Loren L. Johns. *Hillel and Jesus: Comparisons of Two Major Religious Leaders.* Minneapolis, Minn.: Fortress Press, 1997.

Charlesworth, James H., Hermann Lichtenberger, and Gerbern S. Oegema, Editors. *Qumran-Messianism: Studies on the Messianic Expectations in the Dead Sea Scrolls.* Tübingen: Mohr Siebeck, 1998.

Chase, Debra A. "A Note on an Inscription from Kuntillet ʿAjrūd." *Bulletin of the American Schools of Oriental Research* 246 (1982): 63-67.

Cohen, Abraham. *Everyman's Talmud.* New York: Schocken Books, 1949; orig. 1931.

_____. "Jesus' Defence of the Resurrection of the Dead." *Journal for the Study of the New Testament* 4, no. 11 (1981): 64-73.

Cohen, Shaye. "The Place of the Rabbi in Jewish Society of the Second Century." In Lee I. Levine, Editor. *The Galilee in Late Antiquity.* New York, N.Y.: Jewish Theological Seminary Press, 1992.

Cook, Edward M. "4Q246." *Bulletin for Biblical Research* 5 (1995): 43-66.

Cutler, Allan. "Does the Simeon of Luke 2 Refer to Simeon the Son of Hillel?" *Journal of the American Academy of Religion* 34, no. 1 (1966): 29-35.

Davies, William David, Louis Finkelstein, & Steven T. Katz (Editors). *The Cambridge History of Judaism.* Volume 4: The Late Roman-Rabbinic Period.

Cambridge: Cambridge University Press, 2006; orig. 1984.

Davies, Philip R. "The Prehistory of the Qumran Community," *The Dead Sea Scrolls: Fory. Years of Research.* Edited by Devorah Dimant and Uriel Rappaport. Jerusalem: Magnes Press, 1992.

DeJonge, Marinus, Editor. *Outside the Old Testament.* Cambridge: Cambridge University Press, 1985.

Delitzsch, Franz. *Isaiah.* Keil-Delitzsch Old Testament Commentary 7. Edinburgh: T. & T. Clark, 1866.

_____. *Jesus und Hillel.* 2nd Revised Edition. Erlangen: Verlag von A. Deichert, 1867.

Del Medico, Henri E. *The Riddle of the Scrolls.* London: Burke, 1958.

DePuy, W. H. *People's Cyclopedia of Universal Knowledge: with numerous appendixes invaluable for reference in all departments of industrial life.* 3 Volumes. New York, N.Y.: Phillips & Hunt, 1883.

Derenbourgh, Joseph Naftali. *Essai sur l'Histoire et la Géographie de la Palestine d'Après les Thalmuds et les Autres Sources Rabbiniques Vol. I: Histoire de la Palestine.* Paris, 1867.

_____. "Mélanges Rabbiniques III: Quelques Observations sur le Rituel." *Revue des Études Juives* 14 (1893):26-32.

DeVaux, Roland. *Archaeology and the Dead Sea Scrolls: The Schweich Lectures 1959*. London: Oxford University Press, 1973.

Dinar (דינר), Eliezer ben Avraham Moshe. יוסף צבי הכהן קאטצבורג מנחם. Berlin: זכרון, 1933.

Driver, Godfrey Rolles. *The Judaean Scrolls: The Problem and a Solution*. Oxford: B. Blackwell, 1965.

Dunn, James D. G. *The Epistles to the Colossians and to Philemon: A Commentary on the Greek Text.* Grand Rapids, Mich.: Wm. B. Eerdmans, 1996.

Dupont-Sommer, André. *The Essene Writings from Qumran*. Translated by Geza Vermes. Oxford: B. Blackwell, 1961.

Edersheim, Alfred. *The Life and Times of Jesus the Messiah*. 2 Volumes. Oxford: Longmans, Green, and Company, 1883.

Eisenberg, Ronald L. *Essential Figures in the Talmud*. Lanham, Md.: Jason Aronson, Inc., 2013.

Eisenman, Robert H. *James the Brother of Jesus: The Key to Unlocking the Secrets of Early Christianity and the Dead Sea Scrolls*. New York, N.Y.: Viking Press, 1997.

_____. "Sicarii Essenes, 'Those of the Circumcision,' and Qumran." *Journal of Higher Criticism* 12 (Spring 2006): 17-28.

Elledge, Casey D. *Resurrection of the Dead in Early Judaism: 200 BCE – CE 200*. Oxford: Oxford University Press, 2017.

Elliott, James Keith *The Apocryphal New Testament*. Oxford: Clarendon Press, 2005; orig. 1993.

Emerton, John Adney. "The Origin of the Son of Man Imagery." Journal of Theological Studies 9 (1958):225-242.

Falk, Harvey. *Jesus the Pharisee: A New Look at the Jewishness of Jesus*. Eugene, Ore.: Wipf & Stock, 2003; orig. 1985.

Farmer, Kathleen A. *Who Knows What is Good? A Commentary on the Books of Proverbs and Ecclesiastes*. Grand Rapids, Mich.: Wm. B. Eerdmans, 1991.

Fiensy, David A., and James Riley Strange (Editors). *Galilee in the Late Second Temple and Mishnaic Periods Life Culture, and Society*. Volume 1. Minneapolis, Minn.: Fortress Press, 2014.

Fischler, Ben-Zion. 5 Jun 2003. "Rabbi Akiva and his Women." *HaAretz*. Online: http://www.haaretz.com/rabbi-akiva-and-his-women-1.90450. Accessed 1 Apr 2017.

Fleury , M. L'abbe. *Ecclesiastical History*. Translated by John Henry Parker. London: J. F. G. & J. Rivington, 1843, orig. 429 CE.

Flusser, David. „Die jüdische Messiaserwartung Jesu." Pages 37-52 in *Das Christentum: Eine jüdische Religion*. Munich, 1990.

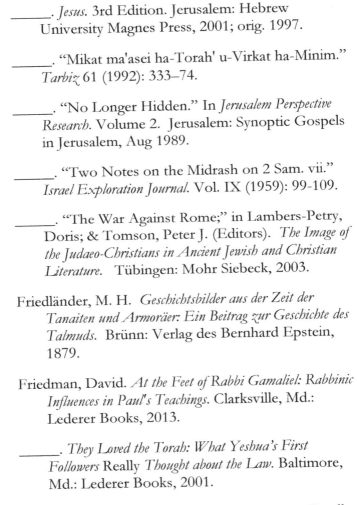

_____. *Jesus*. 3rd Edition. Jerusalem: Hebrew University Magnes Press, 2001; orig. 1997.

_____. "Mikat ma'asei ha-Torah' u-Virkat ha-Minim." *Tarbiz* 61 (1992): 333–74.

_____. "No Longer Hidden." In *Jerusalem Perspective Research*. Volume 2. Jerusalem: Synoptic Gospels in Jerusalem, Aug 1989.

_____. "Two Notes on the Midrash on 2 Sam. vii." *Israel Exploration Journal*. Vol. IX (1959): 99-109.

_____. "The War Against Rome;" in Lambers-Petry, Doris; & Tomson, Peter J. (Editors). *The Image of the Judaeo-Christians in Ancient Jewish and Christian Literature*. Tübingen: Mohr Siebeck, 2003.

Friedländer, M. H. *Geschichtsbilder aus der Zeit der Tanaiten und Armoräer: Ein Beitrag zur Geschichte des Talmuds*. Brünn: Verlag des Bernhard Epstein, 1879.

Friedman, David. *At the Feet of Rabbi Gamaliel: Rabbinic Influences in Paul's Teachings*. Clarksville, Md.: Lederer Books, 2013.

_____. *They Loved the Torah: What Yeshua's First Followers Really Thought about the Law*. Baltimore, Md.: Lederer Books, 2001.

Friedman, Shamma. "A Good Story Deserves Retelling – the Unfolding of the Akiva Legend." *Jewish Studies: An Internet Journal* 3 (2004): 55-93. Online: http://www.biu.ac.il/JS/JSIJ/3-2004/Friedman.pdf. Cited 11 May 2017.

Friedman, Shammai. *Sefer Beit Shammai*. Krakow, Poland, 1930.

Galambush, Julie. *The Reluctant Parting: How the New Testament's Jewish Writers Created a Christian Book*. New York, N.Y.: HarperOne, 2006.

Geiger, Abraham. *Das Judenthum und seine Geschichte in zwölf Vorlesungen*. Breslau: Verlag der Schletter' schen Buchhandlung, 1864.

Gershfield, Edward M. "Hillel, Shammai, and the Three Proselytes." *Conservative Judaism* 31, no. 3 (Spring 1967): 29-39.

Gilat, Yitzhak D. R. *Eliezer ben Hyrcanus: A Scholar Outcast*. Bar-Ilan Studies in Near Eastern Languages and Culture. Bar-Ilan University Press, 1984.

Ginsberg, H. L. "The Oldest Interpretation of the Suffering Servant," *Vetus Testamentum* 3 (1953): 400-404.

Gmirkin, Russell. 1996. "The War Scroll and Roman Weaponry Reconsidered." *Dead Sea Discoveries* 3(2): 89-129.

Goldingay, John. "Biblical Narrative and Systematic Theology." In *Between Two Horizons: Spanning New Testament Studies and Systematic Theology*. Edited by Joel B. Green and Max Turner; Grand Rapids, Mich.: Wm.B. Eerdmans, 2000. Pages 123-42.

Goldwurm, Hersh, and Meir Holder. *History of the Jewish People: The Second Temple Era.* Brooklyn, N.Y.: Mesorah Publications: 1982.

Goodblatt, David. *Rabbinic Instruction in Sasanian Babylonia.* Leiden: E. J. Brill, 1975.

Goodman, Martin David. "Sadducees and Essenes after 70 CE." 1994; reproduced on pages 153-162 in Martin David Goodman. *Judaism in the Roman World: Collected Essays.* Leiden: E. J. Brill, 2007.

Goshen-Gottstein, Alon. "God and Israel as Father and Son in Tannaitic Literature." Ph.D. dissertation; Hebrew University of Jerusalem, 1986.

Grätz, Heinrich. *Geschichte der Juden von den ältesten Zeiten bis auf die Gegenwart.* Improved and extended edition. Leipzig: Oskar Leiner, 1900.

Gundry, Robert H. *Matthew: A Commentary on His Literary and Theological Art.* Grand Rapids, Mich.: Wm. B. Eerdmans, 1982.

Hahn-Tapper, Aaron J. *Judaisms: A Tweny.-First-Century Introduction to Jews and Jewish Identities.* Oakland, Calif.: University of California Press, 2016.

Harris, Stephen L. *Understanding the Bible.* Palo Alto, Ca.: Mayfield, 1985.

Harvey, Ralph V. *Rabban Gamaliel.* Xulon Press, 2005.

Hegg, Timothy J. *The Letter Writer: Paul's Background and Torah Perspective.* Marshfield, Mo.: First Fruits of Zion, 2002.

Helyer, Larry R. *Exploring Jewish Literature of the Second Temple Period.* Downers Grove, Ill.: InterVarsity Press, 2002.

Hengel, Martin. "The Effective History of Isaiah 53 in the Pre-Christian Period." In *The Suffering Servant: Isaiah 53 in Jewish and Christian Sources.* Edited by Bernd Janowski & Peter Stuhlmacher. Grand Rapids, Mich.: Wm. B. Eerdmans, 2004.

_____. *Judentum und Hellenismus: Studien zu ihrer Begegnung unter besonderer Berücksichtigung Palästinas bis zur Mitte des Zwei Jahrhunderts vor Christus.* Wissenschaftliche Untersuchungen zum Neuen Testament 10. Tübingen: Mohr Siebeck, 1969.

Henshke, David. "Minhag mevatel halakha? (Le-ishushah shel hash'arah)." *Dine Israel* 17(1994): 135-54.

Hertz, J. H. *The Pentateuch and Haftorahs.* 2nd Edition. London: Soncino Press, 1985; orig. 1971.

Heschel, Abraham Joshua. *Torah min haShamayim baAspaklaria shel haDorot.* 3 Volumes. London: Soncino Press, 1962-65.

Hézser, Catherine. *The Social Structure of the Rabbinic Movement in Roman Palestine.* Tübingen: Mohr-Siebeck, 1997.

Hidary, Richard. *Dispute for the Sake of Heaven: Legal Pluralism in the Talmud.* Brown Judaic Studies 353. Providence, R.I.: Brown University, 2010.

Hirschman, Yizhar. *Qumran in Context: Reassessing the Archaeological Evidence.* Peabody, Mass.: Hendrickson, 2004.

Holder, Meir. *History of the Jewish People: From Yavneh to Pumbedisa.* Brooklyn, N.Y.: Mesorah Publications, 1986.

Holtz, Barry W. *Rabbi Akiva: Sage of the Talmud.* Jewish Lives. New Haven, Conn. and London: Yale University Press, 2017.

Horbury, William. *Messianism among Jews and Christians: Twelve Biblical and Historical Studies.* London and New York: T & T Clark, 2003.

Horner, Barry E. *Future Israel: Why Christian Anti-Judaism Must be Challenged.* NAC Studies in Bible & Theology; Nashville, Tenn.: B&H Academic, 2007.

Hurtado, Larry W. *One God, One Lord: Early Christian Devotion and Ancient Jewish Monotheism.* 2nd Edition. London and New York: T & T Clark, 1998.

Hurtado, Larry W. and Paul L. Owen, Editors. *Who is This Son of Man'? The Latest Scholarship on a Puzzling Expression of the Historical Jesus.* London and New York: T & T Clark, 2011.

Hutterer, Natan. *Die Mittelalterlichen Jüd: Komentare zu den Ebed-JHWH-Liedern des Jesaja.* S. Jacobowitz, 1938.

Isaacs, Nathan. "The Law and the 'Law of Change.'" *University of Pennsylvania Law Review* 65 (1917): 659-79, 748-63.

Jacobovici, Simcha. "Jesus Discovered in Dead Sea Scrolls," *Times of Israel.* 25 Mar 2016.

Jacobs, Louis. *The Jewish Religion: A Companion.* Oxford: Oxford University Press, 1995.

Jastrow, Morris Jr. *Hebrew and Babylonian Traditions: The Haskell Lectures.* New York, N.Y.: Charles Scribner's Sons, 1914.

Juel, Donald. *Messiah and the Temple: The Trial of Jesus in the Gospel of Mark.* SBLDS 31; Missoula, Mont.: Scholars Press, 1977.

Karo, Yosef of Safed. *Shulchan Arukh.* Israel, ca. 1560.

Kasher, Aryeh. *Jews, Idumæans, and Ancient Arabs: Relations of the Jews in Erets-Israel with the Nations of the Frontier and Desert during the Hellenistic and Roman Era (332 BCE – 70 CE).* Texte und Studien zum Antiken Judentum 18; Tübingen: J. C. B. Mohr, 1988.

Kennedy, David B. Course lectures. *BBL-642: Old Testament Exegesis III – Prophets & Writings.* Grand Rapids, Mich.: Grand Rapids Theological Seminary, Fall 2009.

Kirsch,Jonathan. *The Woman who Laughed at God: The Untol History of the Jewish People*. New York, N.Y.: Penguin Group, 2001.

Kimelman, Reuven. "Birkat Ha-Minim and the Lack of Evidence for an Anti-Christian Jewish Prayer in Late Antiquity." In E. P. Sanders, et al., Editors. *Jewish and Christian Self-Definition Volume 2: Aspects of Judaism in the Greco-Roman Period*. London, 1981.

Klausner, Yosef Gedaliah. *Mi-Yeshu ad Paulus* . London: Allen & Unwin, 1939.

_____. "The Rise of Christianity." In Michael Avi-Yonah, & Zvi Baras, Editors. *The World History of the Jewish People: Society and Religion in the Second Temple Period*. Jerusalem: Massada Publishing Ltd., 1977.

_____. *Yeshu ha-Notzri: Zemanno, Chayyav ve-Torato*. Jerusalem: Shtibel, 1922.

Koch, Klaus. „Der König als Sohn Gottes in Ägypten und Israel." In „*Mein Sohn bist Du" (Ps 2,7): Studien zu den Königspsalmen*. Edited by Eckart Otto and Erich Zenger. Stuttgarter Bibel-Studien 192. Stuttgart: Verlag Katholisches Bibelwerk, 2002.

_____. „Messias und Menschensohn." In *Vor der Wende der Zeiten: Beiträge zur apokalyptischen Literatur*. Neukirchen-Vluyn: Neukirchener, 1996.

Koppel, Moshe. *Meta-Halakhah*. Northvale, N.J.: Jason Aronson, Inc., 1997.

Krummacher, Friedrich Adolphus. *Parabeln.* Essen und Duisburg: G. D. Badefer, 1817.

Lange, Armin, Emanuel Tov, and Matthias Weigold. *The Dead Sea Scrolls in Context: Integrating the Dead Sea Scrolls in the Study of Ancient Texts, Languages, and Cultures.* Leiden: E. J. Brill, 2011.

Langer, Ruth. *Cursing the Christians? A History of the Birkat HaMinim.* Oxford: Oxford University Press, 2012.

Lapide, Pinchas. *The Resurrection of Jesus: A Jewish Perspective.* Eugene, Or.: Wipf & Stock Publishers, 2002.

Lapide, Pinchas and Jurgen Moltmann. *Jüdischer Monotheismus, christliche Trinitätslehre: Ein Gespräche.* Munich: Chr. Kaiser Verlag, 1979.

Levey, Samson H. *The Messiah: An Aramaic Interpretation – The Messianic Exegesis of the Targum.* Hebrew Union College Monographs 2. Cincinnati, Oh.: Hebrew Union College/Jewish Institute of Religion, 1974.

Levine, Amy-Jill. "A Jewish take on Jesus: Jesus was smack in the middle of the Jewish tradition of his time. Remembering that can make you a better Christian, says this Jewish scholar of the New Testament." *U.S. Catholic* 77, no. 10 (Oct 2012): 18.

_____. *The Misunderstood Jew: The Church and the Scandal of the Jewish Jesus.* New York, N.Y.: HarperOne, 2006.

Levine, Lee. *Judaism and Hellenism in Antiquity: Conflict or Confluence?* Peabody, Mass.: Hendrickson Publishers, 1999; orig. 1998.

Lichtenstein-Herschensohn, Yechiel Tzvi. *Kommentar zum Neuen Testament in 8 Heften.* Leipzig: Institutum Judaicum Delitzschianum, 1904.

Lightfoot, John. *Horæ Hebraicæ et Talmudicæ: Hebrew and Talmudical Exercitations Upon the Gospels, the Acts, Some Chapters of St. Paul's Epistle to the Romans, and the First Epistle to the Corinthians.* 4 Volumes. Oxford: Oxford University Press, 1859; orig. 1675.

Lightner, Robert P. *Handbook of Evangelical Theology: A Historical, Biblical, and Contemporary Survey and Review.* Grand Rapids, Mich.: Kregel Publications, 1995.

Lipschits, Oded. *The Fall and Rise of Jerusalem.* Winona Lake, Ind.: Eisenbrauns, 2005.

Long, Phillip J. 7 Sep 2011. "Paul: At the Feet of Gamaliel?" *Reading Acts.* Online: http://readingacts.com/2011/09/07/paul-at-the-feet-of-gamaliel/.

Lorberbaum, Yair. "*Imago Dei* in Judaism: Early Rabbinic Literature, Philosophy, and Kabbalah." Pages 57-74 in Peter Koslowski, editor. *The Concept of God, the Origin of the World, and the Image of the Human in the World Religions.* Dortrecht: Kluwer Academic, 2001.

_____. *In God's Image: Myth, Theology, and Law in Classical Judaism*. New York, N.Y.: Cambridge University Press, 2015.

MacDonald, John. *The Theology of the Samaritans*. SCM Press, 1964.

Marmorstein, Arthur. *The Doctrine of Merits in Old Rabbinical Literature*. No. 7. Oxford: Oxford University Press, 1920.

McCall, Thomas S. Mar 1996. "Was Luke a Gentile?" *Levitt Letter* 18(3). Online: http://www.levitt.com/essays/luke. Cited 23 Mar 2014.

McRay, John. *Paul: His Life and Teaching*. Grand Rapids, Mich.: Baker Academic, 2003.

Mendelssohn, Moses. *Jerusalem, or On Religious Power and Judaism*. Translated by Allan Arkush. Waltham, Mass.: Brandeis University Press, 2013; orig. 1783.

Mettinger, Tryggve N. D. *A Farewell to the Servant Songs: A Critical Examination of an Exegetical Axiom*. CWK Gleerup, 1983.

Mitchell, David C. "Messiah bar Ephraim in the Targums." *Aramaic Studies* 4 (2006): 225-245.

_____. "Messiah ben Joseph: A Scacrifice of Atonement for Israel." *Review of Rabbinic Judaism* 10 (2007): 77-94.

Mohrmann, Douglas C. Course lectures. *New Testament Survey*. Grand Rapids, Mich.: Cornerstone University, Fall 2004.

Moseley, Ronald Wayne. *Yeshua: A Guide to the Real Jesus and the Original Church*. Clarksville, Md.: Lederer Books, 1996.

Nesbit, Edward Planta. *Jesus an Essene*. London: Simpkin, Marshall, Hamilton, Kent, & Co., 1895.

Neusner, Jacob. *Early Rabbinic Judaism: Historical Studies in Religion, Literature, and Art*. Studies in Judaism in Late Antiquity 13. Leiden: E. J. Brill, 1975.

_____. *First-Century Judaism in Crisis: Yohanan ben Zakkai and the Renaissance of Torah*. Augmented Edition. Eugene, Ore.: Wipf & Stock, 2006; orig. 1975.

_____. *Judaism when Christianity Began: A Survey of Belief and Practice*. Louisville, Ky.: Westminster John Knox Press, 2002.

_____. *A Life of Rabban Yochanan ben Zakkai: Circa 1-80 CE*. 2nd Edition. Leiden: E. J. Brill, 1970.

_____. *The Mishnah: An Introduction*. Lanham, Md.: Jason Aronson, Inc., 1994.

_____. *Narrative and Document in the Rabbinic Canon: The Two Talmuds*. 2 Volumes. Lanham, Md.: University Press of America, 2010.

_____. *A Rabbi Talks with Jesus: An Intermil-lenial, Inter-faith Exchange.* New York, N.Y.: Doubleday, 1993.

_____. *Rabbinic Literature: An Essential Guide.* Nashville, Tenn.: Abingdon Press, 2005.

_____. *Rabbinic Traditions about the Pharisees before 70.* 2 Volumes. Eugene, Ore.: Wipf & Stock, 2005; orig. 1971.

Nickelsburg, George W. E. *Jewish Literature between the Bible and the Mishnah: A Historical and Literary Introduction.* 2nd Edition. Minneapolis, Minn.: Fortress Press, 2005.

North, Christopher R. *The Suffering Servant in Deutero-Isaiah: An Historical and Critical Study.* Oxford: Oxford University Press, 1956.

Novak, David. *The Sanctity of Human Life.* Washington, D.C.: Georgetown University Press, 2009.

Oakes, Christina. *God: Getting to Know Him – Experiencing God through His Names and Titles.* BookBaby, 2016.

Pardee, Dennis and S. David Sperling. *Handbook of Ancient Hebrew Letters: A Study Edition.* Society of Biblical Literature Sources for Biblical Study 15. Chico, Calif.: Scholars Press, 1982.

Pasachoff, Naomi E. & Littman, Robert J. *A Concise History of the Jewish People.* Lanham, Md.: Rowman & Littlefield, 2005.

Pick, Bernhard. Apr 1886. "Old Testament Passages Messianically Applied by the Ancient Synagogue." *Hebraica* II(3): 129-139.

Pines, Shlomo. "The Jewish Christians of the Early Centuries of Christianity According to a New Source." In *Proceedings of the Israel Academy of Sciences and Humanities.* Volume 2, No. 13. Jerusalem, 1966.

Pfeifer, Gerhard. *Ursprung und Wesen der Hypostasenvorstellungen im Judentum.* Arbeiten zur Theologie 31. Stuttgart: Calwer Verlag, 1967.

Polhill, John B. *Paul and his Letters.* Nashville, Tenn.: B&H Academic, 1999.

Porter, Stanley E. *The Criteria for Authenticity in Historical-Jesus Research: Previous Discussion and New Proposals.* London: T & T Clark, 2004.

Price, Nelson L. *The Chronicles of Nicodemus.* Metairie, La.: Journey Publications, 2008.

Reed, Annette Yoshiko. "Old Testament Pseudepigrapha and Post-70 Judaism." In Simon C. Mimouni, Bernard Pouderon, and Claire Clivas, Editors. *Les Judaïsmes dans tous Leurs États aux Ier-IIIe Siècles (Les Judéens des Synagogues, les Chrétiens et les Rabbins).* Judaïsme Ancien et Origines du Christianisme 5. Paris: Brepols, 2015.

Regev, Eyal. *Sectarianism in Qumran: A Cross-Cultural Perspective.* Berlin: Walter de Gruyter GmbH., 2007.

Rendsburg, Gary A. "The Galilean Background of Mishnaic Hebrew." Pages 225-40 in Lee I. Levine, Editor. *The Galilee in Late Antiquity*. New York, N.Y.: Jewish Theological Seminary Press, 1992.

_____. "Rise of the Jewish Sects." *Dead Sea Scrolls*. Chantilly, Va.: The Great Courses, 2010. DVD.

Richards, E. Randolph and Brandon J. O'Brien. *Misreading Scripture with Western Eyes: Removing Cultural Blinders to Better Understand the Bible*. Downers Grove, Ill.: IVP Books, 2012.

Roth, Cecil. *Historical Background of the Dead Sea Scrolls*. Oxford: B. Blackwell, 1958.

Sagan, Carl. *Broca's Brain: Reflections on the Romance of Science*. New York, N.Y.: Presidio Press, 1980 orig. 1974.

Salway, Benet. 1994. "What's in a name? A Survey of Roman Onomastic practice from c.700 B.C. to 700 A.D." Pages 124-45 in *Journal of Roman Studies, 84.*

Sanders, E. P. *Judaism: Practice & Belief, 63 BCE – 66CE*. London: SCM Press, 2005; orig. 1992.

Saunders, Ernest W. "The Colossian Heresy and Qumran Theology."*Studies in the History and Text of the New Testament in honor of Kenneth Willis Clark* (1967): 133-45.

Schäfer, Peter. *Der Bar Kokhba Aufstand: Studien zum zweiten jüdischen Krieg gegen Rom*. Texte und Studien zum antiken Judentum 1. Tübingen: Mohr Siebeck, 1981.

_____. *Jesus in the Talmud*. Princeton, N.J.: Princeton University Press, 2007.

_____. *Rivalität zwischen Engeln und Menschen: Unter-suchungen zur Rabbinischen Engelvorstellung*. Berlin & New York: Walter de Gruyter GmbH & Co., 1975.

Schaff, Philip. *History of the Christian Church: Volume I*. 3rd Revised Edition. New York, N.Y.: Charles Scribner's Sons, 1890; orig. 1858.

Schauss, Hayyim. *The Jewish Festivals: A Guide to their History and Observance*. New York, N.Y.: Schocken Books, 1938.

Schiffman, Lawrence H. "Merkavah Speculation at Qumran: the 4Q Serekh Shirot `Olat HaShab-bat." Pages 15-47 in *Mystics, Philosophers, and Politicians: Essays in Jewish Intellectual History in Honor of Alexander Altmann*. Edited by J. Reinharz and D. Swetschinski. Duke University Press, 1982.

Schiffman, Lawrence H., Emanuel Tov, James C. VanderKam, Editors. *The Dead Sea Scrolls Fifty Years After Their Discovery*. Jerusalem: Israel Exploration Society, 2000.

Schiffman, Lawrence H. and James C. VanderKam, Editors. *The Encyclopedia of the Dead Sea Scrolls*. Oxford: Oxford University Press, 2000.

Schofer, Jonathan Wyn. *The Making of a Sage: A Study in Rabbinic Ethics.* Madison, Wisc.: University of Wisconsin Press, 2005.

Schürer, Emil. *Geschichte des jüdischen Volkes im Zeitalter Jesu Christi.* 5 Volumes. Leipzig, Germany: J. C. Hindriks'sche Buchhandlung, 1898.

Shalit, Ioseph ben Iacob *Mantua Haggadah.* 2nd Edition. Padua, 1568.

Shapira, Itzhak. *Return of the Kosher Pig: The Divine Messiah in Jewish Thought.* Clarksville, Md.: Lederer Books, 2013.

Sjöberg, Erik. *Der Menschensohn in dem Äthiopischen Henochbuch.* Lund: C. W. K. Gleerup, 1946.

Skarsaune, Oskar. *In the Shadow of the Temple: Jewish Influences on Early Christianity.* Downers Grove, Ill.: IVP Academic, 2002.

Sneed, Mark R. *The Social World of the Sages: An Introduction to Israelite and Jewish Wisdom Literature.* Minneapolis, Minn.: Fortress Press, 2015.

Soloveitchik, Joseph B. *The Rav Speaks.* Brooklyn, N.Y.: Judaica Press, 2002.

Spolsky, Bernard. *The Languages of the Jews: A Sociolinguistic History.* Cambridge: Cambridge University Press, 2014.

Steinsaltz, Adin. *Talmudic Images.* Northvale, N.J.: Jason Aronson, Inc., 1997.

Stendahl, Krister. *The School of St. Matthew and its Use of the Old Testament.* Uppsala: Almqvist & Wiksell, 1954.

Stern, David H. *Jewish New Testament Commentary.* Clarksville, Md.: JNTP. 1992.

Strack, Hermann Lebrecht & Günter Stemberger, *Einleitung in Talmud und Midrasch.* München: C. H. Beck'sche Verlagsbuchhandlung, 1921; orig. 1887.

Strelan, Rick. *Luke the Priest: The Authority of the Author of the Third Gospel.* Burlington, Vt.: Ashgate Publishing, 2008.

Stuart, Moses. *A Commentary on the Apocalypse.* Andover, N.Y.: Allen, Morrill, and Wardwell, 1845.

Sweeney, Marvin A. *Tanak: A Theological and Critical Introduction to the Jewish Bible.* Minneapolis, Minn.: Fortress Press, 2012.

Tabor, James D. 1992. "A Pierced or Piercing Messiah? - The Verdict Is Still Out." *Biblical Archaeology Review* 18(6): 58-59.

Taylor, Charles. *Sayings of the Jewish Fathers.* Cambridge, UK: Deighton, Bell, & Co., 1877.

Telushkin, Joseph. *A Code of Jewish Ethics Volume 1: You Shall Be Holy.* New York, N.Y.: Crown Publishing, 2006.

_____. *A Code of Jewish Ethics Volume 2: Love Your Neighbor as Yourself.* New York, N.Y.: Crown Publishing, 2009.

_____. *Hillel: If Not Now, When?* New York, N.Y.: Schocken Books, 2010.

Thiering, Barbara E. *Jesus and the Riddle of the Dead Sea Scrolls: Unlocking The Secrets of His Life Story.* New York, N.Y.: Doubleday, 1992.

Tice, Brian. "Eden as a Garden Temple." *Emunah BiY'shua.* 2011. Online: https://adiakrisis.files.wordpress.com/2014/10/eden-as-a-garden-temple.pdf.

_____. "'Names' of False Deities in the Bible." 15 Nov 2011. Online: https://www.facebook.com/notes/brian-tice/names-of-false-deities-in-the-bible/10150365099831825.

_____. "The Sayings and Prayer of Agur: The Possibility of Gentile Wisdom in Proverbs 30:1-14." Written for BBL-501 – Biblical Hermeneutics. Grand Rapids, Mich.: Grand Rapids Theological Seminary, 2008 unpublished.

_____. "Who or What were the Nephilim?" *Emunah BiY'shua.* 2011. Online: https://adiakrisis.files.wordpress.com/2014/10/imti-sons-of-g-d-study.pdf.

Tripolitis, Antonía. *Religions of the Hellenistic-Roman Age.* Grand Rapids, Mich.: Wm. B. Eerdmans, 2002.

Tsedaka, Benyamin. *The Israelite Samaritan Version of the Torah*. Grand Rapids, Mich.: Wm. B. Eerdmans, 2013.

Tov, Emanuel. *Textual Criticism of the Hebrew Bible*. Minneapolis, Minn.: Fortress Press, 1992.

Tucker, Wade Dennis Jr. "Daniel: History of Interpretation." Pages 123-132 in *Dictionary of the Old Testament Prophets*. Downers Grove, Ill.: IVP Academic, 2012..

Urbach, Ephraim E. *The Sages: Their Concepts and Beliefs*. Jerusalem: Hebrew University Magnes Press, 1971.

van der Horst, Pieter Willem. "The Birkat ha-minim in Recent Research." *Hellenism – Judaism – Christianity: Essays on their Interaction*. 2nd Edition. Leuven: Peeters, 1998.

Van Pelt, Miles V. *Basics of Biblical Aramaic*. Grand Rapids, Mich.: Zondervan, 2011.

VanderKam, James C. *The Dead Sea Scrolls Today*. Grand Rapids, Mich.: Wm. B. Eerdmans, 1994.

Vizetelly, Frank H, Editor. *Jewish Encyclopedia*. Funk & Wagnall, 1906.

Wallace, Daniel B. 2 Jun 2004. "Why I Do Not Think the King James Bible Is the Best Translation Available Today." Bible.org. Online: https://bible.org/article/why-i-do-not-think-king-james-bible-best-translation-available-today. Cited 18 May 2014.

Waltke, Bruce K. "Agur's Hebrew Words for "Words". Pages 137-39 in Milton Eng and Lee M. Fields, editors. *Devotions on the Hebrew Bible: 54 Reflections to Inspire and Instruct.* Grand Rapids, Mich.: Zondervan, 2015.

Wein, Berel. "Rabbi Akiva." *The Voice of Jewish History.* Cited 25 Mar 2014. Online: http://rabbiwein. com.

Weitzman, Steve. "Why did the Qumran Community write in Hebrew?" *Journal of the American Oriental Society* 119 (1989): 35-45.

Welker, Bill. 13 Apr 2017. Personal Correspondence.

Welker, Carmen. *Should Christians be Torah Observant?* 2nd Edition. Sedro-Woolley, Wash.: Netzari Press, 2008.

Wilson, Marvin R. *Our Father Abraham: Jewish Roots of the Christian Faith.* Grand Rapids, Mich.: Wm. B. Eerdmans, 1989.

Wimpfheimer, Barry Scott. Narrating the Law: A Poetics of Talmudic Legal Stories. Philadelphia: University of Pennsylvania Press, 2011.

Witherington, Ben III. *Jesus the Sage: The Pilgrimage of Wisdom.* Minneapolis, Minn.: Augsburg Fortress, 2000.

Wood, Leon J. *A Survey of Israel's History: Revised and Enlarged Edition.* Grand Rapids, Mich.: Zondervan, 1986; orig. 1970.

Wright, N. T. *What Saint Paul Really Said: Was Paul of Tarsus the Real Founder of Christianity?* Grand Rapids, Mich.: Wm. B. Eerdmans, 1997.

Yadin, Azzan. "Rabban Gamliel, Aphrodite's Bath, and the Question of Pagan Monotheism." *Jewish Quarterly Review* 96, no. 2 (2006): 149-79.

Yitzchaqi, Shlomo (Rashi). *Tractate Sanhedrin with Rashi commentary and Tosafot.* Italy: Gershom ben Moshe Soncino, 1497.

_____. "Commentary on *Yeshayahu* 53." Online: http://www.chabad.org/library/bible_cdo/aid/1 1598/jewish/Chapter-53.htm#showrashi=true. Cited 21 Mar 2014.

Young, Brad H. *Jesus the Jewish Theologian.* Peabody, Mass.: Hendrickson Publishers, 1995.

_____. *Meet the Rabbis: Rabbinic Thought and the Teachings of Jesus.* Grand Rapids, Mich.: Baker Academic, 2007.

_____. *The Parables: Jewish Tradition and Christian Interpretation.* Grand Rapids, Mich.: Baker Academic, 1998.

Zetterholm, Karin Hedner. *Jewish Interpretation of the Bible: Ancient and Contemporary.* Minneapolis, Minn.: Fortress Press, 2012.

Zetterholm, Magnus (Editor). *The Messiah in Early Judaism and Christianity.* Minneapolis, Minn.: Fortress Press, 2007.

Zevit, Ziony. *The Religions of Ancient Israel: A Synthesis of Parallactic Approaches.* London and New York: Continuum, 2001.

REFERENCE WORKS

Bauer, Walter, F. W. Danker, W. F. Arndt, and F. W. Gingrich. *A Greek-English Lexicon of the New Testament and other Early Christian Literature*. 3rd Edition. Chicago, Ill.: University of Chicago Press, 2000; orig. 1957.

Boyd, James P. *Dennison Bible Dictionary*. Baltimore, Md.: Ottenheimer Publishers, 1958.

Brown, Francis, Samuel Rolles Driver, and Charles A. Briggs. *The Brown-Driver-Briggs Hebrew and English Lexicon*. Boston, Mass.: Houghton, Mifflin, and Company, 1906.

Cohn-Sherbok, Daniel M. *Dictionary of Jewish Biography*. London: Continuum, 2005.

Crum, Walter Ewing. *A Coptic Dictionary*. Oxford: Clarendon, 1939. Online: http://www.greeklatin. narod.ru/coptic/index.htm. Cited 21 Mar 2017.

Even-Shoshan, Avraham. קוֹנְקוֹרְדַּנְצְיָה חֲדָשָׁה לְתַּנַ"ךְ. Jerusalem: Kiryat Sepher, 1983.

Harris, R. Laird, Gleason L. Archer, Jr., and Bruce K. Waltke, Editors. *Theological Wordbook of the Old Testament*. 2 Volumes. Chicago: Moody Press, 1980.

Hawthorne, Gerald F., & Martin, Ralph P., editors. *Dictionary of Paul & His Letters*. Downers Grove, Ill.: InterVarsity Press, 1993.

Holladay, William L. *A Concise Hebrew and Aramaic Lexicon of the Old Testament*. Leiden: E. J. Brill, 1988.

Jastrow, Marcus. *Dictionary of the Targumim, the Talmud Babli and Yerushalmi, and the Midrashic Literature*. New York, N.Y.: Title Publishing, 1943; orig. 1903.

Kiraz, George Anton. *Lexical Tools of the Syriac New Testament*. London: Sheffield Academic, 1994.

Kittel, Gerhard. *Theologisches Wörterbuch zum Neuen Testament*. 5 Volumes. Stuttgart: Verlag Von W. Kohlhammer, 1932.

Köhler, Ludwig and Walter Baumgartner. *The Hebrew and Aramaic Lexicon of the Old Testament: Study Edition*. Volume 1. New York: E. J. Brill, 2001.

Köhler, Ludwig and Walter Baumgartner. *Supplementum ad Laxicon in Veteris Testamenti Libros*. Leiden: E. J. Brill, 1958.

Kunze, Wolfgang P., editor, et al. *German-English Dictionary of Theological and Philosophical German*. Berrien Springs, Mich.: Andrews University, 2009. Online: http://www.dictionary-theologicalgerman.org/.

Leslau, Wolf. *Concise Dictionary of Ge'ez (Classical Ethiopic)*. Wiesbaden: Otto Harrassowitz Verlag, 2010.

Lisowsky, Gerhardus. *Konkordanz zum Hebräischen Alten Testament.* 2nd Edition. Stuttgart: Württembergische Bibelanstalt, 1958.

Martin, Ralph P., & Davids, Peter H., editors. *Dictionary of the Later New Testament & Its Developments.* Downers Grove, Ill.: InterVarsity Press, 1997.

Sokoloff, Michael. *A Dictionary of Jewish Palestinian Aramaic.* Ramat-Gan: Bar-Ilan University Press, 1990.

Steinberg (Штейнбергъ), Yehoshua N. *Еврейский и халдейский этимологический словарь к книгам Ветхого Завета.* Vilna: Tipographia L. L. Matsa, 1878. Online: http://www.greeklatin.narod.ru/ hebdict/img/_00001.htm. Cited 4 May 2017.

Thomas, Robert L. and Stanley N. Gundry. *The NIV Harmony of the Gospels.* San Francisco, Calif.: Harper Collins, 1988.

Weiser, Chaim M. *Frumspeak: The First Dictionary of Yeshivish.* Lanham, Md.: Jason Aronson, Inc., 2004; orig. 1995.

GRAPHICS & ILLUSTRATIONS

Drawing of Rabban Gamli'el haZaqen. *Rylands Haggadah*. Catalonia,Spain, ca. 1330. In holdings of John Rylands Library, Manchester. Public Domain. [used on page 52]

Drawing of Rabban Gamli'el haZaqen. „Gamaliel mit Schülern." *Sarajevo Haggadah*. *Ca.* 1350. In holdings of Zemaljski Museum, Sarajevo, Bosnia and Hercegovina. Public Domain. [used on page 226]

Drawing of Rabbi Aqiva ben Yosef. *Rylands Haggadah*. Catalonia,Spain, ca. 1330. In holdings of John Rylands Library, Manchester. Public Domain. [used on page 104]

Drawing of Yavneh Sages. *Rylands Haggadah*. Catalonia,Spain, ca. 1330. In holdings of John Rylands Library, Manchester. Public Domain. [used on page 86]

Mosaic of Sha'ul Paulos haTarsi. 4th–5th Century CE. In the holdings of Capella di Sant'Andrea d'Museo Arcivescovile, Ravenna, Italy (1st Floor ceiling). Public Domain. [used on page 55]

"Sanhedrin." In DePuy, W. H. *People's Cyclopedia of Universal Knowledge: with numerous appendixes invaluable for reference in all departments of industrial life*. 3 Volumes. New York, N.Y.: Phillips & Hunt, 1883. Public Domain. [used on page 265]

Shevo, Aharon (designer). "Jerusalem of Gold"
    Souvenir Sheet. Tel Aviv-Yafo: Post of Israel,
    issued 14 May 2008. Used by courtesy of the
    Israel Philatelic Service, Israel Postal Company.
    Usage rights granted 23 Apr 2017. [back cover]

Sketch of Rabbi Aqiva ben Yosef. In Shalit, Ioseph
    ben Iacob *Mantua Haggadah*. 2nd Edition. Padua,
    1568. Public Domain. [used on page 94]

Tice, Brian (graphic artist). "Reflecting on the Rabbis"
    cover art. Copyright 2017. All Rights Reserved.
    [front cover]

_____. Ebedlieder Graph. Based on commentary
    from Franz Delitzsch and David B. Kennedy.
    2009. Entered into Public Domain. [page 151]

_____. ben Yosef, Aqiva. Tomb (sketch). 2016.
    Entered into Public Domain. [page 116]

_____. ben Zakkai, Yochanan. Tomb (sketch). 2017.
    Entered into Public Domain. [page 90]

_____. First-Century Eretz-Israel (map). 2017.
    Entered into Public Domain. [page ב]

_____. haZaqen, Hillel. Tomb (sketch). 2016.
    Entered into Public Domain. [page 48]

_____. haZaqen, Shammai. Tomb (sketch). 2016.
    Entered into Public Domain. [page 29]

_____. "Judges Cycle" (graphic). 2011. Entered into
    Public Domain. [page 7]

Vespasiana Iudaea Capta denarius (photograph). "Iudaea Capta Coinage." Wikimedia Creative Commons, 31 Dec 2001. Online: https://upload.wikimedia.org/wikipedia/commons/b/ba/Sestertius_-_Vespasiano_-_Iudaea_Capta-RIC_0424.jpg. Used under terms of GNU Free Documentation License, Version 1.2. Cited 21 May 2017. [used on page 81]

Zuzim coins (photograph). "Bar Kokhba Coin." Wikimedia Creative Commons, 22 Sep 2007. Online: https://commons.wikimedia.org/wiki/File:Bar_Kokhba_Coin.jpg. Edited by Brian Tice. Used under terms of GNU Free Documentation License, Version 1.2. Cited 19 Apr 2017. [used on page 39]

COMPREHENSIVE INDEX
מַדָּד מָלֵא

ABOUT THE AUTHOR

Professor Brian Tice is an active member of the Adat Eytz Chayim congregation of Grand Rapids, Michigan, where he has served as a *moreh* and occasional *chazzan*. He has served other congregations in the capacity of *chazzan*, musician, *zaqen*, and congregational consultant, since receiving *semikha* in 2000. He has been composing and/or performing original worship music since 1991 and has filled in as a guest speaker on the "Torah Foundations of Faith" cyber-radio program on the Hebrew Nation network.

Professor Tice's formal education includes studies in Modern Languages and Music at Kalamazoo Valley Community College; Bible, Ancient Languages, and Youth Ministry at Cornerstone University; Divinity at Grand Rapids Theological Seminary; and

Higher Education at Kaplan University with emphasis on Classical Hebrew Andragogy... culminating in Bachelor's and Master's degrees. He has also taken additional post-graduate Jewish Studies courses through Tel Aviv University/Coursera.

Over the past several years, Professor Tice has taught Biblical Hebrew, Biblical Aramaic, Tanakh Survey, Tanakh Exegesis, Biblical Hermeneutics, and Apologetics during his tenure at Cornerstone University (graduate assistant), Take Hold Ministry School (professor), and Messianic Jewish Rabbinate Yeshiva (where he is presently a professor of Biblical Languages and Jewish Studies and founding Rosh Yeshiva).

Professor Tice's contributions to *tiqun 'olam* include service as an advocate for victims of violence crime, a board member for Habitat for Humanity and a frequent volunteer at Little Mary's Hospitality House (which serves families with children battling life-threatening, terminal, or debilitating illnesses or conditions). He has volunteered with America's Promise, the Willing to Wait abstinence education program, Boys & Girls Clubs of Greater Kalamazoo, Ministry with Community (a homeless drop-in center), and other outreaches to the homeless and/or disenfranchised.

This book stands as Professor Tice's first contribution to the body of literature on Jewish Studies. He also has a work on Jewish involvement in the American Civil War pending publication.

https://mjrabbinate.org/publishing
publishing@mjrabbinate.org

Made in the
USA
Monee, IL

15862764R00213